Imaginary Companions
and the Children
Who Create Them

Imaginary Companions and the Children Who Create Them

Marjorie Taylor

New York   Oxford
OXFORD UNIVERSITY PRESS
1999

Oxford University Press

Oxford New York
Athens Auckland Bangkok Bogotá Buenos Aires
Calcutta Cape Town Chennai Dar es Salaam
Delhi Florence Hong Kong Istanbul Karachi
Kuala Lumpur Madrid Melbourne Mexico City
Mumbai Nairobi Paris São Paulo Singapore
Taipei Tokyo Toronto Warsaw

and associated companies in
Berlin Ibadan

Copyright © 1999 by Oxford University Press, Inc.

Published by Oxford University Press, Inc.
198 Madison Avenue, New York, New York 10016

Oxford is a registered trademark of Oxford University Press, Inc.

Library of Congress Cataloging-in-Publication Data

Taylor, Marjorie.
Imaginary companions and the children
who create them / by Marjorie Taylor.
p. cm. Includes bibliographical references and index.
ISBN 0-19-507704-0
1. Imagination in children.
2. Play. I. Title.
BF723.I5T38 1999 155.4'133—dc21 98-7753

3 5 7 9 8 6 4 2

Printed in the United States of America
on acid-free paper

To my mother Edith, Doug, and Amber

Contents

▼
▼

Imaginary Companions
and the Children
Who Create Them

1

Introduction

▼

I MAGINARY companions often get bad press. In movies and novels, they tend to be equated with psychological disturbance. Look what happens to Danny Torrance, the child character in the movie based on Stephen King's novel *The Shining*.[1] Near the beginning of the story, Danny describes Tony, a small invisible boy who lives in his mouth and gives him advice whenever he needs it. This movie is filled with shots of a haunted hotel, an elevator filled with blood, and violent deaths, yet one of the most psychologically chilling scenes occurs when Danny becomes so traumatized by the unfolding events that he is no longer able to function. In this scene, Danny's mother finds him in a trancelike state and tries to rouse him by shaking him, repeating his name, and telling him to wake up. When the boy responds, it is in the distinctive monotonic voice of Tony saying, "Danny can't wake up, Mrs. Torrance . . . Danny's gone away, Mrs. Torrance."

Although, even in the movies, pretend friends don't usually commandeer children's bodies, they are often depicted as the inventions of lonely, unhappy children. In the movie *Bogus*, about a boy who creates an imaginary friend at a time of personal crisis, the child protagonist is laughed at by other children, runs away from home, and for a time seems lost in a fantasy world. The popular comic strip, *Calvin and Hobbes*, presents a humorous depiction of imaginary companions, but still raises questions about the type of child who has one. We enjoy Calvin's wild imagination and his exploits with his stuffed tiger, Hobbes, but in real life, we wouldn't laugh at a boy who did so poorly in school and had no real-life friends. Calvin's long-suffering teacher counts the days until retirement, his mother reads child psychology books to find out where she went wrong, and his father questions whether they should have become parents at all! Even Bill Watterson, the creator of *Calvin and Hobbes,* says he wouldn't want a child like Calvin in his home.[2]

No wonder some parents worry about the implications of their children having imaginary companions. And it is not just popular culture that gives imaginary companions a bad reputation. Early psychological research on this topic often suggested negative implications.[3] The silver lining in these studies was that imaginary companions also tended to be interpreted as signs of special intelligence or creativity, a possibility that shows up in some portrayals in the media. A comedy sketch on *Saturday Night Live* some years ago depicted two parents fighting over whose child had the better (i.e., more unique, detailed, creative) imaginary companion. In fact, some parents have expressed concern to me about their children not having imaginary companions. They wonder if this is a negative sign regarding their children's intellectual or creative potential.

So what does having an imaginary companion mean? What is the likelihood that a child might become so engrossed in an imaginary world as to lose touch with reality altogether? Is the creation of an imaginary companion the first sign of mental illness? Is it an early marker of special intelligence? These are some of the questions addressed in this book. The answers come from an analysis of psychological research with young children. Many of the older studies that painted a negative picture of imaginary companions had methodological problems. More reliable information collected in recent years indicates that fantasy play is an important component of children's cognitive and emotional development. More specifically, the creation of an imaginary companion is healthy and relatively common.

This is not to say that the stereotype portrayed in movies is without basis in reality. A child like the boy in *Bogus* who lost his mother and had to move to a new and strange place would be a likely candidate for having an imaginary companion. The creation of a pretend friend in such cases can be an adaptive response on the part of the child for dealing with difficult issues in his or her life. Fantasy allows a child to work on a variety of concerns, fears, and problems. More often, though, children pretend to have an imaginary friend simply because it is fun. The view that is emerging from recent research is that the children who create pretend friends are very social people who particularly enjoy interacting with others. When no one is around to play with, these children make someone up.

Chapter 2 is devoted to defining "imaginary companion." Thus far I have used the term as if everyone knows exactly what I am talking about, but there are lots of play activities that parents and others might consider having an imaginary friend. Does the friend have to be invisible to count as an imaginary companion or are children's teddy bears and other toys also potential candidates? Does the imaginary friend have to be nice? What about imaginary friends whose mean or scary behavior makes them more like imaginary enemies?

Although for research purposes, children tend to be categorized as either having or not having an imaginary companion, I consider this dichotomy to be misleading or at least simplistic. Many children have several imaginary friends at a time, and some acquire new ones as others disappear. Children may also have sustained and elaborate fantasies that do not easily fit into what we label as an "imaginary companion." For example, many preschool children pretend to *be* an animal or another person on a regular basis—they take on the imaginary character and act it out, rather than pretend it is a separate entity from themselves. Chapter 2 provides descriptive information about the kinds of pretense that might be considered examples of imaginary companions, as well as some variations on the theme.

Chapter 3 describes the research investigating possible differences between children who create imaginary companions and those who do not. The importance of the definitional issues discussed in Chapter 2 immediately becomes clear when we consider this literature. One of the challenges of interpreting the research findings is that there has been considerable variation from study to study in what is included in the category "imaginary companion." However, the general picture emerging from recent studies is that, in most respects, the similarities between the two groups of children are more striking than their differences. When differences are found, they tend to turn the stereotype of children who have imaginary companions on its head. Children with imaginary companions appear to be *less* shy, more able to focus their attention, and to have advanced social understanding when compared with other children.

Another type of potential difference between children with and without imaginary companions that is explored in Chapter 3 concerns the role played by parental attitudes and cultural beliefs about fantasy play. Although North American parents sometimes worry about imaginary companions, in general they tend to promote children's pretend play, and our culture provides a wealth of fantasy material that is often incorporated into children's private fantasy creations. For example, many young children have imaginary companions similar to characters they have seen on television or in movies, such as the Little Mermaid or Ninja Turtles. However, not all children are encouraged to engage in fantasy play. There are substantial cultural differences in parental reaction to, and interpretation of, childhood fantasies that are likely to affect children's engagement in pretense, as well as their understanding of the distinction between fantasy and reality. The experience of childhood can be quite different in cultures in which fantasy is actively discouraged because it is viewed as a waste of time, equivalent to deceit, or even evidence of demonic possession.

Chapter 4 deals with the reasons children create imaginary companions. There is currently considerable interest in the possibility that one of the special functions of pretend play is to help children control and master their emotions.[4] The research on imaginary companions supports this view, suggesting that pretend friends may be created to serve a variety of emotional needs, including a desire for companionship, a way to work through fears, or a method of dealing with actual or perceived restrictions. Children also create imaginary companions as a response to traumatic life situations—which is why clinicians have sometimes linked imaginary companions with psychological distress.

In Chapter 5, I start by asking if children think their imaginary companions are real, but answering this question requires a much broader discussion of the general distinction between fantasy and reality. Overall, I think children's grasp of this distinction tends to be underestimated, but it's a tricky question because fantasy comes in a variety of forms. The topics covered in this chapter include children's beliefs in fantasy characters such as Santa Claus, their understanding of fantasy material on television and in movies, their comprehension of joint pretend play with others, and their conception of dreams, as well as their beliefs about their imaginary companions. Sometimes the boundary between fantasy and reality is not entirely clear to children, but when it comes to pretend friends, children seem to know exactly what is going on. They might think Santa Claus and the Tooth Fairy are real, but they are quite knowledgeable about the fantasy status of the people, creatures, and objects that are the figments of their own imaginations.

In Chapter 6, I discuss the ultimate fate of imaginary companions. What happens to them? When and why are they given up? Not much is known about how these fantasies end, but the available evidence suggests that children simply move on to other things. In most cases, no well-marked event leads to the imaginary companion's disappearance—it simply fades away. Many parents report that children abandon their imaginary companions at about 6 years of age when they start school, but there is reason to question this commonly held assumption. Some pretend friends are retained much longer, and sometimes imaginary companions first appear when the children are well beyond the preschool years. For some of these older children, fantasies about imaginary characters become increasingly elaborate until entire fantasy worlds are created for them to inhabit. The imaginary companions of older children are described in Chapter 7, along with adult behaviors that I consider similar to having an imaginary companion.

In Chapter 8, I summarize some of the main points of this book and discuss the larger issues raised by the study of imaginary companions. The bottom line is that although imaginary companions and other fantasies have sometimes been interpreted as signs of emotional disturbance, a break with reality, or even the emergence of multiple personalities, they really are just a variation on the theme of all the pretend play that is going on in the preschool years, a period sometimes referred to as "the high season of imaginative play."[5] I hope this book will help explain some of the reasons for our misconceptions about imaginary companions, while stressing the important role played by such fantasies in the cognitive and emotional development of healthy children.

2

What Are Imaginary Companions Like?

▼

O NE 4-year-old who participated in our research told us about two invisible birds named Nutsy and Nutsy (a male and a female) who lived in a tree outside her bedroom window. According to the child, the two Nutsys had brightly colored feathers, were about 12 inches tall, and talked incessantly. Sometimes the little girl was irritated by the clumsy and generally raucous behavior of these birds, but usually their silliness made her laugh. The child's parents were well aware of the Nutsys; they regularly observed their daughter talking and playing with them, and they were frequently informed about the Nutsys' opinions and activities. In fact, Nutsy and Nutsy were almost like part of the family. The birds went along on outings by riding on top of the car, they had their own places set at the dinner table, and their antics were enjoyed by all. I met the Nutsys myself one day when they accompanied the little girl to my lab. I provided a chair for them, and the little girl laughed at how funny they looked as they stood on tiptoe to peer over the table at her. Two years after she first told us about Nutsy and Nutsy, the child still remembered them, and her mother reported that she and her daughter sometimes reminisced about their exploits.

Elaborate invisible creatures like Nutsy and Nutsy who are played with for an extended period of time and are described consistently by both the child and her parents would fit almost anyone's definition of an imaginary companion. However, there are many variations on the imaginary companion theme. The animals and people who populate children's fantasy lives differ in their vividness, personality development, and the extent to which they have some basis in the real world. Some children have an imaginary version of a real friend or adopt a character from a movie or book as an imaginary companion (e.g., Ariel from the Walt Disney movie *The Little Mermaid*). Other children use a favorite stuffed toy, their own image in a mirror, or their hands as props in their pretense. Sometimes the props are more idiosyncratic. There is one documented case of a child who had an ongoing (and rather stormy) relationship with the chest of drawers in his bedroom, speaking to it as if it were aware of his thoughts and behaviors.[1] In another case, a little girl had friends she called Leafies who lived in an aspen tree in her backyard.[2]

Fantasy people and animals also vary in the length of time they inhabit a child's imagination. Sometimes imaginary companions are stable, long-lived, and played with regularly. They may even be passed down from one child to the next in a family, like outgrown but still serviceable clothes. Other pretend friends have a much more transitory existence, drifting in and out of the child's fantasy life. In our research, we have encountered children whose lives were crowded with imaginary people and animals, none of which lingered for long. Other children had only one or two imaginary companions at a time, but they updated their friends frequently, for example, trading in a blue-eyed blond boy named Tompy for a mischievous female mouse named Gadget. In some cases, children have described an army of Martians or a host of lizards rather than a solitary individual.[3] In fact, it is common for children to have two or more imaginary companions.

Given the diversity in children's fantasy play, parents are often unsure if their own child would be considered to have an imaginary companion. This makes it difficult for parents to decide if the research findings about imaginary companions are relevant to their children. In this chapter, I discuss in some detail what imaginary companions are like, and the different sources of information that researchers have used to identify the children who have them.

What counts as an "imaginary companion"?

Invisible friends versus stuffed animals

Many young children endow a stuffed animal, doll, or other toy with a stable personality and treat it as if it were real—talking to it, making a special voice for it, and consulting it about problems. This type of pretend play is the basis of Bill Watterson's comic strip *Calvin and Hobbes* about a small boy and his stuffed tiger companion. One might also think of Winnie the Pooh, the teddy bear friend of Christopher Robin in A. A. Milne's children's books, or the toy bunny in *The Velveteen Rabbit*. Parents often ask if special toys are examples of imaginary companions.

Experts on childhood fantasy differ in their opinions about toys. In the past, the term "imaginary companion" was restricted to fantasy friends who were invisible, excluding cases in which toys were used as props. For example, in one of the first widely read articles on the subject, published in 1934, Dr. Margaret Svendsen of the Institute for Juvenile Research in Chicago defined an imaginary companion as "an invisible character, named and referred to in conversation with other persons or played with directly for a period of time, at least several months, having an air of reality for the child but no apparent objective basis. This excludes that type of imaginative play in which an object is personified, or in which the child himself assumes the role of some person in his environment."[4] In order to be absolutely clear about her definition, Svendsen gave the following real life example:

> Shortly before her second birthday Mary referred to "Tagar," her imaginary companion. She led Tagar around on an imaginary string. Food was kept for it under the radiator where it also slept; she always fed it on the floor. It was particularly fond of ice cream, as she was. "Berrie and Auntie" followed Tagar, appearing when she was about 3-1/2 years of age. They were two persons, but lived together. Mary would set places for them at the family table. Although dishes and silver were laid and Mary would ask if they had enough, real food was never offered them. On other occasions, she would seize the opportunity at meal-time to tell her father all the things which they had done. Mary might be punished but they never were, and never did anything wrong. Berrie and Auntie frequently accompanied her and her parents on outings, and on several occasions she attempted to draw her real companion into play with them, by insisting that she talk with them on the telephone.[5]

Of the 111 children in Svendsen's sample, 13.4 percent were identified as having imaginary companions. Her estimate is quite low, in part because the children ranged in age from 3 to 16 years, and it is likely that at least some of the older children had forgotten the imaginary friends they had when they were younger. And what about the omission of stuffed animals and other toys? It seems to me that at least in some cases, toys function quite well as imaginary companions. Certainly if a little boy similar to Watterson's Calvin participated in my research, I would want him to be in the group of children described as having imaginary companions.

One argument for excluding stuffed animals is that they have an existence and physical appearance that is independent of the child's imagination. Perhaps a companion is only truly imaginary when it exists solely in the mind's eye of the child and none of the details are specified by the environment. The trouble with this reasoning is that play with stuffed animals and play with invisible imaginary companions are not as different as one might think with regard to how much imagination is involved. According to Kendall Walton, professor of philosophy at the University of Michigan, the experience of imagining an entity such as an imaginary bear is apt to be *more* vivid if an actual object serves as a prop.[6] And clearly, children use their imaginations to embellish the appearance of toys that serve as imaginary companions. In the child's mind, the imagined friend based on a toy might look quite different from the way the toy appears to a more impartial observer. The mother sees a scruffy little stuffed dog that she would like to whisk away for a quick cycle through the washing machine, but to the child, the dog appears large, fluffy, and graceful.

This insight is captured in Watterson's technique of drawing the stuffed tiger in his comic strip very differently depending on whether the reader is seeing Hobbes as he appears to Calvin (i.e., a large, expressive, and lifelike beast) or as he appears to another character in the cartoon (i.e., a small inert toy). Ronald Benson and David Pryor of the Department of Psychiatry at the University of Michigan described this kind of discrepancy in perspective when they asked a 16-year-old girl to show them the stuffed dog that had served as her childhood companion.[7] When she located the dog in the back of her closet, she was shocked to see how tattered and worn it was. She felt she was seeing the toy for the first time as it appeared to other people.

The distinction between stuffed animals and invisible imaginary companions is also blurred because parents frequently respond to their child's expression of interest in a particular kind of animal by supplying him or her with a toy version of it. One adult who participated in my research recalled that her mother asked her lots of questions about the imaginary companion she had as a small child (an invisible "Mouse-Mouse") and then made a stuffed animal to her daughter's specifications, complete with brown fur and blue-flowered super-hero cape.

More commonly, parents simply buy toys that correspond to the type of animals their children are imagining in their play. One 5-year-old in our research began creating fantasies about dolphins when she was 2 years old. Her father reported that she used to pretend to hold tiny dolphins in her hands and to give them to family members. Because of her interest in dolphins, the parents gave her a stuffed dolphin that became the prop for an imaginary companion named Dipper. When asked to describe Dipper, the child did not describe the physical attributes of her toy (a small, gray plush dolphin), but instead reported that Dipper was "the size of a door," had sparkles and stripes (unlike "a regular dolphin"), and lived far away on a star. These same details were repeated when the child was interviewed a year later. In her pretend play with dolphins, this child moved flexibly between interacting with an entirely invisible friend and using a toy as a prop in her play. I also know cases in which a child first used a toy as an imaginary companion and later invented an invisible version of the friend.

If we decide that stuffed animals, dolls, and other toys sometimes function as imaginary companions, a new problem arises. How do we distinguish between toys that are imaginary companions and toys that are not? After all, the majority of children have a stuffed animal or a doll. A toy that is played with from time to time, but spends most of its time on the shelf, would obviously not warrant the label "imaginary companion." Other toys are special, but not in the same way as an imaginary companion. For example, some children have a teddy bear that they habitually cling to, sleep with, and use for comfort. Toys, blankets, and other items used in this way by young children are referred to as "transitional objects."[8] Transitional objects are of interest to psychologists because they are believed to help some children work out the distinction between self and other, but enjoying the comfort of a soft toy is not the same as creating a distinct personality for it.

Professors Dorothy Singer and Jerome Singer, leading authorities on children's imagination and authors of *The House of Make-Believe*, chose to include stuffed animals and dolls as possible imaginary companions in their research conducted at Yale University. They distinguished the toys serving as imaginary companions from other playthings in the following way: "Our data do include parents' reports of their children's transformations of stuffed animals, which assume human-like properties. We did not, however, count teddy bears or dolls where these were simply carried around or treated in the concrete fashion of the transitional object. Rather, to be included they had to be endowed by the child with definite human qualities and be treated as a friend or playmate."[9] The inclusion of toys helps to account for why Singer and Singer report that about 65 percent of children have imaginary companions, an estimate more than four times higher than Svendsen's.

Dr. Jennifer Mauro, a clinical psychologist who is an expert on imaginary companions, explicitly mentioned toys when explaining to the children in her research what she meant by a pretend friend. "Pretend friends are like dolls or toys that you pretend are real or people that you pretend are real. They are make-believe friends. Do you have a pretend friend?"[10] Of the imaginary companions described in response to this question, 41 percent turned out to be invisible people, 19 percent were invisible animals, and 39 percent were dolls or stuffed animals. Like Singer and Singer, Mauro estimated the incidence of imaginary companions to be quite high— more than 50 percent of young children.

Clearly, the decision to include or exclude stuffed animals or dolls as imaginary companions has a large effect on how common one believes the phenomenon to be. Some psychologists have taken an intermediate stance when it comes to stuffed animals, resulting in estimates that fall between Svendsen's and Singer and Singer's. For example, John and Elizabeth Newson, two British psychologists who have conducted extensive research on the lives of young children, estimated that 22 percent of 4-year-olds have imaginary companions.[11] For the most part these researchers excluded stuffed animals or dolls as imaginary companions, but in a few cases they relented. "It was clearly necessary to admit a character to the fantasy category because, although having a 'real' origin, so extensive a saga had been built upon this foundation that fantasy had long since out-stripped reality." In fact, the Newsons' own daughter had such elaborate fantasies about her doll Susanna that they decided to interview the child about her 4-year-old daughter (the doll) in the same way that they interviewed real parents about their children. The transcript—a 4-year-old's view of her supposedly 4-year-old child and her opinions on its upbringing—is published as an appendix at the end of Newson and Newson's book *Four Years Old in an Urban Community*.

This example indicates that young children sometimes build detailed fantasies involving their toys. The pretense can go well beyond play with one special stuffed animal or doll. One of my graduate students recently told me about an elaborate network of social relationships involving the many stuffed animals she had as a young child:

> I attributed various personality traits to each animal and treated them according to my beliefs about each one. For example, one of the animals was a stuffed bear who was far older and considerably more tattered than my other animals. I worried that he would think I liked the other animals better because of their more attractive appearance, so I made a special effort to reassure him that I loved him just as much as the others. I also had concerns about the larger animals bullying the smaller ones. I remember telling these larger animals to remember to be extra kind and gentle to the littler ones.
>
> Occasionally, conflict arose in my relationships with the animals. The conflicts usually centered around one of two events: my receiving a new stuffed animal or toy, and times when I left home on a trip and had to choose which animal would travel with me. In the case where I was given a new stuffed animal for Christmas or my birthday, I reassured the other animals that I still loved them as much as I always had, and that an "addition to the family" would have no impact on my relationships with them. I would then engage in an elaborate procedure of introducing the new animal to each of the older ones. I presumed that the new animal would be shy in his new home, and reassured him that we would all get along with each other.
>
> When I traveled away from home with my family, I was allowed to take only one animal. I remember agonizing over the decision, not wanting to hurt anyone's feelings. I eventually developed a rotating system that allowed each animal to essentially go on the same number of trips as any other animal. Before each trip, I carefully selected the animal who would accompany me, and then proceeded to have a "meeting" with all of the animals together. I would tell them to the best of my ability where I was going, how long I would be gone, and what I expected to do on the trip. I reassured the animals who were staying behind that I would take them all if I could, but due to parental constraints I had been forced to choose one of them. I tried to make it clear to all of them that I was doing my best to be fair, and that they would all eventually go on a trip with me. In addition to this elaborate clarification of my motives for choosing the animal that I had, I felt the need to protect the animal who was going with me from possible retaliation from the other animals upon our return. I

pleaded with the other animals to be kind to the one who had been selected. I also advised the animal who had been selected to refrain from bragging about how much fun the trip had been, as this would only provoke the other animals.

Such reports from adults remembering their childhoods, together with observations of young children, demonstrate that pretense involving the animation of toys can be elaborate, vivid, and important to young children. Perhaps these examples will help parents determine if their own child's toy serves as an imaginary companion. This decision is harder for researchers who have more limited information about the way the child plays with the toy. There is a blurry line between toys that serve as props for imaginary companions and other more run-of-the-mill playthings. We also do not know the extent to which imaginative play with toy props has the same sorts of emotional and cognitive consequences as play with invisible beings.[12] Perhaps inventing an invisible friend is not exactly the same kind of experience as creating a personality for a special toy, but in most current research on imaginary companions, special toys are included.

Imaginary identities

Another kind of play that seems very similar to having an imaginary companion occurs when children create an imaginary personality or character that they act out themselves. For example, one child we originally thought had an imaginary companion named Applejack (based on the report of the child's mother), turned out to have an imagined character that she impersonated, rather than one she interacted with as a separate individual. The child corrected us over the course of the interview by responding to questions such as "How much do you play with Applejack?" by saying, "No, I *am* Applejack."

Of course, most children act out a variety of roles in their pretend play with other children. On any given day, one child might be the firefighter, another the monster, and so on. This kind of role playing is common. But some children engage in a kind of impersonation that is much more enduring, for example, a child who pretends to be Superman every day for months. The completeness of the identification and the persistence with which the impersonated identity is maintained distinguishes impersonation from common role playing.[13]

Surprisingly little has been written about children's impersonation of animals and people. One exception is an old study by Louise Ames and Janet Learned conducted at Yale University.[14] Ames and Learned gathered information by interviewing parents and observing children at play. Their data include several fascinating reports of children such as the girl described below, who had some imaginary companions that were invisible and some based on props, and who also impersonated imagined characters.

> Imaginary play started around 2 years. She animated her hands and had the fingers talk to each other, before she herself could talk well. Outdoors she used sticks as imaginary people. Later when she could talk she called her hands "hand-duds" when they were acting as imaginary companions. She dressed up her hands with ribbons between the fingers for hair.
>
> At 33 months she talked to imaginary beings in the corners of the room. She would sit at supper and make faces at the corner of the room near the ceiling. Had long conversations with this imaginary friend and was oblivious of the rest of the family. Would talk to the companion, and then makes faces and slight grunting noises in her throat when other person was supposed to be talking to her.
>
> Her most familiar companions are Hankea, Jellia and Honia. Hankea is a little girl with a "hanky" around her head. Honia is full of honey, Jellia is full of jelly. Honia had a hole in her tummy and a door popped open and the honey popped out. Then all the bees came buzzing around and got the honey. In fact, that is how one gets honey. . . . Sometimes this child changes places with her imaginary friends and she is one of them.[15]

Ames and Learned considered the creation of an imaginary character that is acted out rather than treated as a separate person as an activity that is closely related to playing with an imaginary friend. As an example of animal impersonation, they described a boy who at 24 months visited his grandmother, who had a kitten: "When he got home, he became a kitten and this continued quite consistently till he was 36 months old. He went around on all fours 'meowing'; lapped up milk. At 30 months he took on, briefly, an additional role, that of his best friend's dog. In this role he went around on all fours and bit people."[16] They also provided an example of a girl who pretended to be a boy from 36 months to 60 months: "Mostly she was a boy named 'Jimmy' and would not answer if addressed by her own name. Would say, 'My name is Jimmy.' If any request were prefaced with 'Jimmy, will you———?' she would accede immediately. Sometimes she was a boy other than Jimmy. Occasionally when she did something she was not supposed to do she was Shisky."[17]

Of the 210 children who participated in Ames and Learned's study, 17 were observed or described by parents as habitually impersonating animals or people. The eight cases of animal impersonation included three dogs, three cats, a horse, a pig, and a "great big grizzly bear." The extent of the activity for two of the children was simply saying they were the animals and wanting to be addressed appropriately. However, four were described as carrying out the pretense extensively —"going around on all fours, saying 'woof woof' or 'meow' instead of talking, lapping up food from a dish on the floor, chasing automobiles, even urinating in animal fashion by standing on one leg."[18]

It is not surprising that the parents in this study reported that impersonation was more troublesome than other kinds of imaginative play. I too have found that regular impersonation of an imaginary character can be particularly vexing for parents. One mother told us that when company was expected, she and her husband worried whether their sons would be children or cats during the evening. The cat possibility was undesirable because the boys would meow instead of talk, try to eat directly from a plate instead of using silverware, and rub against the legs of the guests in feline fashion.

One of the frustrations is that animals do not understand English and do not talk. When asked to do something (e.g., "Pick up your things and go to bed"), the animal-child is apt to bark or look quizzically at the parent rather than comply. One evening I took my 4-year-old to the home of two clinical psychologists for dinner. As soon as she saw their dog, she became one herself. My requests for her to stop being a dog became pleas, then whispered threats. Amber responded with whimpering dog sounds and licks. I was reluctant to force the issue in front of my colleagues, so I ended up smiling foolishly, while my friends exchanged glances and politely tried to ignore my daughter's behavior.

Sometimes a child might impersonate a machine rather than an animate being. In his autobiography Sir Peter Ustinov, the British actor, playwright, and director, recalls this type of childhood activity.

> I was a motor-car, to the dismay of my parents. Psychiatry was in its infancy then, both expensive and centered in Vienna. There was no one

yet qualified to exorcise an internal combustion engine from a small boy. . . . I switched on in the morning, and only stopped being a car at night when I reversed into bed, and cut the ignition."[19]

Parents of children who behave this way might be helped by the advice Ustinov's grandfather gave to his mother: "Don't think of it as the sound of an automobile, but rather as the sound of his imagination developing, and then you will see it will become bearable."[20]

Imaginary "friends" that aren't so friendly

Most invisible entities in children's fantasy lives embody the desirable characteristics of a loving friend, but a few might more accurately be called "imaginary enemies." In fact, Singer and Singer think that Samuel Clemens's (a.k.a. Mark Twain) childhood imaginary companion was a devil. They base this speculation on the following facts about Clemens: (1) He often included material from his childhood in his novels; (2) In *The Mysterious Stranger,* Satan is an invisible character that communicates with young boys; and (3) Clemens's mother referred to Satan frequently in the home.[21]

Other imaginary companions, if not downright evil, can be unruly, difficult, or scary. For example, a 14-year-old boy who was in bed recovering from a long illness imagined that a picture facing him showed a giant that sometimes stepped out from the wall intent on cutting off his hands. The boy slept with his hands covered for three years.[22] Similarly, Russian psychologist Eugene Subbotsky describes a 4-year-old who developed a fear of a "bamzeli," a monster who came to the child when he was alone in his bed at night. The child developed a ritual for freeing himself from the bamzeli by holding a rolled-up blanket in his hands, which allowed him to sleep peaceably.[23] One mother told me about her son from age 3 to 5 having an imaginary "bad guy" who lived in the bedroom closet. The invisible "Barnaby" was a large man with a black mustache who liked to scare people. Whenever she was asked to check the closet for Barnaby, she always told her son there was no sign of him, but the child continued to complain about Barnaby. During a plane trip to Denver, she announced that Barnaby would not be around anymore because he didn't know where they were going, but the little boy informed her that Barnaby was following them on the next plane.

Are these examples of imaginary companions? Maybe not. The

descriptions of these particular cases suggest that the imagined creatures did not have much interaction with the children beyond scaring them. But sometimes frightening imagined characters serve other functions as well. According to the mother of a 4-year-old in Newson and Newson's research, the child imagined monkeys who "live in the cellar, and that's why he won't go down the cellar, because they might get him; and if there's something wrong, it's always a monkey that's come up from the cellar and done it." Another child had a pet dragon who played with him, "but the dragon gets in the way sometimes when Alistair's frightened. If he wants to go upstairs and it's dark, he says 'The dragon might get me if I go upstairs, won't you, Dragon?'"[24]

Frances Wickes reports a case in which an ominous being appeared to help a child overcome her fear of the dark or the unknown. Typically, imaginary companions that help children overcome fears are the friendly, docile sort, such as a gentle tiger who can be bossed around by a child who is afraid of animals (this type of function is discussed in Chapter 4). However, in this case, an invisible menacing figure referred to as "it" helped the child conquer her fears.

> She deliberately let this figure go with her. She walked into the dark places where she believed it was and faced it. She let it walk with her on the street, she deliberately took it as her companion until she found that not only had it lost its terrifying power but that also her unreasoned fears of dark places and of being alone were dropping from her.[25]

My impression is that invisible entities who are primarily disliked or feared but who have other characteristics associated with imaginary companions (e.g., a relatively stable personality), are relatively rare. However, children sometimes express negative feelings about imaginary companions who, in most respects, are good friends. Mauro reported that 34 percent of the children with imaginary companions said they sometimes were angry with their friends, and many parents report having witnessed their children engaged in arguments with imaginary companions.

We found that when we asked children if there was anything they did not like about their imaginary companions, they had plenty of complaints. "She puts yogurt in my hair." "He hits me on the head." "She won't share." Some imaginary companions don't show up when the child wants them to, whereas others are annoying because they never go away. Pretend friends have been known to bite, throw tem-

FIGURE 1. *B. Hickerson.*
Copyright 1994. Distributed
by The Los Angeles Times
Syndicate. Reprinted
with permission.

per tantrums, and make their child creators do bad things, such as toss a sister's beloved doll in the toilet.[26] Sometimes they are overly free with negative comments and criticisms. For example, as a young boy, Ben Hogan had a pretend friend named Hennie Bogan who sat on his shoulder and made fun of the way he played golf. Perhaps Ben took Hennie's criticisms to heart because he grew up to become one of the greatest golfers of this century, winning the Masters, the U.S. Open, and the British Open in 1953.[27]

Sources of information about imaginary companions

Who are the best informants about imaginary characters, the parents or the children themselves? What about retrospective reports—the memories of adults for the imaginary characters they created as young children? Each source of information has drawbacks and advantages.

Interviews with parents

In general, parents are not particularly good sources of information about imaginary companions. There often are large discrepancies in the descriptions of imaginary companions given by parents and by their children.[28] For example, one parent told us that her son had a playmate named Nobby, a little invisible boy. The child also mentioned Nobby when he was asked about pretend friends, but when we asked how often he played with Nobby, he scowled and replied, "I don't *play* with him." We learned that Nobby was a 160-year-old businessman who visited the child between business trips to Portland and Seattle, whenever the child wanted to "talk things over." The boy's mother was as surprised as we were.

More commonly, parents simply don't know many details about the imaginary friend. Sometimes it's because they are reluctant to ask their children about the imaginary companions. Parents often tell us that although they are comfortable with their children having pretend friends, they don't want to actively encourage this type of play. They allow their children to "do their thing," but they don't ask about the pretend friends or participate in the pretense. Especially as they get older, children are quite sensitive to this sort of ambivalence. One 6-year-old told us all about her imaginary companion, but when we were leaving the interview room, she asked us not to repeat to her mother anything she had said. In fact, many parents are completely unaware that their children have imaginary companions. In our work with 6- and 7-year-olds, we found that parents were aware of only seven of 32 imaginary companions created after the age of 4. Even with younger children, many parents in our research learned about their children's imaginary companions for the first time when the children participated in our study. (The effect of parents' attitudes about imaginary companions on children's play will be discussed more fully in Chapter 3.)

It is not necessarily the case that parents who do not know about their children's imaginary companions are uninvolved in their children's lives or harbor negative feelings about imaginary companions. Sometimes pretend friends have commonplace names that the child mentions, in passing, along with the names of real children at the local day care or in the neighborhood. When my daughter was 3, she sometimes referred to a person named Michael Rose. Amber seemed to enjoy her time with Michael Rose, and I became curious about him. When I asked her preschool teachers to point him out to me, they had no idea whom I was talking about. I subsequently pressed my daughter for details and learned, among other things, that he had a barn full of giraffes. Somewhat belatedly, I figured out that Michael Rose lived only in her imagination.

A similar case involved a 3-year-old boy who created an imaginary companion when he started attending a play group. His mother was a little worried about how her son would adjust to the group because he was quite apprehensive about leaving her for an extended period. She was relieved to find him relaxed and happy when she picked him up after his first day. He explained that he had met a little girl named Margarine who was really nice to him. After hearing several references to the kindness of Margarine over the next few weeks, the mother decided to contact Margarine's parents to convey how much she appreciated their daughter's thoughtfulness and caring behavior toward her son. Clearly, Margarine had been a big factor in his easy transition to a group play experience. It turned out to be a challenge to locate Margarine or her parents. The play group leader and the boy's mother searched the list of children in the play group, but couldn't find any name with even a passing resemblance to "Margarine." The mother asked her son to describe what the girl looked like, and learned that Margarine had long yellow braids that dragged behind her on the floor. It soon became apparent that Margarine was imaginary. Over time, Margarine evolved into a stable personality who remained with the family for several years, accompanying them on a move from the East Coast to the West Coast. When the boy's little sister started going to preschool, Margarine was on hand to ease her transition as well. The brother drew the picture of Margarine on the left, and his little sister drew the one on the right.

I don't want to be too negative about the usefulness of asking parents about their children's imaginary companions. When parents are aware of these friends, they can sometimes provide information that a child might fail to mention, such as the events that were taking place in the child's life when he or she first started playing with an imaginary friend. It is also reassuring when the child's report is corroborated by the parents'. However when it comes to answering some kinds of questions about imaginary companions (e.g., how common are they?), parental reports have severe limitations. It is not surprising that estimates of the incidence of imaginary companions based on parental report are much lower than Singer and Singer's estimate of 65 percent. For example, in a study by Martin Manosevitz and his colleagues at the University of Texas at Austin, 28 percent of the parents of 222 children ages 3 to 5 years reported that their children had an imaginary companion.[29] It is quite likely that some parents in this study were unaware of the existence of their children's pretend friends.

FIGURE 2. *Drawings of Margarine, an invisible girl shared by brother (left drawing) and sister (right drawing).*

Interviews with children

Children are the best source of information about imaginary companions, but this doesn't mean that there are no problems interpreting what they have to say. Sometimes children are not completely sure what you mean when you ask if they have a pretend friend. They might say "yes," and then describe a real friend instead of an imaginary one. Other children might mention a stuffed animal that actually spends most of its time in the toy box. An even trickier problem is that some children make up imaginary companions in response to questions about them. A pretend friend? What a good idea! And they invent one on the spot. Once when we pointed out to a child that the imaginary companion he was describing was not the same one he had told us about the week before, he replied that if we asked him 20 times, he would have 20 different imaginary companions. No doubt this child was quite imaginative, but it would have been inaccurate to describe him as having an imaginary companion.

Some researchers have openly discussed such confabulation. In an early monograph, Arthur Jersild, Frances Markey, and Catherine Jersild of Columbia University found that some children made up responses to the research question: "Did you ever have an imaginary playmate, someone who seemed to be with you but who really was not a real person?"[30] While some of descriptions elicited by this question were imaginary companions that seemed to be vivid and well-developed fantasy creations, many children described characters which were much less permanent and could be revised or changed entirely on any passing whim. "It became apparent that the children's replies could serve only as a record of the kinds of characters children most frequently entertain in their imagination rather than as an adequate appraisal of the peculiar phenomenon of imaginary companions."[31] Thus, Jersild and his colleagues interpreted the children's answers to their questions as a record of the types of creatures children imagine rather than as an account of the characteristics of imagined entities that played an enduring role in the child's fantasy life.

Even when children clearly are describing an imaginary companion that they play with on a regular basis, inconsistencies in their descriptions suggest that they are making up details as they go along. When we first started interviewing children about imaginary companions, the discrepancies and spontaneously created details bothered us. We wondered if the information we were gathering was telling us anything meaningful about the children's fantasy lives. Now we view this aspect of children's reports as part of the phenomenon we are researching and something to be expected.[32] After all, although the adult's goal is to find out about the imaginary companion, for the child, the interview might be just another opportunity to pretend. Probably every time children think about their imaginary companions, they invent new details. Some are transitory, some remain as part of the core representation of the imaginary companion. On occasion children may try out a whole new way of thinking about the imaginary companion. Jean Piaget, the famous Swiss psychologist, reported that his own daughter had an imaginary animal friend named Aseau who changed on a daily basis.[33] Sometimes it was a dog, but it could also be an insect, a bird, or even a huge beast with nails on its feet. This is a particularly extreme example; more commonly, the core representation of the imaginary companion is relatively stable, and some details are variable.

When we first interviewed the child who had Nutsy and Nutsy, we witnessed the dynamic character of imaginary companions in the fantasy lives of children. The mother had previously told us that there were two Nutsys, a male and a female. When we asked the child how many pretend friends she had, she said she had many and held up both hands to indicate 10.

> EXP.: You have 10 Nutsys?
> CHILD: Yes, *lots* of Nutsys!
> EXP.: Are they boys or are they girls?
> CHILD: One is a boy, and one is a girl.

Now she was back to the usual way she thought about her pretend friends which continued throughout the rest of the interview. These sorts of inconsistencies do not make the child's report any less interesting, and should not be taken as evidence that there is nothing substantive in what the child says about his or her fantasy life. However, in contrast to children who alter the details of an imaginary friend from one time to the next, some children *completely* change the description, or cannot remember anything about an imaginary companion they discussed a week earlier. For example, one child we interviewed described a wonderful giant penguin who tended to get into trouble for knocking over lampposts (his mother, who was watching the interview from behind a one-way mirror, was absolutely transfixed!). A week later, he said he didn't have an imaginary companion, and looked at us blankly when we asked him about the penguin. We suspect that the penguin made a cameo appearance in the child's fantasy life on the day that we brought up the topic of imaginary companions.

Adult memories of imaginary companions

Another way to find out about imaginary companions is to ask adults about their own childhoods. Adults often provide interesting and thoughtful accounts of their childhood imaginary companions. The insight gained from maturity allows them to speculate about why they created the imaginary companion, and they can often provide information about how long the fantasy friends lasted and why they disappeared. This account of two childhood imaginary companions, provided by a man in his 40s, exemplifies the rich detail that adults are sometimes able to report:

> Sometime before my sixth birthday, possibly when I was 3 or 4, I began to have two imaginary companions. These two folks were named Digger and Dewgy. They were with me for several years, and I remember them mostly as playmates, more specifically playing with me in the backyard, enough so that I would consider from this perspective of time and space, that they lived in the backyard. I don't remember them ever coming into the house, though I don't think it was forbidden or anything, it's just that I mostly remember going into the backyard to find them, like you would go to the neighborhood playground to meet your friends.
>
> Digger was my twin. He looked like me and spoke in pretty much the same voice. The major difference was that he was more serious. He was the leader, the person who initiated the games, designed the roads in the sandbox, tempted me to stay when my mother called me home. He was very smart and knew many answers to complex questions, like Why are there trees? Or where do you really come out if you dig straight down? I say he was my twin, but he was also bigger and stronger than me. We never fought. He was there to protect me from the unknowns of the woods. He was very brave and sometimes even daring. He looked out for the rest of us. He had a dog that wasn't really a dog. The dog's name was Dewgy. Dewgy was more than a mere dog. He was sort of a superdog. He was at least half human. He could talk and he liked to make jokes. He laughed a lot. Sometimes when Digger got too serious, Dewgy and I would smile at each other and nod knowingly. Dewgy walked mostly on his hind legs. He reminds me most closely of a cartoon character, maybe modeled after Goofy, only he wasn't clumsy or stupid. Dewgy was black with short hair, and he smelled like a dog only I don't remember him having dog breath. Sometimes Dewgy and I would rumble together, play tag, fall asleep next to each other in a thicket of red cedar. I was much more physical with Dewgy than I ever was with Digger. Dewgy and I loved each other freely and openly like a boy loves a dog. Digger and I were on more of an intellectual plane. Digger was the thinker and doer. Dewgy liked to play for the sheer joy of playing. He laughed for the joy of laughing. On the other hand, you always got the feeling that Dewgy would be there growling if there was ever any real danger. Together Dewgy and Digger watched the woods for you, they made it safe to go up the hill into the Kaschel's farm with the Big Rock and all the scary dairy cows.

I have found that the great variety in the descriptions collected from children is also present in the descriptions collected from adults. For example, one retrospective report described an imaginary companion created when our Iranian informant was 4 years old and growing up in Israel. His friend lived in the mirror, was always well dressed and professional looking, had a positive attitude about life, and liked to talk about business-related matters. He never slept because he was busy with work. Another adult remembered an invisible imaginary companion named Hermie who looked like a big fluffy cotton ball with facial features. Hermie appeared whenever the child tugged twice on her earlobe. Adults have also told us about The Green Gunkies (small green furry monsters who were funny, but tended to steal things from around the house), miniature bears, stone turtles, an invisible pidgeon named Che-Che, and many other interesting imaginary friends.

The problem with retrospective reports is that many children forget about their imaginary companions once they no longer need them (see Chapter 6). Even a few months later, children sometimes claim not to remember the friends they used to enjoy so much. For this reason, it is likely that memories for a large number of imaginary companions do not survive into adulthood. As a consequence, estimates of the incidence of imaginary companions based on adult memories tend to be quite low. Charles Schaefer, a psychologist at Fordham University in New York, asked 800 high school students, "As a child, did you ever have any imaginary companions (e.g., friends, animals)?"[34] (They did not specify if stuffed animals were to be included.) In this study, 18.25 percent of the students reported they had had an imaginary companion.

Another problem with retrospective reports is that the source of the memory is not clear. Many adults report that they don't remember firsthand having had an imaginary companion, but their parents tell them they did and have the anecdotes to prove it. Thus, adult answers to questions about their childhood imaginary companions are sometimes based on family stories, rather than actual memories of interacting with a pretend friend.

Multiple sources and repeated interviews

Now that I have described some of the complexities in trying to come up with believable information about imaginary companions, I'll describe the strategy that Stephanie Carlson and I used in a study with 152 3- and 4-year-olds.[35] We interviewed the parents and the children twice, with the two interviews occurring about one week apart.

By having two sources of information and asking about imaginary companions on two occasions, we avoided some of the problems I have described above.

At the time of the first meeting we asked the child about imaginary companions in the following way:

> Now I'm going to ask you some questions about friends. Some friends are real like the kids who live on your street, the ones you play with. And some friends are pretend friends. Pretend friends are ones that are make-believe, that you pretend are real. Do you have a pretend friend?

If the child answered "yes," he or she was asked a series of questions about the friend, including questions about its name, whether it was a toy or completely pretend, its gender, age, physical appearance, what the child liked and did not like about the friend, and where the friend lived and slept.

Here is the way we asked parents about imaginary companions at the time of the first interview:

> An imaginary companion is a very vivid imaginary character (person, animal) with which a child interacts during his/her play and daily activities. Sometimes the companion is entirely invisible; sometimes the companion takes the form of a stuffed animal or doll. An example of an imaginary companion based on a stuffed animal is Hobbes in the popular comic strip "Calvin and Hobbes." Does your child have an imaginary companion?

A week later, both the children and the parents were interviewed again. This time we used information we had collected a week earlier to clarify the responses of both the parents and the children. When we talked to the children, we first asked if they had an imaginary companion in exactly the same way as before. We were interested in finding out if children would be consistent in their descriptions of imaginary companions mentioned at the first interview. Some children said they didn't have an imaginary companion, but their parents had provided descriptions of imaginary companions a week earlier. If the child again reported that he or she did not have an imaginary companion, we asked about the one described by the parent (e.g., "Who is Baintor?"). These follow-up questions in which the pretend friend was mentioned by name were uniformly successful in eliciting descriptions from the children. Maybe these children simply had not understood our original question.

The information from the parents gathered at the first interview also helped to clear up another source of confusion. Some children have their own idiosyncratic way of referring to an imaginary companion. At the time of the first interview, parents sometimes told us that their child used another term, such as "fake friend," "ghost sister," or "friends who live in my house." In these cases, we used the child's own term to ask about imaginary companions at the time of the second interview.

We also used the information provided by the child in our second interview with the parent. If the child had named an imaginary companion that was not mentioned by the parent, we asked the parent if the description corresponded to any real friend or if they had any idea who the child was talking about. If the child had mentioned a stuffed animal or doll at the first interview, the parent was asked a series of questions about the extent of the child's interaction and play with the named toy.

On the basis of all the information collected from the parents and the children, children were categorized as having an imaginary companion if:

(1) the child provided a description of an imaginary companion at Session 1, named the same imaginary companion at Session 2, and the parent said the description did not correspond to a real friend or (in the case of stuffed animal) the parent said the child played with the toy a lot and treated it as if it were real (the parent did not have to independently identify the imaginary companion).

(2) the child said "yes" at Session 1 or Session 2 and named an imaginary companion described independently by the parent. or

(3) the child described different imaginary companions at the two sessions and the parent said the child had lots of imaginary companions (the parent might describe a third).

The child was categorized as not having an imaginary companion if:

(1) the child said "no" at both sessions, even if the parent said "yes."

(2) the parent said the child did not play much with a stuffed animal named as an imaginary companion by the child. or

(3) The child said "yes," but could not give any details (e.g., a name) for the imaginary companion.

Twenty-eight percent of the 152 children (42 children) met our criteria for having an imaginary companion. (The parents of an additional 19 children reported that their children had imaginary companions, but these children did not name the imaginary companions independently, and when asked about the imaginary companion named by the parent, they did not provide any information.) Twenty of the imaginary companions were invisible, and 22 were based on toys. The descriptions were tremendously varied. One child created pretend versions of her real friends, so that she could continue to play with them when they were not around (e.g., she had Rachel, her real friend, and "Fake Rachel," her pretend friend). Similarly, another child played regularly with MacKenzie, an imaginary companion based on her real cousin MacKenzie, who lived in another state. Here are some other examples of imaginary companions:

- Derek—a 91-year-old man who is only 2 feet tall but can "hit bears"
- Bobo—a monkey who plays hide-and-seek and sometimes messes up the bed
- Station Pheta—a boy with "big beady eyes and a big blue head"; his job is to hunt for sea anemones and dinosaurs at the beach
- The Girl—a 4-year-old girl who is "a beautiful person" and "wears pink all the time"
- Joshua—a possum who lives in San Francisco
- Baintor—an invisible boy who "lives in the light"; you can't see him because he is white
- Hekka—a 3-year-old invisible boy who is very small but "talks so much" and is "mean" sometimes

The table on the opposite page shows the number of boys and girls who created imaginary companions. In addition, this table shows that many of the children impersonated imaginary characters. We asked the children about impersonation in the following way:

- Do you ever pretend to be an animal?
  (What animal do you pretend to be?)
- Do you ever pretend to be a different person?
  (What person do you pretend to be?)
- Have you ever pretended to be anything else like a machine, airplane, or something like that?
  (What sort of thing did you pretend to be?)

Imaginary companions (IC) of preschool children

	IC only	Impersonation only	Both IC and impersonation	Neither IC nor impersonation
Girls n=77	21 (27%)	4 (5%)	6 (8%)	46 (60%)
Boys n=75	9 (12%)	13 (17%)	6 (8%)	47 (63%)
Total n=152	30 (20%)	17 (11%)	12 (8%)	93 (61%)

Almost all the children reported that they sometimes pretended to be a person or an animal. Some of the imagined characters that were impersonated were quite unique (e.g., Mr. Electricity, Flashman of the World). Others were more mundane (e.g., cats, tigers, woodpeckers). Some children also pretended to be a machine (e.g., a vacuum cleaner), but this was much less common. To identify children who impersonated an imagined character on a regular basis, we had to rely on their parents' reports. Parents were asked the same questions as the children and, in addition, were asked:

- How often did your child pretend to be this animal (person, object)—only once or twice, occasionally, frequently, or every day?
- At what age and for what period of time?

The parents frequently reported this type of play, but for some children it seemed particularly important. Children were categorized as impersonators if the parent reported that their child pretended to be an animal or person *every day* for a period of at least one month. Nineteen percent of the 152 children (29 children) were categorized as impersonators. Twelve of these children also had imaginary companions. The 17 impersonators who did not have imaginary companions included four children whose parents reported a previous imaginary companion that was not mentioned by the child (e.g., one parent reported that her son had created an imaginary pet rat that went everywhere with him for several months). The table shows the number of boys and girls who were categorized as impersonators and the extent that this category overlapped with having an imaginary companion.

Our estimate that 28 percent of preschool children create imaginary companions may be a little low, reflecting our conservative approach to identifying children who had imaginary companions. Perhaps we should have included children who did not corroborate their parents' descriptions of imaginary companions. Some of these children may not have wanted to share their private fantasies with us, or may have forgotten about an imaginary companion, even though at one time it was important to them. It is also possible that some of the toys that were rejected as imaginary companions on the basis of the parent interview played a more significant role in the children's fantasy lives than the parents realized.

Despite these caveats, we think that 28 percent is a reasonable estimate for the incidence of imaginary companions for children up to 4 years of age. I used to think this number was a more global estimate of how common pretend friends are because 4 is the age that is usually mentioned as the peak time for imaginary companion production. However, I learned differently when Lynn Gerow, Carolyn Charlie, and I interviewed 100 of these same children when they were 6 and 7 years old. This group included 69 children who did not have an imaginary companion as preschoolers. A large number of these children (32 of the 69, or 46 percent) had created an imaginary companion after 4 years of age. The majority of these later-developing imaginary friends were invisible (81 percent). They included ordinary types of invisible boys and girls, along with a variety of interesting and exotic individuals. One girl described a blue-skinned friend named Simpy. Our first cases of an imaginary companion with a pierced ear, an invisible snowman, an invisible elephant, and an invisible squirrel were in this group.

If we consider all cases of imaginary companions created up to the age of 7, 63 percent of the children in our study had them. If we include only the invisible friends, 43 percent of the children had them. Any way you look at it, lots of children have imaginary companions. It is an elaborate type of imaginative activity that is surprisingly common. What are they like? What stands out most to me is how extremely varied they are. I have been talking to children, parents, and other adults about imaginary companions for several years now, and I am always hearing about new and different kinds. When it comes to imaginary companions, variability is the name of the game. Now that we have discussed what counts as an imaginary companion and how to figure out who has one, let's turn our attention to the children themselves. Who are these big-time pretenders?

3

The Characteristics of Children Who Create Imaginary Companions

▼

From the wildness of my heart I cannot exclude the question whether railway-engineers, if they had been brought up on more fantasy, might not have done better with all their abundant means than they commonly do.

— J.R.R. Tolkien

Nот all children create imaginary companions. What can be said about the children who do? Is there any truth to the idea that these children are especially bright and creative, but perhaps too shy or socially awkward to develop friendships with real children? What about the Hollywood portrayal of such children as emotionally damaged or lacking a firm grasp of reality? The purpose of this chapter is to describe what the most recent research has revealed about children with imaginary companions. Along the way, I will point out why overly negative stereotypes of these children have been generated and perpetuated.

Personality and behavior

One of the earliest papers published on imaginary companions described the children who created them as tending to have a "nervous temperament."[1] Other researchers have generated much longer lists of the shortcomings and problems believed to characterize children with imaginary companions. For example, Margaret Svendsen reported that 35 of 40 children with imaginary companions (ages 3 to

16 years) were described by their parents as having some type of personality problem, including "timidity in the presence of other children; a domineering manner with other children, fear in physical activity, sensitivity; an undemonstrative manner and reserved demeanor; evasiveness and irresponsibility; eagerness for being in the limelight and fear of being outdone, and evidence of dissatisfaction with the role of his sex."[2]

In another commonly cited (but dated) study, Ames and Learned assert, partly on the basis of parent interviews, that all children with imaginary companions must have some personality defect, with the type of imaginary companion indicative of the particular problem. They were especially negative about the children whose imaginary friends were animals:

> It appears to be characteristic of children who have imaginary animals as playmates that they are children who have adjustment difficulties, particularly difficulties in social, i.e., interpersonal, adjustments. The animals seem to some extent to take the place of unsatisfactory or unacquired human friends. The following phrases descriptive of personality occur in the records of their cases: "gets along badly with children"; "very fearful of new people"; "dependent on mother and aversion to children, slow to adjust to a group and plays quietly by herself"; "dictatorial, plays poorly with contemporaries"; "moody, negative, explosive, slightly dependent"; "a very dependent child, a lone wolf in school"; "negative, strong tendency to react by opposites, slow to adjust to new people."[3]

From all this, one might conclude that children with imaginary companions have a lot of problems. But there is a fundamental flaw in these early studies. What they share, in addition to negative views on the personalities and behaviors of children with imaginary companions, is a failure to compare the characteristics of these children with those of children who do not have imaginary companions. How many of these personality characteristics and behavior problems might have been generated by the parents of children who did not have imaginary companions? This is a crucial piece of missing information because we are not interested in whether children with imaginary companions have problems, but whether those problems are actually more common among children with imaginary companions than children without imaginary companions. Any group of parents—those of musical children, of red-headed children, of children who live in Nova Scotia, as well as the parents of children with imaginary companions—would be able to generate a list of less-than-desirable attributes of their offspring. However, such lists provide *no* information about whether these problems are uniquely associated with being musical, having red hair, living in Nova Scotia, or having an imaginary companion. The lack of an appropriate comparison or control group makes a list of problems generated by any single group of parents impossible to interpret.

One might argue that although it would be nice to have a control group, the negativity in these descriptions of children with imaginary companions is striking, and unlikely to be neutralized when compared with descriptions of other children. But many early studies have a second problem that helps to explain why these children sound out of the ordinary. Researchers tended to recruit for their studies children who were particularly likely to have emotional or behavioral problems. For example, about half of the children in the Ames and Learned study were enrolled in a guidance nursery at the Yale Clinic of Child Development, and the other half were recruited from the private practice of a mental health professional. In another well-known study conducted in the 1940s, the children were patients on the Children's Ward of Bellevue Psychiatric Hospital.[4]

What happens when a nonclinical random sample of children is studied (instead of the outpatients of a clinic or some other biased group) and when children who have imaginary companions are compared with children who do not have fantasy friends? A much more positive picture emerges. For example, no significant differences between the two groups of children are detected in the incidence of a wide range of behavior problems (e.g., restlessness, masturbation, jealousy, thumb sucking, fearfulness, attention seeking, hair pulling, etc.), and some positive behaviors are more common among children with imaginary companions (e.g., more cooperative with adults, less aggressive play).[5]

Perhaps the most comprehensive study comparing the personalities of children with and without imaginary companions was conducted by Jennifer Mauro.[6] In her research, children with imaginary companions were interviewed three times over a period of three years, beginning when the children were about 4 years of age.[7] Their responses were compared with those of a group similar in age, gender, and socioeconomic background who did not have imaginary companions.

Mauro assessed temperament by asking the parents to fill out the

Child Behavior Checklist, a questionnaire about children's reactions to common childhood situations. The checklist includes assessments of 15 aspects of temperament that vary among young children and are related to personality characteristics in adults.[8] On 13 of the 15, children with and without imaginary companions did not differ.[9] The two groups were markedly similar in most respects. Interesting differences emerged, however, between the two groups of children in shyness and attentional focusing. Each of these differences will be discussed in turn.

Shyness

Thirteen questions on the Child Behavior Checklist concern shyness. Parents were asked to indicate on a scale from 1 to 7 whether statements such as the following were true of their children: "sometimes prefers to watch rather than join other children playing," "gets embarrassed when strangers pay a lot of attention to her/him." The parents of 4-year-old children with imaginary companions rated their children as *less* shy than the parents of children who did not have imaginary companions, debunking the myth that children who create imaginary companions are too shy to make real friends.

Other studies have yielded similar findings. Jerome Singer and Dorothy Singer observed 111 children playing at day cares over the course of a year and found that children who were identified as having imaginary companions were less fearful and anxious in their play with other children. They were also described as smiling and laughing more than children without imaginary companions.[10] In another study, college students who remembered having imaginary companions in childhood were found to be less neurotic, less introverted, more dominant in face-to-face situations, more self-confident, and more sociable than college students who did not remember any childhood pretend friends.[11]

Differences in shyness do not show up in every study. At the University of Texas in Austin, Martin Manosevitz and his colleagues found that preschool children with imaginary companions were rated as being more adept at talking and interacting with adults, but there were no differences between the two groups in the extent that parents described the children as shy and reserved as opposed to open and outgoing.[12] In addition, when the children in Mauro's research were retested at age 5, the difference between the two groups was less pronounced and failed to reach significance. By 7 years of age, the difference in shyness between the two groups of children had disappeared. Given that children with imaginary companions are not observed to be less shy than other children in every study and that the result does not hold up after the preschool years, it is best to think of this finding as intriguing but preliminary and in need of replication. In any case, it is not true that children with imaginary companions are typically *more* shy or introverted than other children.

Attentional focusing

Mauro also found a difference between children with and without imaginary companions in attentional focusing. Children were considered to be high on attentional focusing if their parents agreed with such statements as the following: "when picking up toys, usually keeps at the task until it's done," "sometimes becomes absorbed in a picture book and looks at it for a long time." In addition, the attentional focusing score was high if parents identified such statements as the following as *not* true of their child: "has a hard time concentrating on an activity when there are distracting noises," "often shifts rapidly from one activity to another."

Overall, the degree of focus detected in children with imaginary companions by their parents was greater than that detected in children without imaginary companions. As in the case of shyness, the differences between children with and without imaginary companions in attentional focusing decreased with age. When the children were tested at age 7, there was no longer a difference between the two groups.

In research related to attentional focusing, J. Singer assessed children's ability to wait quietly in the context of a game.[13] He was interested in the possibility that imaginative children, who presumably have a rich inner life, would be able to sit quietly doing nothing for longer periods of time than other children. Although being imaginative is not the same as having an imaginary companion, the two are closely related in the context of this research. In fact, the question "Do you have a make-believe friend?" was one of four questions designed to identify children as high in imaginative predisposition.

In one of these studies, children between the ages of 6 and 9 were asked to pretend to be spacemen by sitting quietly in a "space cap-sule" for as long as possible. As predicted, the children who had been categorized as high in imaginative predisposition were able to sit qui-etly for longer than the other children. Singer and Singer concluded, "The predisposition of fantasy play as a personality trait may play an important part in children's capacity to tolerate delay or wait quietly in situations in which external stimulation is minimal. . . . Imagina-tive play may be an important asset in the socialization process, which eventually helps children to develop the capacity for deferring immediate satisfaction that is part of growing up."[14]

It should be noted that not every study has found a difference in waiting ability between children with and without imaginary com-panions. Manosevitz and his colleagues assessed waiting ability by seating children (average age was 5 years, 9 months) on the floor sur-rounded by heavy cardboard.[15] The child was instructed that to be a "good driver, you have to sit real still, watch the road, and not talk or turn around." The researcher said, "Go," and then recorded the number of seconds children remained seated without moving or speaking. Although children with imaginary companions were able to sit still a little longer than children without imaginary companions (215.4 seconds compared with 171.3 seconds), this difference was not statistically significant.[16]

In summary, comparisons of children with and without imaginary companions suggest that children who have pretend friends are bet-ter able to focus their attention than other children, but as was found for shyness, the difference between the two groups of children is not found in every study. These results, combined with Mauro's finding that the two groups of children were rated as equivalent on 13 out 15 aspects of temperament, indicate that, overall, the per-sonality similarities between children with and without imaginary companions are far more striking than their differences.

Intelligence

Although in the past the personalities of children with imaginary companions have been maligned, their intellects have been seen in a more positive light. Early researchers linked the creation of an imag-inary companion with superior intelligence, and several studies have shown that children with imaginary companions tend to score above average on IQ tests.[17] In addition, when children with imaginary companions are compared with children who do not have imaginary companions, some studies have reported small but significant differences in intelligence.[18] Despite these results, the evidence for an association between imaginary companions and superior intelligence is not compelling. Although many of the older studies report higher levels of intelligence for children with imaginary companions, not all of them do, and one of the most carefully conducted recent studies shows no difference in intelligence.[19]

Why are the research results so inconsistent? Probably the answer has to do with variability in the assessment of intelligence, in the socioeconomic backgrounds of the children who participated in the studies, as well as in the criteria used to categorize children as having imaginary companions. Intelligence has many facets, only some of which might be related to the ability to create an imaginary friend.[20] For example, there is some evidence that the link between having an imaginary companion and doing well on intelligence tests might be limited to tests of verbal abilities. Mauro found that children with imaginary companions scored significantly higher on the vocabulary subtest of the WISC-R, a comprehensive test of intelligence designed for use with young children, but there was no difference in scores on the block design subtest, which assesses spatial abilities.[21] Stephanie Carlson and I found a similar difference in verbal intelligence between children with and without imaginary companions, as assessed by the Peabody Picture Vocabulary Test, a widely used test of verbal intelligence in which the child's task is to point to the picture considered to illustrate best the meaning of a word presented orally by the experimenter.[22] However, the studies which report differences in verbal intelligence tend to include children from a range of socioeconomic backgrounds. When predominantly upper-middle-class children are tested, no differences between children with and without imaginary companions are found in verbal intelligence.[23]

In summary, despite some results suggesting that children with imaginary companions might be superior in intelligence, it is not true that all intelligent children create imaginary companions nor that only highly intelligent children create them. Not all studies show a difference between children with and without imaginary companions, and when a difference is found, it tends to be small and pertain only to verbal intelligence. It probably takes some degree of intelligence to create an imaginary friend—we have found that children who are well below average in intelligence are unlikely to have one. But many children of average intelligence invent pretend friends, and the absence of an imaginary companion says *nothing* about the child's intellectual abilities.

Creativity

Children can be extremely creative, and nowhere is this more apparent than in their invention of pretend beings endowed with curious names, odd details, and strange characteristics. The capacity of children to entertain themselves for long stretches of time by interacting with pretend friends reflects an impressive imagination. Whether such children are more creative than those who do not have imaginary companions is unclear. Although some research suggests a small difference in creativity, this difference has been extremely difficult to document.

A major problem is the challenge of devising methods for measuring creativity in young children. One commonly used test is to ask children to state all the ways they can think of to use a common object (e.g., a cup, knife, newspaper, coat hanger) and then to score their responses for number and uniqueness (the Uses test). Another way of assessing creativity is to show children a series of abstract patterns and ask them to report what they see in the patterns (the Abstract Patterns task). Children's responses are scored for quality, originality, and fluency. On these tests, children with and without imaginary companions score about the same.[24] Other tasks in which children respond to a series of pictures (Torrance's Thinking Creatively with Pictures, Penguin Picture Stories) also show no differences in creativity between children with and without imaginary companions.[25]

On the other hand, children with a proclivity for fantasy (categorized partly on the basis of whether they had an imaginary companion) tell more novel stories in responses to a set of verbal stimuli than children who are less interested in fantasy play, and children who have imaginary companions, particularly boys, are described as more imaginative in their free play than other children.[26] Charles Schaefer compared 400 adolescents who were categorized as creative on the basis of teacher evaluations and performance on two tests of creative thinking with 400 adolescents who were categorized as less creative. The majority of the adolescents who reported having had an imaginary companion (90 out of 146) were in the creative group.[27]

Perhaps the strongest evidence for differences in creativity is from Mauro's longitudinal study. When the children were 7 years old, she asked them to make a picture using a set of 48 geometric shapes and to describe it to her (the Gross Geometric Forms Test). The forms made by the children with imaginary companions were more recognizable to the experimenter, were given more appropriate names by the children, and were more likely to imply some action than the forms created by the other children. In addition, children who had imaginary companions were better able to describe the forms they had designed to the experimenter.

When differences in creativity are found, they favor children with imaginary companions, but overall, the differences in creativity, as measured on standard tests, are not overwhelming. Probably we do not find strong and consistent differences because, quite apart from the measurement problems, having an imaginary companion is only one of many ways to express creativity. I am always impressed with the imaginations of children who invent pretend friends, but not all highly creative children engage in this type of play. Certainly, parents should not interpret the absence of an imaginary companion as a negative reflection of their child's creative potential.

Family structure

Although children from families of every size create imaginary companions, first born and only children are somewhat more likely to do so.[28] In a questionnaire study with parents, children who were identified as having imaginary companions included significantly more firstborns (40 percent) than children who did not have imaginary companions (23 percent).[29] Although the difference in the percentages of only children in the two groups of children was not statistically significant in this study (33 percent vs. 26 percent), other samples of children with imaginary companions have tended to include many only children.[30] In fact, the majority of the children with imaginary companions studied by Svendsen had no siblings. There is mixed evidence regarding the extent that imaginary companions are associated with other types of family structures—the biological parents being divorced, separated, or deceased. In several studies, the breakup of a nuclear family has not been reliably associated with the creation of a pretend friend. However, the Yawkeys at Pennsylvania State University found that children in single-parent families showed more evidence of having active imaginations, including a greater number of imaginary companions.[31]

Many parents report that they first noticed the imaginary companion shortly after the birth of the second child in the family, a timing which suggests that the imaginary companion might have been created to help the child cope with the reduced access to parents or the general upheaval that accompanies a new birth (see Chapter 4). In addition, the finding that firstborn and only children are more likely to have imaginary companions suggests that children might turn to this kind of pretense when other play partners are not readily available. This also might be true for families in which children are spaced by several years. I know of one family in which the firstborn child is nine years older than the second child, who is four years older than the third child. All three children created a pair of invisible imaginary companions: The oldest child had Ratter and Tatter, the middle child had Mousey and Squirrel, and the youngest child had Sheagle and Beagle.

Overall, there does seem to be some relation between the number and spacing of children in a family and the inclination to create imaginary companions. However, it is not solely children who are firstborn or who have no siblings who create imaginary companions, and the appearance of an imaginary companion in the lives of these children is not necessarily a sign of loneliness or psychological distress. It is quite possible that children who do not have siblings close to their own age are simply more likely to have the kind of unstructured time alone that promotes this type of play.

Television viewing

Children with imaginary companions watch significantly less television than children without imaginary companions. That was the finding of a study by Singer and Singer, who asked parents to keep a log of the television their children watched over the course of a year.[32] The same finding was replicated in our own recent study, in which parents estimated the number of hours a day their children watched television.[33]

The relation between having an imaginary companion and watching less television is not surprising for a couple of reasons. When children talk about why they watch television, it becomes clear that television serves some of the same functions as imaginary companions—both are fun and provide company. A child who is bored or lonely can turn on the television set. Another solution would be to create a pretend friend. In addition, some of the impulses toward imaginative play might be displaced by television watching, which substitutes an externally generated fantasy world for one of the child's own invention.

It is also possible that children who watch a lot of television simply do not have time for imaginative play. According to Singer and Singer, watching television is not a bad thing in and of itself, but it does take away time from other kinds of activities. In order to develop imaginative kinds of play, children need unstructured time, but too often children with nothing to do are tempted to turn on the television. For some children this turns into a regular habit of watching television for several hours a day—hours that could be spent reading, playing outdoors, or in imaginative play. In fact, the average preschooler watches about 21 hours of television a week.[34] Although watching television can be an enjoyable way to pass the time, parents should remember that children who complain of having nothing to do eventually develop ways of entertaining themselves.

Theory of mind

During the preschool years, children acquire a considerable body of knowledge about their own mental life and that of others. For example, they become aware of mental states such as belief and desire, and begin to use their understanding of these mental states to explain and predict behavior. This type of knowledge is so fundamental to social understanding it has become a major area of developmental research known as children's developing "theory of mind."[35]

Developmental change in the child's theory of mind has been documented in a variety of ways, but the first important demonstrations were conducted by Heinz Wimmer, Josef Perner, and their colleagues in Salzburg, Austria.[36] In a "false belief" task which is now used in child development laboratories around the world, children are shown a box (e.g., a Band-Aid box) that typically contains objects familiar to young children. When the child opens the box, he or she discovers that it does not have the expected contents. For example, there might be crayons in the box. Then children are asked questions about what a person who saw the box, but not its contents, would think was inside and what the children themselves thought was in the box before they looked inside. Most 3- and many 4-year-olds make a striking kind of error when they answer these questions. They seem to have difficulty appreciating that it is possible to have a belief that does not correspond to the true state of the world, that is, a belief that is false. For example, once they learn that a Band-Aid box contains crayons, they predict that another person will think there are crayons in the box even before the person looks inside. They also report that they, themselves, originally thought the box contained crayons. (See the dialogue below for an example involving the discovery of pencils in a Smarties box, a candy familiar to Canadian and British children.) In contrast, older preschoolers have no difficulty realizing that they earlier had a false belief about the contents of the box, as would another person who had not had the opportunity to look inside the box.

Although the false belief task is the most common measure of theory of mind development, young children make other kinds of related

Interaction between researcher administering a false belief task and a child participant

Researcher:	Look, here's a box.
Child:	Smarties!
Researcher:	Let's look inside.
Child:	Okay.
Researcher:	Let's open it and look inside.
Child:	Oh . . . holy moly . . . pencils!
Researcher:	Now I'm going to put them back and close it up again. (Does so) Now . . . when you first saw the box, before we opened it, what did you think was inside it?
Child:	Pencils.
Researcher:	Nicky (child's friend) hasn't seen the box, what will he think is inside it?
Child:	Pencils.

(from J. W. Astington & A. Gopnik, *Knowing you've changed your mind: Children's understanding of representational change*, in A. W. Astington, P. L. Harris, & D. R. Olson [eds.] *Developing theories of mind* [pp. 193–206]. New York: Cambridge University Press, 1988, p. 195.)

FIGURE 3. *Picture of elephant shown in restricted view task. The section enclosed in the dotted lines is the nondescript part that many children think is sufficient for a person to be able to identify the whole as an elephant.*

errors that demonstrate their difficulty distinguishing between mental representations and the objects in the world that are being represented. For example, young children tend to have difficulty taking the perspective of someone who knows less than they do. They equate their own subjective interpretation of an event with an objective reality that is external to themselves and is shared with other people. Thus, when a child is shown a picture of an elephant that is then covered so that only the tip of the elephant's trunk is showing (as depicted above), the child tends to claim that the elephant is recognizable to a new person who sees only the small nondescript part.[37]

Children also equate appearance with reality when asked to make judgments about trick objects. For example, John Flavell and his colleagues at Stanford University showed children objects that looked like one kind of thing, but turned out to be something quite different (e.g., a piece of sponge that looks like a rock). Once the children figured out what the object really was, they incorrectly reported that it had the appearance of that sort of thing (e.g., they said that the fake rock looked like a sponge). They had a lot of difficulty reporting that an object had a misleading appearance.[38]

Children's ability to distinguish appearance from reality, to take false beliefs into account when reasoning about another person's behavior, and to appreciate that another person might interpret an object or event differently from themselves all develop during the preschool years and are interpreted as markers of children's developing "theory of mind." Does having an imaginary companion or engaging in other types of elaborate pretense promote the development of these insights? After all, imaginary companions frequently take part in family life—joining the family at the dinner table, the children at bath time and story time, and going along on family excursions. On these occasions, the child is the official commentator on the imaginary companion's activities and the translator of what it has to say. Perhaps there are cognitive consequences of becoming practiced in negotiating interactions between imaginary companions and real people. Once the distinction between internal mental representations of external stimuli and the stimuli themselves is mastered in pretend play, children might be better equipped to think about similar distinctions in other situations or contexts. In other words, they might have an advanced understanding of mental life.

Stephanie Carlson and I tested this hypothesis by giving children with and without imaginary companions a series of the tasks described above (e.g., the appearance/reality, false belief, and restricted view tasks), which all require the insight that mental representations may not constitute an accurate reflection of the external world.[39] We found that children who had imaginary companions did better on the theory of mind tasks than the other children. They were more likely to report that the fake rock looked like a rock although it was a sponge, to predict that another person would mistakenly think Band-Aids were in the Band-Aid box and that they themselves had originally thought the box contained Band-Aids, and that another person would not know an elephant was in a picture when only a small, nondescript part of the trunk was showing.[40]

The knowledge that mental representations are distinct from the objects and events that they represent is an insight which is fundamental to our understanding of other people. People act on the basis of how they believe the world to be (i.e., their subjective understanding), not on the actual state of the world (i.e., the objective reality). The possibility of a mismatch between what a person thinks to be the case and what actually is the case must be taken into account when we try to predict or explain the behavior of other people. Children with imaginary companions seem to be better able to imagine the perspective of another person in theory of mind tasks. This result complements other research showing that engaging in pretend play helps children make distinctions that can be applied more generally in understanding other people.[41]

Gender

One of the most frequently made claims about the differences between children with and without imaginary companions concerns their gender. In many studies, girls are reported to be more likely to create imaginary companions than boys.[42] Why do we find this gender difference? Is it because girls play with dolls, which are apt to be included as imaginary companions? Are boys less interested in imaginative play or more reluctant to reveal their fantasies to an experimenter?[43]

None of these possibilities accounts for the gender difference. Girls' fondness for dolls explains nothing: Studies with varying definitions (e.g., including or excluding stuffed animals and dolls) have found gender differences. In fact, boys seem to have as many imaginary companions based on toys as girls do.[44] It is also not the case that preschool boys are less involved in fantasy play than their female counterparts, or less likely to tell a researcher about their pretend play. We found that preschool boys and girls reported imaginary characters equally often. The gender difference may be partly due to how the children play with the character. Girls tend to create an imaginary character that functions as a companion; whereas many preschool boys impersonate imaginary characters instead of treating them as separate entities. For example, instead of pretending that Batman is a friend, a preschool boy might be likely to pretend that he is Batman.

One might ask if impersonating an imagined character is fundamentally different from having an imaginary companion. As I said in Chapter 2, I do not equate the two types of play, but consider them to be closely related. In our study, we collected information about both kinds of play and thus were able to compare children who had imaginary companions with children who impersonated and with a control group of children who engaged in neither type of pretend play. We found that children who had imaginary companions and children who impersonated imaginary characters were very similar in ways that distinguished both groups from the other children. For example, both impersonators and children with imaginary companions did well on theory of mind tasks, many of which involved taking the perspective of another person. Their theory of mind scores did not differ from each other, but both groups scored significantly higher than children in the control group. In addition, both groups of children scored significantly higher than children in the control group on a task used to assess the developmental level of the child's pretend play.[45]

In addition to the tendency of boys to impersonate imaginary characters, boys might be under-represented in groups of preschoolers identified as having imaginary companions because the boys haven't created them yet. While it is true that many more preschool girls than boys have imaginary companions, we found that the gender difference narrowed when we followed children up to the age of 7. Of the 32 children we interviewed who created imaginary companions between ages 4 and 7, over half were boys. And when adults are asked about the imaginary companions they had as children, men report having created an imaginary companion at older ages than women.[46]

In summary, the commonly stated claim that more girls than boys have imaginary companions is somewhat misleading. Gender differences in this type of play exist, but they might be partly due to the timetable for creating imaginary companions, with boys tending to create imaginary companions at older ages than girls. In addition, although both preschool boys and girls create imaginary characters, many of the boys impersonate the character, instead of imagining it as a companion. Reasons for a gender difference in how preschool children interact with an imaginary character will be discussed further in Chapter 4.

Attitudes of parents

Not surprisingly, there are substantial differences in adult reaction to and interpretation of childhood fantasy activities in general, and imaginary companions in particular. Some adults view imaginary companions in an extremely positive light and may even attempt to introduce the idea of an imaginary person to children who don't already have one. For example, Dr. Spock advises that children without a father might benefit from creating an imaginary one. Similarly, in an article in *Sesame Street Magazine*, parents are provided suggestions for introducing invisible guests into the child's pretend play (e.g., when the parent and child are pretending to drink tea, the parent might say, "Oh, Aunt Jane has come to see us! Could we pour her some tea?").[47]

Many parents would not go so far as to plant the idea of an imaginary companion in the child's head, but once they discover their child has one, they support the fantasy in a variety of ways. One of the children in our study began to express her interest in dolphins as soon as she was old enough to talk and created the first of several imaginary dolphin friends at about age 3. When I visited this child's home, the large collection of dolphin toys and dolphin pictures on the walls of her bedroom were obvious evidence of her parent's supportive attitude. At the time of this visit, the mother was wearing a dolphin T-shirt, which she had put on to please her daughter.

Sometimes the child involves family members in her game of pretense. A colleague of mine has a daughter who as a 3-year-old enjoyed fantasy games of impersonation that required the cooperation of the entire family. On her request, everyone shifted to alter identities on Wednesdays. The girl became a boy named Rainbow Cutter, the younger brother became a girl named Rainbow Cut, the mother became a little girl named Sweet Flower, and the father (who got the raw end of things, I think) became a piece of string named Hagar. The child's music lessons were also on Wednesdays, which was a little embarrassing for the mother, who didn't want other parents to think that she had named her child Rainbow Cutter (even the music teacher called her by this name), or that the little girl had only one outfit of clothing (the dress and vest she insisted on wearing whenever she assumed the identity of Rainbow Cutter).[48]

In another family, a 3-year-old insisted upon being known both at home and at school as Rabbit. For almost a year he routinely wore a sock pinned to the back of his pants to serve as a tail. His mother told me that when she attended events at her son's preschool, she wore a name tag that said "Rabbit's Mother" at his request. Parents often are drawn into the fantasy in some sort of way. One mother whose son had an imaginary dog described her involvement with the pretense: "He has Candy, a dog. When I go for a walk with *my* dog, we take Candy; we have to take Candy to the edge of the pavement. I think he can really see this dog. In fact, I said to my husband, I think *I* can see this dog!"[49]

The parents in these families and many others like them go along

FIGURE 4. *This scenario happens in real life. A friend told me recently that she is quite attached to her daughter's stuffed "Ernie" (a constant companion since the child was a toddler), and when he is lost, she often finds herself calling him by name as she searches. CALVIN AND HOBBES © 1987 Watterson. Dist. by UNIVERSAL PRESS SYNDICATE. Reprinted with permission. All rights reserved.*

with such games because they value imagination and hope to cultivate it in their children. And there is no question that parental support and encouragement promote children's engagement in fantasy. After decades of studying the development of imagination, Singer and Singer place the support of fantasy behavior by a key person in the child's life at the top of their list of common threads in early childhood that are linked to the development of fantasy. They base this conclusion on the results of their own empirical studies, as well as their extensive review of childhood memories reported in biographies of creative adults. These sources provide extensive evidence that adults can promote imagination in their children by treating children's inventions with delight and respect, and by providing children with time, a place, and simple props to stimulate their pretend play.[50]

However, not all parents are supportive of fantasy play. First of all, there are substantial cultural differences in the extent that play is viewed as a valuable activity. For example, when JoAnn Farver and Carolee Howes of UCLA compared the responses of 30 mothers in a community in northern California with those of 30 mothers in a small town in southern Mexico, they found that the American mothers believed play to be important for the educational benefits it provided their children, whereas the Mexican mothers considered play to be of no value in their children's development.[51] More research is

needed to document these types of cultural differences and investigate their implications.

There is also considerable variation within American culture in
attitudes about play. More specifically, I have encountered a variety
of reactions to imaginary companions, including many negative
ones, in the literature and in my own research with American children. Sometimes parents simply object to the nuisance factor of having an invisible entity in the household who must not be sat upon
and requires its own space at an already crowded dinner table.[52]
Other parents have more substantive concerns about imaginary
companions. They worry that pretend friends reflect some underlying confusion about fantasy and reality, that talking about a pretend
friend is equivalent to lying, or that this type of play is actually a
more serious activity involving communication with spiritual beings.
What impact do these negative attitudes have on children's fantasy
behavior? Do children create pretend friends even when their parents actively discourage it?

First let's consider the case of children whose parents worry that
an imaginary companion is indicative of fantasy/reality confusion or
psychological disturbance of some kind. In Newson and Newson's
British sample, many working-class parents in particular believed
that "there might be something disturbing about the mental health
of a child who seems to this extent out of touch with reality." These
parents, the Newsons wrote, "distrust an imagination which, they
believe, might later lead the child into plain dishonesty; or . . . regard
the child's stories as already constituting a threat to their control of
his behavior."[53] Here are some examples of parents expressing such
concerns:

> He's got a . . . I'll tell you what it is—it worries me sometimes—he's got
> a vivid imagination; and it goes on and on until he *lives* it; and sometimes,
> these imaginary people, you have to *feed* them with him, do you see what
> I mean? It worries me.

> Well, yes, I've often been worried about that. He—you know if he's on his
> own, he starts these imagining games; and he'll start talking to hisself,
> and then being the other guy you know, talking back, and I worried a bit
> about it; till, you know, I sort of thought . . . listened to him one day, and
> he says, "That was a good game of mine, wasn't it, Mom?" And I thought,
> well all right, he realizes it is a game, and I might as well let him go on.[54]

Often this concern is related to the parents' beliefs about the types of behavior that are appropriate for particular ages. Even parents who have some admiration for the creativity involved in a preschooler's invention of a pretend friend might express concern when the child is still playing with the imaginary companion beyond the preschool years. In Chapter 6, I will discuss the evidence that children become more and more secretive about their imaginary companions as they sense their parents' disapproval. In any case, Newson and Newson's work provides a number of examples of children who have imaginary companions despite the disapproval of their parents.

Child educators, as well as parents, have sometimes voiced concerns about the effects of children's involvement in fantasy. Maria Montessori, the first woman to receive a medical degree in Italy, espoused a view of early childhood education in which children were to be provided with materials that would help them discover real-world variations in shapes, sounds, and textures as a preparation for the learning of reading, writing, and mathematics. Although Montessori made important contributions to early childhood education and many of her ideas continue to be influential today, one of the major criticisms of her approach is the total focus on intellectual exercises and exclusion of imaginative play. "In the strictly utilitarian atmosphere of the Montessori classroom, there are none of the usual toy animals, dolls, trucks or dress-up costumes. Children in 'pure' Montessori schools are virtually restricted to materials she devised, which are intended to suppress fantasy and imaginative play. Children should not make believe, Montessori proclaimed; to encourage them along such lines is to encourage defects of character."[55]

Kornei Chukovsky, a well-known author of books for children in the former Soviet Union, describes a period of time in Russia in which a similarly negative view of fantasy was held in academic circles. Parents and educators were discouraged from telling fairy tales to young children because of the potential for confusing children about the real world. Chukovsky received the following letter criticizing the imaginative nature of the poetry he wrote for children.

> Shame on you, Comrade Chukovsky, for filling the heads of our children with all sorts of nonsense, such as that trees grow shoes. . . . Why do you

distort realistic facts? Children need socially useful information and not fantastic stories about white bears who cry cock-a-doodle-doo. This is not what we expect from our children's authors. We want them to clarify for the child the world that surrounds him, instead of confusing his brain with all kinds of nonsense.[56]

In response Chukovsky wrote that the nonsense that seemed so harmful to the author of the letter

> not only does not interfere with the child's orientation to the world that surrounds him, but, on the contrary, strengthens in his mind a sense of the real: and that it is precisely to further the education of children in reality that such nonsense verse should be offered to them. For the child is so constituted that in the first years of his existence we can plant realism in his mind not only directly, by acquainting him with the realities in his surroundings, but also by means of fantasy.[57]

Chukovsky's view of how children's understanding of reality and fantasy proceed hand in hand is echoed in more recent theorizing to be discussed in Chapter 5, when we turn to children's grasp of the fantasy/reality distinction. For now, I want to note that Chukovsky believed that the negative adult attitudes about fantasy did not substantially curb children's own pretend activities. He gives the example of the son of a noted Soviet authority on children's education who discouraged fantasy because he believed that it had a negative impact on children's understanding of the real world. Despite his father's views, the boy created a host of imaginary animals, including a red elephant who lived in his room, a bear named Cora, and a tiny baby tiger that sat in his hand and ate from a small plate beside his own at the dinner table. Chukovsky used this example to support his view that children will create their own fantasy tales to supplement any deficit in the stories provided by adults.

Some of the negativity expressed about imaginary companions concerns the view that fantasy behavior is similar to deceit and could lead to habitual lying if not monitored very carefully.[58] In fact, when lower-middle-class mothers were asked to rate different kinds of child behaviors, their ratings for incidences involving imaginary companions were similar to their ratings for incidences involving lies. The authors concluded that for these mothers, "fantasy and deceit were part of the same global category of children's behavior."[59]

Shirley Brice Heath of Stanford University found some evidence of a relation between a concern for truthfulness and negative attitudes about fantasy in her ethnographic work in a rural southern white community. Her observations on this topic primarily concern parental attitudes about their children's storytelling. From an early age, young children are taught culturally defined ways of telling stories that are acceptable to their community. The children in this study were strongly discouraged from telling any sort of story that did not conform closely to actual events. Stories with made-up or fanciful characters and imagined happenings were not enjoyed as evidence of the child's growing imagination. Instead, they were considered to be "lies, without a piece of truth."[60] If children described any event in which they interacted with a fantasy character, they were severely admonished. "To do so would shock the adults and cause them to accuse her of 'telling a story,' i.e., changing a real incident to make it a lie. In general, only children and the worst scoundrels are ever accused of lying. 'Thou shalt not lie' is an adage on the tip of everyone's tongue, and the community is on the lookout for offenders. 'Don't you tell me a story' means 'Don't tell me a lie.'"[61]

Heath provides some examples of children pretending even though their parents tended to equate pretending with lying. She describes how one small boy tried to claim that a toy truck that he had taken from another child had been made by another truck: "He got a big truck, it makes lotsa li'l trucks, 'n I got this one." When he was scolded for his lie, he replied, "Digger Dan talks."[62] He had recently seen a storybook at nursery school in which a mechanical crane named Digger Dan was personified. It had a face, a personality, and acted like a hero to little boys and other trucks. The boy seemed to be saying to his mother that his story was no more exaggerated than stories like the one about Digger Dan. In his play at nursery school, this boy created extended fantasies about trucks that flew, talked, and produced other trucks.

Cindy Dell Clark of DePaul University also found evidence of parental concern about fantasy as deceitful in an ethnographic study on culturally shared forms of fantasy.[63] In particular, parents who identified with fundamentalist Christianity were uncomfortable with cultural myths such as the one about Santa Claus because they were concerned that once their children found out the truth, they would start to question the existence of God. After all, if parents lied about Santa, how was the child to know the parents were not also lying about Jesus? Actually, many young children do seem to think Santa and God are connected in some way.[64] Children in Clark's research suggested that God and Santa must live next door to each other and be friends, that God made Santa, that Santa knows whether children have been good or bad because God told him, and that God is the one who asks Santa to give presents to children.

Although Clark found no evidence that when children learn there is no Santa, they routinely lose their faith in God, parents are sometimes directly questioned on this issue. "One father told of his son asking him if he was really Santa Claus. The father had admitted that he was, after which the boy thought for a while, and then asked if his father was also the Tooth Fairy. Again the father admitted that he was. The son then asked if the father was also the Easter Bunny, and when the father said yes, the son asked, 'Are you God, too?'"[65] Jehovah's Witnesses explicitly discourage parents from teaching children about Santa Claus because they believe that the Santa Claus myth will ultimately have a negative impact on children's belief in God. Clark provides the following quote from *The Watch Tower:* "One little fellow, sadly disillusioned about Santa Claus, said to a playmate: 'Yes, and I'm going to look into this "Jesus Christ" business too.'"[66]

Clark found that with only one exception, all the children of fundamentalist Christian parents in her study believed that Santa Claus was real, despite the influence of their churches and parents. The exception involved a mother who believed it was better to tell children the truth about Santa and that it was wrong to give Santa credit for gifts and blessings that should be credited to God. Her son's behavior had raised concerns at school because he told many of the other children that Santa was fake and he refused to join the other children in drawing Santa Claus on decorations for Christmas. When interviewed for this study, he pointed out to the interviewer that Santa was Satan with the letters changed.

The mention of Satan brings up the second type of concern that members of some fundamentalist groups have about fantasy, in general, and imaginary companions, in particular. This concern is espoused by fundamentalists who have a particular interest in or preoccupation with spiritual warfare. Parents with this belief system are very concerned about protecting their children from evil forces in the spiritual world. Imaginary companions are sometimes explicitly discussed in this context. For example, in one book on spiritual protection for children, parents are given the following advice: "Many children have imaginary 'friends' they play with. It can be harmless unless the imaginary friend is talking back. Then it is no longer imaginary. . . . A child's dependence on spirit 'friends' will eventually result in spiritual bondage. This must be identified as soon as possible. Satan disguises himself as an angel of light, so young children probably won't see the danger."[67] These authors go on to provide a prayer that parents should teach their children in which they confess to God that they have had an imaginary companion and they renounce this type of activity.

How common is it for parents to worry that an imaginary companion could result in spiritual harm via the devil? There are no studies that accurately document the prevalence of this point of view. In my research with 7-year-old children and their parents, two parents who identified themselves as fundamentalist Christians voiced this kind of concern. One mother told us, "Around our house we try to keep our kids from having imaginary companions. I think they are associated with the devil, and it would be very bad if they had imaginary companions. I try to emphasize that imaginary companions are bad so he doesn't have an imaginary companion." Another mother stated that imaginary companions were anti-Christ and that she was very concerned about her 6-year-old daughter's fantasies involving unicorns. Sometimes the little girl pretended to be a unicorn, shaking invisible wings and making fluttering sounds, and sometimes she seemed to be playing with an imaginary unicorn. According to her mother, this child played with a unicorn because "she wants to be free. She also wants to be a bird for the same reason." The mother told us that she sometimes played along with her daughter because she loved her, but she tried to hide her daughter's vivid imagination from other people and prayed every day for the devil to leave her child. This little girl was clearly very engaged with pretense, despite her mother's strong objections. Actually this was also the case for the little boy whose mother was quoted above. While his mother was telling the interviewer that imaginary companions are associated with the devil, the boy was telling a research assistant in the next room about his pretend moose friend. In this case, the mother was totally unaware of her son's fantasy.

Our finding that 2 percent of our sample associated imaginary companions with the devil is likely to underestimate the prevalence, because it is probable that fundamentalist parents are dubious about participation in psychological research. Certainly this was true when we conducted research in a Mennonite community.[68] We were interested in the Mennonite faith because our reading of the Men-

nonite literature suggests that this community has quite negative attitudes about children's fantasy. The nature of their objections differs from those of fundamentalist Christians concerned about
communications with the devil. Instead, in Mennonite society pretend play is seen, at best, as a waste of time. Mennonites believe that
free time or "idleness" is detrimental to children's development. At
worst, pretend play is considered a potential threat to the cohesion
of the group because of its association with individual freedom of expression.

A general rule in Mennonite communities is that personal development must not intrude upon the concerns of the group.[69] Thus,
adults discourage individual incentive for nonphysical activities because they are viewed as harmful to the group and might lead to personal pride and pompousness. This attitude reflects a concern for
any activity that makes one stand out from the crowd, including
imaginative play. Thus, Mennonite children are discouraged from
engaging in any fantasy play that is not directly related to their future
roles in the community as mothers, fathers, and farmers. Acceptable
reading material for children would be stories that represent an
American rural way of life and teach a moral lesson (such as the
value of hard work). Stories that have a play or fantasy orientation
are considered unacceptable. Mennonite parents "do not want their
children to read fairy tales or myths; many object to any stories that
are not true such as those in which animals talk and act like people
or stories that involve magic, such as 'The Pied Piper of Hamlin.'"[70]

Very little research has been conducted on the pretend play of
Mennonite children, with the exception of our small ethnographic
study designed to learn how attitudes about play vary as a function of
religion.[71] Carlson interviewed 18 teachers from Mennonite and
non-Mennonite private Christian elementary schools in rural Pennsylvania about their attitudes toward fantasy play, as well as their
practices relating to children's imagination. We were particularly interested in imaginary companions because restrictions on children's
activities or in their lives sometimes actually stimulate this kind of
private fantasy activity (see Chapter 4). For example, in her account
of growing up in a Mennonite community, Laura Weaver recalled
that she and many of her friends had imaginary companions who
were "fancy," and thus allowed to wear clothes and play with toys
that were off-limits to the children themselves.[72]

Although, overall, the Mennonite teachers were not as positive about *social* pretense as the non-Mennonite teachers, the reports concerning *private* fantasy activities painted a different picture. Specifically, the Mennonite teachers were more likely than the other teachers to say that they share their dreams and/or daydreams with their class and that they themselves have active imaginations. They also were more positive about imaginary companions. Unlike their non-Mennonite counterparts, at least some of the Mennonite teachers did not believe that imaginary companions were best grown out of as soon as possible. These teachers were also the only ones who reported that their students, or even they themselves, had imaginary companions. They tended to view having an imaginary companion as making up for a lack of social contact with real friends or siblings. Thus, some of these teachers agreed that they would talk to an imaginary companion for a child's benefit and believed that children would end this type of play on their own as they acquired real friends.

The most detailed account of an imaginary companion was a young Mennonite teacher's description of her own make-believe friend which she "kept" until age 15. The friend's name was "Rachel," and she was the same age and size as "Laura," the teacher. Rachel had blond hair, dark brown eyes, and pretty clothes (but not too fancy). She and Laura had the same abilities and did all the same things; they were inseparable best friends. Laura's favorite activities with Rachel were riding horses and working together as clerks in a store that she imagined their families owned (in reality her parents were farmers). Laura had four sisters and four brothers living at home while she was growing up, which suggests that, in this case, the imaginary companion was not an antidote to loneliness.

What about the Mennonite children? Does their behavior in any way reflect the attitudes documented by Carlson et al.? Carlson observed that these children did not seem to have the conceptual understanding of pretense that would be expected in most mainstream American 6-year-olds. For example, the children appeared to have difficulty with the language used to describe pretense. One day when the children gathered around to inspect a doll brought to school by one of the girls, a child said repeatedly, "It's not a right baby." When questioned by Carlson, it became apparent that the child meant to communicate that the doll was not real. This was only one of several incidences suggesting that the children did not have the vocabulary for talking about fantasy. In fact, one child asked, "What's pretend?"

when he came across this word in a book, and he appeared puzzled
by the researcher's attempts to explain its meaning.

Carlson found that on the playground Mennonite children's play
themes adhered more closely to everyday family roles and activities
than did children's play in the non-Mennonite Christian group, but
some of the Old Order Mennonite teachers suspected that a few of
the children in their classes had imaginary companions. For example, one teacher reported that she saw a third-grade boy talking to an
invisible friend and another boy talking to an imaginary dog. It is
possible that the children in orthodox Mennonite communities recognize what is acceptable—or at least tolerable—behavior in the
realms of social and nonsocial fantasy play.

The non-Mennonite Christian teachers in this study were more
suspicious of imaginary companions. Two of them voiced the concerns about psychopathology or demonic possession that we have
discussed as characterizing their fundamentalist orientation. One
teacher stated that although she encourages her class to be creative
(e.g., imagining their favorite place to be and writing about it), she
likes them to be realistic too. "I'd watch out for an imaginary friend.
Children should have real friends," she said. She added that a broken
home life can lead to the "wrong kind" of imagination. Another
teacher from a non-Mennonite Christian school reported that imaginary companions could lead a child into "demon occultist activity."
This teacher believed that manipulating make-believe entities in the
mind is like witchcraft and thus contrary to a true God.

Overall, it seems clear that the supportive attitudes of parents and
other adults are not *required* for children to create pretend friends.
The examples I have described indicate that parents' attempts at
curbing their children's fantasy behavior are not entirely successful;
at least some children engage in elaborate pretense anyway. The research with Mennonites points to the importance of examining religious and cultural influences on adult attitudes about both social
and nonsocial forms of pretense and fantasy. Although Mennonites
do not overtly encourage social pretend play, their views concerning
imaginary companions suggest that they are more approving of private, nonsocial fantasy.

In this chapter I have described some of the similarities and differences between children who do and do not create imaginary companions. Although children with imaginary companions might be

somewhat advanced in their social understanding, and at younger ages they seem a little less shy and more able to focus their attention, they are not much different from other children in most respects. I hope this discussion helps to dispel some of the myths about these children. In Chapter 4, I discuss the diverse roles imaginary companions play in children's lives. Why do children create them? One possibility suggested by the finding that children with imaginary companions tend to have fewer brothers and sisters is that children create pretend friends so they will have someone to play with when nobody else is around. This possibility along with a variety of other answers to this question will be considered next.

4

Why Do Children Create Imaginary Companions?

▼
▼

*T*HE *Cat in the Hat* by Dr. Seuss begins with two bored children who can't go outside to play because it is too cold and wet.[1] They are sitting around with nothing to do, when suddenly a tall black cat in a red top hat walks through the door and saves the day by entertaining the children for hours with his peculiarities. Everyone has a great time messing up the house until the grownups return. Scholars of popular culture differ in their interpretations of the title character of this story, but he sounds like an imaginary companion to me. For many children, someone like the Cat in the Hat would be an ideal solution to the problem of being stuck in the house on a rainy day, and it is likely that many imaginary companions have their beginnings in scenarios like the one described in Dr. Seuss's story. As discussed in Chapter 3, children who create imaginary companions tend to enjoy social interaction. It makes sense that they would invent companions when no one else is around and they want something interesting to do.

But imaginary companions can be much more than partners in play. They are all-purpose, extraordinarily useful beings. Not only can they provide companionship, they can bear the brunt of a child's anger, be blamed for mishaps, provide a reference point when bargaining with parents (e.g., "Bla Bla doesn't have to finish his dinner, why should I?"), or serve as a vehicle for communicating information that a child is reluctant to say more directly (e.g., "Poh is afraid he will go down the drain when he takes a bath"). The purpose of this chapter is to discuss all the various reasons a child might create imaginary companions and the purposes they serve in everyday life.

Outlining the needs met by imaginary companions is a complex task because the companions themselves are so diverse. However, it is often possible to tell a plausible story about the services an imaginary companion provides beyond the primary function of companionship by examining the match between child and companion on a case-by-case basis. The forms that they take, their activities—even their names—provide lots of clues about what the child is attending to in his or her environment. Singer and Singer report several examples of imaginary companions with revealing names—"Phena" and "Barbara Tall" were created by a preschooler who must have heard references to the medication used by her father, "Fetiss" was created by two girls whose mother was pregnant, and "Pigsty" was created by a child whose untidy room was a source of annoyance for the mother.[2]

Imaginary companions can also help children cope with psychological needs that are more substantive than a desire to escape blame or bargain with parents. In fact, many have design features that appear customized to meet the idiosyncratic psychological needs of the child creators. The descriptions of these imaginary companions are fascinating and make up the bulk of this chapter. I have had to rely primarily on case histories because, as far as I know, no comprehensive large-scale studies have systematically matched groups of children with specific kinds of imaginary companions. The problem with case histories, however, is that most have been collected by therapists trying to piece together an understanding of the inner experiences of troubled children. The insights of skilled clinicians are interesting and instructive, but these are exactly the kinds of writings that have contributed to the association of imaginary companions with emotional disturbance. Although some of these authors stress that the children were not referred because of their imaginary companions and the imaginary companions did not play a significant role in the children's treatment, the negative impression created of imaginary companions is hard to avoid.

The fact is many children with emotional problems and children living in stressful situations do have imaginary companions. Why? Because children use fantasy to help cope with problems. Imaginary companions love you when you feel rejected by others, listen when you need to talk to someone, and can be trusted not to repeat what you say. No wonder children who have been traumatized or abused often have them. The tricky point here is that although children with

FIGURE 5. *Drawing of the Butcher Shop Guy.*

problems often have imaginary companions, having an imaginary companion does not mean that the child has problems. With this point firmly in mind, let's consider some of the reasons children create imaginary companions.

Fun and companionship

I believe that fun and companionship are the primary reasons most children create imaginary companions. Some of the imaginary beings who fulfill these purposes are zany characters like the Cat in the Hat. They reflect the child's idiosyncratic interests, have characteristics that are not particularly logical or internally consistent, and evolve to suit the whims of their creators. One boy I know created the Butcher Shop Guy at age three. He was called the Butcher Shop Guy because he was fat, although he never worked in a butcher's shop. His appearance was a little strange—green skin and only one eye—but the Butcher Shop Guy was a very friendly person and a world traveler. Until the child was about 5 years old, he daydreamed about taking trips with him. A young girl who spent a lot of time practicing her violin provides another example of unusual pretend friends who provided great companionship. "I pretend that Bee-thoven, the Two Strausses, Wagner, and the rest of the composers are still living, and they go skating with me, and when I invite them to dinner, a place has to be set for them; and when I have so many that the table won't hold them all, I make my family sit on one side of their chair to make room for them."[3]

Other imaginary companions are more closely modeled after playmates of the child's own age, size, and gender—happy, active, and loving children with everyday names like Joel or Susan. Who could be a better partner in play than an imaginary friend? Unlike real children, they can be depended upon to play the game of the child's choice, go along with the child's spontaneous rules, and let the child win. They do not make unwelcome suggestions or insist on taking their turn when the child wants to extend her own. The child doesn't have to worry about an imaginary companion getting cranky and threatening to take his or her toys and go home. On the other hand, the child can walk out on the imaginary companion at any point without repercussion—the companion will be cheerfully ready to start up again at a moment's notice.[4]

Of course, interacting with an imaginary being is not every child's idea of fun. Children differ considerably in how much they enjoy pretending, with some children showing a distinct preference for fantasy play at a very early age. In fact, when Linda Acredolo and her colleagues at the University of California at Davis studied the play behavior of a group of children from infancy through the preschool years, they found that children who at age 4 created imaginary companions showed signs of being more interested in fantasy play than their peers even as infants.[5] These results suggest that children who create imaginary companions may have a long history of pronounced interest in fantasy play.

Loneliness

> They (a brother and sister imaginary companion) come when I am very lonely, not when I am playing with the boys. . . . They are a great comfort to me when I am all alone. (10-year-old child)[6]

Perhaps the claim that children create imaginary companions because they are lonely is only another way of saying that pretend friends provide companionship, but it has a more hollow sound to it. The case histories that have been used to document loneliness as a reason for creating an imaginary companion tend to describe a deeper aloneness than having no one to play with one day. Certainly, fantasy activities have helped many children through periods of profound loneliness in their lives. For example, fantasy probably played an important role in helping Francis Ford Coppola, the director of *The Godfather* and many other films, survive a year spent alone in his room as an eight-year-old recovering from polio.[7] He passed the time by reading and acting out stories with his puppets, an unusually intensive fantasy experience that may well have contributed to his choice of career.

According to Dr. Humberto Nagera, a professor of psychiatry at the University of Michigan Medical Center who has published many insightful accounts of the children in his clinic, feelings of loneliness, neglect, and rejection frequently motivate the creation of imaginary companions.[8] This claim has been made by several psychologists[9] and is consistent with some research findings. For example, the finding that only and firstborn children are more likely to have imaginary companions (as discussed in Chapter 3) suggests that when play partners are usually available (as is the case when one has siblings), children are less likely to create imaginary companions. Although most of the parents in my research have not been able to identify a specific cause for their children's imaginary companions, some have mentioned that one appeared when a new baby joined the family, a time when most children receive less attention from parents and may feel lonelier than usual. In fact, Nagera's case histories include several in which the child developed an imaginary companion when a sibling was born.

Tony was about three years old when his first sibling, a boy, was born. He was totally unprepared for this event. When Tony saw the baby for the first time, he looked away and from then on continued to ignore the baby. Immediately after the brother's birth, Tony pretended to have an imaginary friend by the name of 'Dackie' with whom he played and talked for hours at a time. Dackie was around most of the day, getting up in the morning with Tony and going to bed when Tony did. Dackie remained with Tony until he was five years old. Yet, at the age of ten, Tony still remembered Dackie, and when he was reminded of his imaginary companion, he laughed in a shy way.[10]

In the next example taken from Nagera's work, loneliness was not due to a lack of potential play partners—the patient was the fifth of seven children. Despite being from such a large family, he was very lonely as a child. He tried to be a good older brother but felt angry when the younger children would not do what he said. The creation of an imaginary blind brother began shortly after he punched one of his brothers and was accused of nearly blinding the boy. Nagera writes:

> The brother is younger, like his own brothers, but his blindness makes him totally dependent on him; he cannot go anywhere without him and never wants to leave him. Being with his older brother, walking with him, feeling his arm over his shoulders, or sitting close to him, is the happiest experience for the blind brother. There is no one else he wishes to be with, not anyone else who understands him as well. As they walk together they arouse everyone's attention. At first people say, "Look at the blind boy," but immediately afterward they say: "How fortunate he is to have this wonderful big brother, what an unusual child he is to be so good and helpful to his blind brother!" This part of the fantasy gave the patient the greatest satisfaction each time he thought of it, as it contained both the gratification of his exhibitionistic wishes—everyone looked—and the relief about his guilt for his destructive wishes, when he was praised for his kindness toward the younger brother.[11]

Although the imaginary blind brother probably provided this child with some relief from his loneliness, it also seems to have served a number of other psychological functions. For example, it suggests a theme of competence which appears in many other descriptions of imaginary companions.

Issues of Competence

Professor Susan Harter and Christine Chao at the University of Denver have argued that a child might fashion an imaginary companion in at least two different ways to help achieve feelings of competence or mastery.[12] One possibility is that a child might create an imaginary companion that is helpless and incompetent, making the child look good in comparison. On the other hand, by creating an imaginary companion that is exactly the opposite—extremely competent—the child acquires a powerful ally that might bolster his or her self-esteem.

Harter and Chao interviewed 40 children with imaginary companions (20 girls and 20 boys) to determine if the imaginary companions tended to be viewed as more or less competent than the children themselves. They found that girls tended to create imaginary companions that were particularly *in*competent—15 of the 20 girls created imaginary companions who were described as less competent than themselves. Boys, on the other hand, were more likely to create imaginary companions that were especially competent—14 of the 20 boys described imaginary companions that were more competent than the boys themselves.

Here are some of the things that girls had to say about their incompetent imaginary companions: "She doesn't know any colors, so I have to tell her"; "She just falls down when she tries to go hop"; "I can run faster than they can, so when they get tired they watch me run"; "I have to teach him his letters every day because he can't remember so good."[13] The following description provides a more detailed portrait of the kinds of imaginary companions typical of girls:

His name is Kitty Cat. When I'm doing puzzles, he gets them undone. He doesn't know how. He doesn't have friends, just me. He's usually bad. He usually falls off [the jungle gym] and I catch him; he's kinda scared so I get him down. He can't tie his shoes so I tie them for him, I tie his paws. He can't count, he just meows. He doesn't know how to swing, so I push him, but he falls off. I have to help him hop. He's scared at night, so I get him waked up and put him in my bed.[14]

In contrast, the spontaneous comments of the boys include: "He can run faster than all the other children"; "He is bigger than me, and he can draw better and skip better"; "On the jungle gym, he gets to the top fastest." Here is the description of a boy's imaginary companion that is given as an example of a competent pretend friend:

His name is Christian the Monster Magician, and he can do lots of things a lot! He's tall, he's big, he's bigger than me. He can jump so high, he can jump from the barbershop, where he cuts his hair, all the way home. He can jump pretty far, can't he? He can jump on both feet and make one foot go up and he can make magic, he can make a stilt come out of his foot! That's hard to walk on, high stilts, but that's what Christian can do, the highest stilts in the world! That's scary, but he's not scared. Not Christian the Monster Magician, no sir![15]

It is important to note that in their ratings of their own competence, the girls and boys did not differ. Thus, the gender difference in the type of imaginary companions the children created did not arise from differences in the children's own self-concepts. Instead, the results seem to reflect the sex-role stereotypes that preschool children already know very well. Girls believe that they need to be able to nurture and help, whereas boys are supposed to be strong and powerful. These themes are also reinforced in fantasy toys. The baby dolls and similar toys that girls typically play with provide a model for incompetent kinds of imaginary companions. In contrast, the doll figures that are given to boys—the action figure, superman type of character—suggest a different kind of fantasy. Although Harter and Chao focus on the imaginary companions that are completely pretend, children might be influenced by the types of fantasy toys that have been provided for them.

These results suggest a different method of dealing with issues of mastery for boys and girls. Boys create an imaginary companion that has the characteristics they would like to have themselves. Girls, on the other hand, play the role of the more competent individual in the relationship between the imaginary companion and self. Obviously, this gender difference is a general tendency, rather than what always occurs—the blind brother example provides a counterexample of a boy who created a less competent imaginary companion. Dipper, the flying dolphin described in Chapter 2, was created by a girl, but was one of the most powerful and competent imaginary companions I have encountered. In Chapter 6, I describe Alice, another extremely competent imaginary companion created by a girl. Alice saved the girl and her sister from a giant crocodile that tried to eat them, and was on hand "when the monstrous rat at my grandmother's was about to bite me and she came out of who-knows-where to save me at the right moment."

Despite these counterexamples, the finding that boys tend to have heroic and competent imaginary companions, whereas girls' imaginary companions tend to be incompetent is interesting. Perhaps Harter and Chao's result is related to the gender difference Carlson and I found in the kinds of fantasy play preschool boys and girls enjoy. In Chapter 3, I discussed our work showing that preschool girls create more imaginary companions than boys, but many boys create imaginary characters that they act out or impersonate. If Harter and

Chao's research can be interpreted as showing general tendencies in the kinds of characters boys and girls enjoy creating, then it is not surprising that many boys might choose to impersonate the imagined character rather than treat it as a separate entity. After all, characters who have special powers and are particularly competent are exactly the sort of beings it would be interesting to act out oneself. On the other hand, if girls tend to create characters that need to be helped and nurtured, then it makes sense that the character would be imagined as a separate individual. Thus, the tendency for girls to have imaginary companions and boys to impersonate an imagined character might be related to gender-linked differences in the characters that populate their imaginations in early childhood.

Restrictions or limitations in one's own life

The imaginary companions in our research have included many that were not subject to the same restrictions as the child (e.g., the imaginary companion did not have to eat foods it didn't like and did not have to go to bed at a particular time). Other imaginary companions were able to surpass their child creators in certain ways (e.g., on the day that one of the children in our study was given a small bowl of fish, the imaginary companion received a huge tank of sharks). These sorts of characteristics are quite commonplace in descriptions of imaginary companions. Another example is provided by Jean Piaget, who described how his daughter consoled herself, after failing to "tame" a grasshopper, by commenting on the ability of her imaginary friend Marecage to do so. "Marecage tamed a grasshopper. She had one that followed her everywhere; it went for walks with her and came home with her."[16]

As children encounter problems in their everyday lives or become frustrated in their efforts to accomplish a goal, they often make up stories about an imaginary companion overcoming the difficulty of the moment. Sometimes, however, the most central traits of the companion correspond to more pervasive types of restrictions or limitations in the child's life. For example, J. Singer and Streiner report that although the play of blind children generally is more reality oriented than the play of sighted children, almost all of the blind children in their sample had an imaginary companion who could see.[17] Although D. Singer did not find a similar pattern in a sample of deaf children, one autobiographical account of a hearing-impaired woman suggests that the imaginary companion she created as a 6-year-old played an important role in the expression of her feelings about being hard-of-hearing. In fact, when as an adult she wrote about her childhood experiences, she dedicated the book to him. Here is an excerpt:

> Wrinkel was invisible and inaudible, which left him free to do and say whatever he wanted. The first time he entered a room he found the exact center of the ceiling and drove in a large invisible staple. He tossed an invisible rope ladder through the staple, festooning it over the tops of pictures, curtain poles, and chandeliers, and climbed over people's heads, listening to their talk and making nonsense of it.
>
> Wrinkel was smarter than anybody—smarter than my sister Ann. For one thing, he was a boy. For another thing, though he could hear as perfectly as Ann could, he didn't care whether he heard perfectly or not. He chose to hear, and to act on what he heard, strictly as he had a mind to. . . .
>
> When people talked and talked and Wrinkel didn't make sense of what they said, that wasn't because he didn't hear it. It was because he liked to make nonsense by weaving his own name in and out of their sentences. . . .
>
> He killed people off for me all the time. He killed off all the ones I didn't like—the ones who cleared their throats pointedly or raised their voices at me, as if they thought I might not hear them. He killed off the deadpans, when they mumbled some question at me.[18]

In her book on play therapy, *Playing for Their Lives*, Dorothy Singer describes a little boy whose attention deficit disorder and hyperactivity affected his language development, making it difficult for him to understand what was being said and to express himself. With his imaginary friend, Petey, he had none of the frustrations involved in trying to communicate with real people. Singer writes:

> I watched as Marty "talked" to Petey. . . . His speech, racing along, was unintelligible to me, filled with nonsense words, his own private vocabulary, but obviously affording him pleasure. He was peaceful as he played—for the longest time he had remained with one game. . . . Petey was Marty's "friend." Petey made no demands on Marty. It didn't matter if Marty used gibberish to communicate with him."[19]

There are several case histories of imaginary companions created by children with different sorts of physical difficulties. For example, Wickes describes cases in which an imaginary companion helped a child compensate by not needing glasses or by being athletic.[20] A 10-year-old child seen as a patient by Bender and Vogel because of behavior problems—partly due to clumsiness, tics, and grimaces— had an imaginary monkey friend named Fatto who was graceful, agile, and strong: "Fatto can swim and jump over the Empire State Building."[21]

Bender and Vogel described Fatto as allowing the child to live out his desire to be physically strong and athletic because he could do things that the clumsy, awkward boy could not. These authors believe that imaginary companions generally play a positive constructive role in personality development because they help children compensate for some lack or deficiency in their experiences. They describe 14 case studies in which children seem to create imaginary companions in response to an unsatisfactory parent-child relationship or unsatisfactory experiences in the world because of unfavorable social or economic conditions. Bender and Vogel write, "Far from representing a willful and malicious 'flight from reality,' this phantasy represents the child's normal effort to compensate for a weak and inadequate reality to round out his incomplete life experiences and to help create a more integrated personality to deal with the conflicts of his individual life."[22]

As suggested above, the restrictions or limitations in children's lives that become thematically related to imaginary companions are not limited to the physical realm. One of the cases described by Frances Wickes concerned a little girl named Sally whose family had recently suffered substantial financial difficulties. The child invented a little girl named Sally the Second who dressed in a blue velvet coat trimmed with fur and whose rich father gave her everything she wanted.[23]

Sometimes the imaginary companion substitutes for a relationship that the child does not have in real life. For example, in their discussion of children's reactions to an absent or dead father, Burlingham and Freud mention the case of a young boy who created an imaginary father.[24] This child's mother was unmarried, and he had never known his father. Machtlinger discusses this case in the following way:

> Bob's fantasy father was better than everyone else ("his feet were bigger than anyone else's"; "he owned a big car with lots of wheels on it"; "he had golden hair and lovely pink eyes," etc.), and he grew very sensitive when anyone appeared not to accept his stories about his "father." What

is interesting about this child's fantasy father is that the change in the fantasies over time reflected the child's own developmental needs and thus mirrored the changes in the role of the father in the course of development.[25]

The fantasy father, one strategy for coping with the absence of a real father, also provides the child with a strong and powerful ally, as discussed in the section on competence. Once again, it is important to note that an imaginary companion can serve a variety of purposes.

Avoiding blame

There's a little girl called Choany he has had since he could talk. I think she must be his naughty self, because every time anything goes wrong, Choany has done it.

It's always Creep-Mouse. "Who's done it?"—"Oh, I haven't—Creep-Mouse has done it!"[26]

Imaginary companions are convenient scapegoats, and most of them probably serve in this way at one time or another. Princess Margaret of the House of Windsor is said to have used her imaginary companion to avoid blame. Whenever she was confronted by her nanny about having done something wrong, she would say, "It wasn't me—it was Cousin Halifax."[27] There are a couple of different interpretations of this function. One view is that using the imaginary companion as a scapegoat is part of the process in which these children develop self-control. In his discussion of this function Nagera writes,

Perhaps we will be less inclined to underestimate the value of the imaginary companion if we take into account that many of the controls that we demand of the very young child are often beyond his limited capacities. In this respect, we can again observe definite similarities with the role played by fantasying and fantasies in later life. Both are used in the attempt to solve conflicts and to restore, at least transitorily, the inner equilibrium before excessive stress forces a path into symptom formation, regression, or other disturbances.[28]

Similarly, Newson and Newson write,

We may look upon play not simply as a way of repeating life experiences in an attempt to master their emotional implications, nor solely as a rehearsal, symbolic or direct, of roles or of desires: but as the means by which the child tries out his emotions in a protected context, in preparation for the time when he will be held responsible for his actions and will be expected to exercise reasonable control over his feelings.[29]

The process of blaming and sometimes punishing the companion might also help children to identify and internalize the expectations of parents.[30] The imaginary companion embodies a characteristic or behavior that is deemed unacceptable and is distanced from the self by attributing it to the imaginary companion. In doing so, children try to avoid criticism from the parents and maintain their self-esteem, even though they have just done something wrong. According to Fraiberg,

> The child acquires a number of companions, imaginary ones, who personify his Vices like characters in a morality play. (The Virtues he keeps to himself. Charity, Good Works, Truth, Altruism, all dwell in harmony within him.) Hate, Selfishness, Uncleanliness, Envy, and a host of other evils are cast out like devils and forced to obtain other hosts. . . . When Daddy's pipes are broken, no one is more indignant than the two-year-old son under suspicion. "Gerald (the imaginary companion), did you break daddy's pipes?" he demands to know.[31]

I have known of several cases in which children have had two imaginary companions, one good and one bad (e.g., a good invisible person named Folkers and a bad invisible person named Favors). In some respects, this use of pretend friends resembles, at least superficially, the psychological process known as "splitting." When splitting occurs, a person's desirable and undesirable characteristics are separated into polar extremes. In psychopathology, splitting tends to be associated with serious disorders, such as borderline personality disorder, in which individuals show disturbances in basic identity or sense of self, and dissociative identity disorder, in which two or more distinct personalities exist within the same individual. These disorders should not be confused with the inclination of some children to associate primarily bad or primarily good characteristics with an imaginary companion. There is an order of magnitude between the two. Some clinicians believe that children's tendency to blame their imaginary companions for their misdeeds might actually help resolve issues about the child's behaviors and characteristics that others deem unacceptable. As Fraiberg suggests, "While a childhood dilemma might initiate the emergence of imaginary figures, suggesting a splitting pattern, an opportunity for the child to use her capacity for fantasy, usually with parental tolerance, may actually help resolve the dilemma and avert a more serious persistence of 'good me' and 'bad me' beliefs."[32]

Research investigating the relation between having an imaginary companion as a child and later-developing pathology shows that patients with borderline personality disorder are actually less likely to recall playing with imaginary companions than patients with other types of disorders. The relation between dissociative identity disorder and having an imaginary companion as a child is more complex and will be discussed later in this chapter. For now, the important point is that having an imaginary companion that embodies some negative characteristics should not be equated with the sort of splitting that occurs in psychopathology.

Fears

> Going to the bass-wood tree was an adventure, but we always felt safe with Aida Paida. She went to walk with us too. There was always a little circle of security about Aida Paida and we moved in it with her. Things that might have got us never could. Aida Paida never did anything to them, but they could never get at us. She made them keep their distance.[33]

Fantasy play of various types can play a powerful role in children's ability to overcome fear. This point was brought home to me by my daughter's reaction at age 3 to the gift of a small box described as containing a "baby ghost." Amber had developed a fear of ghosts that disrupted her sleep and made her anxious when left alone at bedtime. However, when asked if she would like to take care of the baby ghost, she was eager to do so. For more than a week she carried the box with its invisible contents with her wherever she went and was very much absorbed in this fantasy.[34] The baby ghost and its box were eventually abandoned for other toys, but Amber was never again bothered by a fear of ghosts. Conceptualizing the ghost in the box as something weak, tiny, and in need of care seemed to remove the scariness from her thoughts about ghosts in general.

The role that fantasy can play in the overcoming of fears is well known to play therapists. One clinical technique, known as emotive imagery, was specifically designed for helping children cope with their fears and anxieties by working hero images into stories involving the child's fears. For example, a child who is afraid of the dark and loves Superman might be told to imagine situations in which he is waiting in a dark place for instructions for helping Superman. Arnold Lazurus has found that the positive aspects of such imagery help children overcome their fears. "Some people may be concerned that the emotive imagery procedure plays tricks with a child's mind and encourages the child to daydream and to dwell on fantasy rather than reality," he writes. "I have treated many dozens of children with emotive imagery and have found no negative side effects. I have never come across a child who failed to differentiate fantasy from reality in the emotive imagery."[35]

Fantasy can be used in therapy in other ways that help children with their fears, as well as other types of issues. Nagera describes a 4-year-old boy who used stuffed animals (a crocodile and tiger) during sessions in which he felt anxious after being aggressive toward the therapist. For example, the child might kick the therapist and then warn that the stuffed animals would defend him if the therapist retaliated. This play developed into what might be described as imaginary companions. Nagera writes,

> Later in treatment when his fear of being smacked by the father increased—a fear that had a reality basis—he began to protect himself further by taking the two powerful allies home. If this was not allowed, he took them in his 'imagination' by pretending that he had put them into his pocket. In the following sessions he would comment spontaneously or in response to my questions how these animals had frightened his father, who then did not dare smack him.[36]

In these examples adults have scaffolded the child's use of fantasy, but children often discover fantasy solutions for dealing with fears by themselves. For example, John Gottman describes two children who frequently pretended to comfort dolls who were afraid of the dark.[37] The game was abruptly dropped when the children themselves were no longer afraid of the dark. The descriptions of many imaginary companions suggest that their creation was motivated at least partly by the need to master a fear.[38] Singer and Singer describe a child who, after being caught outside during a heavy rain, replaced her regular imaginary companion. When asked if a place should be set at the table for Louisa, the child announced, "Louisa was drownded in the big puddle!" Then she requested that a place be set for her new imaginary companion, Frogman, who was "not afraid of puddles."[39]

Anna Freud described a case of a boy (age 7) who had an imaginary tame tiger who loved and obeyed the boy but scared everyone else.[40] In another case study reported by Selma Fraiberg, a child created an imaginary companion named Laughing Tiger at a time when she was very afraid of animals, especially some dogs who lived nearby. The important thing about Laughing Tiger was that he laughed instead of growled and was extremely gentle and compliant. He was quite afraid of children, especially his creator, who tended to boss him around. The child's fear of animals immediately abated when Laughing Tiger first appeared, and by the time he disappeared the fear was essentially gone. Fraiberg notes that the child might have coped with her fears in much less productive ways, such as avoiding animals, not leaving the home, or staying close to her parents. "If we watch closely, we will see how the imaginary companions and enemies fade away at about the same time that the fear dissolves, which means that the child who has overcome his tigers in his play has learned to master his fear." [41]

A means of communicating with others

Sometimes it is easier to ask questions about a "friend's" situation or to describe the reactions of a "friend," than to talk about yourself. Hence, communications to doctors, psychologists, and other professionals are often prefaced by "I have a friend who wants to know . . ." or "I have a friend who has this problem . . ." Often it is clear to everyone involved in such communications that the person is actually talking about him or herself. There are many situations in which imaginary companions can provide a veil in just this way to make communication easier for a young child. For example, maybe the child is reluctant to admit being afraid of something, but wants some reassurance relevant to his or her fear. Singer and Singer describe a child whose imaginary companion, Poh, took baths with him. The child often asked the parent supervising the bath to make sure Poh did not go down the drain. The parents believed the child was using the companion to express his own fear of the drain, an interpretation that is consistent with their observation that he was very much relieved after hearing Mister Rogers sing the "You can't go down the drain" song.

One of the children studied by Newson and Newson used her companion for expressing negative emotions in a way that cushioned their possible impact. When upset with her mother, this child would say to her, "I don't love you, but Noddy (the imaginary companion) does!"[42] The continued love of Noddy may have seemed to the child to weaken the blow of her angry communication or indicate that in some part of herself she still loved her mother. Similarly, when Jean Piaget's daughter Jacqueline was upset with him, she would sometimes talk about the mean father of her imaginary companion Marecage. "Marecage has a horrid father. He calls her in when she's playing. . . . Her mother chose badly."[43] By maligning the father of an imaginary companion, this child was able to communicate all sorts of nasty feelings about her own father in an indirect, thinly disguised way that nevertheless felt safe. Another example is provided by a 3-year-old boy who claimed to have a pretend friend who lived in his throat. This boy had a habit of saying things like "My Throat says I don't like peas" or "Throat says I'm not sleepy." The mother sometimes asked her son to open his mouth so she could have it out with Throat directly.[44]

Parents can exploit the imaginary companion for their own communicative purposes. If you want to know how your child feels about a sensitive topic, you might try asking about the imaginary companion's feelings. It also can sometimes be easier for children to express difficult things by whispering to an imaginary companion in the presence of an adult, rather than by telling the adult directly. Therapists often use this technique: they suggest that the children whisper what they want to say to a stuffed animal in the therapy room.[45]

Response to trauma

> She gave me her undivided attention as I poured out all my hurts, all my betrayals, all my goodness and my badness. She never told. She never scolded me.[46]

This is how Mary Jane, a pretend girl with "the most beautiful chocolate skin, great big happy eyes, a million dollar smile and long black curly hair" was remembered by the woman who had created her as a child to help cope with life in a dysfunctional and chaotic family. No wonder she also recalled deep feelings of love for the little invisible girl. Many children use pretend play to help cope with terrible life events related to war, medical conditions, abuse, poverty, and loss.

In fact, children in the Auschwitz concentration camps were observed to play a game called "going to the gas chamber."[47]

Reports of the use of pretense by children who have been traumatized sometimes include descriptions of imaginary companions. In one case study, a 6-year-old boy whose paralytic mother actively rejected him and whose father was retarded developed a fantasy about being the leader of a gang.

> I got a gang. I got friends—three, six. They run away so I got running away (the child had run away from home). The biggest one is 14 years. I'm the littlest. I am the leader. They want me to be. They just sit there. They don't do anything else. The big boy got the idea first. His mother isn't good to him. That is why he runs away. His mother killed his father with a knife. I don't like my mother because the other boys don't like their mothers. I'm afraid my mother will kill my father. She doesn't like my father, nor me, or the baby—not anybody.[48]

Another example of an imaginary companion taken from Nagera's cases is Susan, an invisible friend created by a 5-year-old girl at the time that her parents divorced and her mother was hospitalized for mental illness.[49] Two older children in the family reacted with school difficulties, sleep disturbances, and regression (bed wetting). Nagera attributes Miriam's lack of these symptoms to the presence of her imaginary companion. Miriam looked after Susan (the imaginary companion), talking with her for hours, often asking questions such as, "What happened to Mummy?" Susan also was consulted for advice and seemed to function as a way for Miriam to express her feelings. Susan eventually faded away when Miriam developed a very close friendship with a child at her school.

In another case study, the child created several imaginary companions as part of her reaction to wartime changes in her life situation. This child lived for 18 months in a nursery set up for children during World War II. After the war she was reunited with her mother and a stepfather. The adjustment was very difficult as she missed her caretaker and the children in the nursery. According to her mother, "She has a brood of imaginary animals, cats and chickens which live with her and share all her activities. It is quite uncanny the way she looks at them, just as though she could really see them. Often she tells me off for clumsily kicking one of them or I have to lift them up over the pavement and am told that 'they are too small,' or 'they can't manage.'"[50]

Until 4 years of age, the little girl surrounded herself with this flock of imaginary animals, supplemented at times with other individuals, such as an imaginary husband. When she was 4, her mother reported, "We now have a pony living with us. It has red ears, a red nose, and red legs, and sleeps in the corner standing on two legs. Of course, he accompanies us everywhere, buses included, but I can generally persuade him to go into my shopping bag when the bus is too full." The interpretation given to these fantasies was that in helping and looking after the needs of these imaginary creatures, the little girl was somehow coping with her traumatic history.[51]

A boy who had been kidnapped and held for ransom at the age of 3 provided a vivid account of his imaginary companion to Lenore Terr, a child psychiatrist who is an expert on childhood trauma:

> I called my fake person "Olive." I named him for a jar of stuffed olives I saw on the table. I made him up a couple of years ago when I was five, and I still have him in my mind. Olive never speaks. . . . I pretend Olive is dead. I look up at the sky now and I see his face. Olive was just my age. He had black hair, a light blue face, and yellow eyes. . . . I made him up because I picked up a rotten olive. . . . On my birthday, Olive died. He was going outside, and he had a heart attack. I called the hospital. And they said they were all filled up. Then I didn't know what to do. Then Olive died.[52]

According to Terr, the child had "split off" the weaker, less positive aspects of himself to create Olive. She suggests that the boy's good adjustment after the kidnapping—his ability to do well in school, have many friends, and be well behaved—was in part due to the Olive fantasy. In therapy, she encouraged him to be more accepting of his own imperfections and accept the characteristics of Olive as part of himself.

When young children are injured in some way and have to spend time in the hospital or have repeated visits to the doctor, they can experience considerable trauma associated with the pain of the injury, fear about medical procedures, and anxiety about being separated from home and family. In her book *The Widening World of Childhood*, Lois Murphy gives a detailed description of how one 3-year-old coped with the traumatic events associated with an accidental amputation of his finger, which included surgery to reattach the finger, being given injections of penicillin over the course of treatment, and repeated visits to the doctor's office to have the dressing changed.

The office visits were particularly difficult for the child, in part because of the doctor's decision not to allow the mother in the treatment room. At the beginning of the appointment, the child typically had to be pried off his mother while screaming, "I want my Mommy!" About a week after these visits began, the boy told his mother that an elf named Woody had appeared in the treatment room to keep him company. After this first appearance, Woody turned up on a regular basis, both at home and at the doctor's office.

> Playing doctor, Sam said to me, "You take your medicine and you won't have to have penicillin." "You have to stay in the hospital all day and all night." When I asked him how I could manage to do that he told me there was a little elf, "Woody," who would stay with me, just like it was at Dr. H's office—Woody was there with him because I couldn't be with him.
>
> At Dr. H's office he cried hard when leaving me and while soaking his finger. . . . I asked him why he had made such a fuss at the doctor's office and he said, "Because Woody wasn't there—he was on vacation."
>
> Later, when we were making brownies he said, "Woody used to make brownies when he was a little boy—he told me that at Dr. H's office."[53]

Woody clearly played an important role in Sam's ability to cope with his injury. Once Woody started showing up in the treatment room, Sam's crying and fussing abated, and he became focused on asking the doctor detailed questions about the stitches, the shaping of the new fingernail, and so on. Later on, when Sam started school he experienced some difficulty with the separation from his mother, and once again Woody helped out by showing up at school when Sam needed him.

Another type of trauma in the lives of some children is physical and sexual abuse at the hands of a parent, neighbor, or relative. According to Dr. Frank Putnam, chief of the Unit on Dissociative Disorders at the National Institute of Health, about 89 percent of the children who are abused have imaginary companions.[54] Thus, it appears that abused children may frequently turn to fantasy as part of their response to their difficult life situations. In cases of severe and prolonged abuse, some individuals go on to develop dissociative identity disorder (previously known as multiple personality disorder).[55] As mentioned earlier, dissociative identity disorder is diagnosed when a person seems to have more than one distinct personality that at times take control of the person's body outside of their awareness. A person with dissociative identity disorder might suddenly realize that he or she cannot remember what has happened over the past few days or even months, a time when the alter personality was active.

What is the relationship between imaginary companions and the personalities of dissociative identity disorder? Unlike the alter personalities of dissociative identity disorder, the imaginary companion does not take over the body of the child, does not operate outside the child's awareness, and is involved in everyday interactions with the child. In some cases, however, an alter personality can be traced back to the imaginary companion a child had when she or he became the victim of abuse, or an imaginary companion that was invented to help the child cope with the abusive situation.[56] This does not in any way suggest that children who have imaginary companions are at risk for developing dissociative identity disorder. First of all, the vast majority of imaginary companions are created for reasons that are totally unrelated to abuse. In addition, although individuals with dissociative identity disorder almost always have a history of abuse, the victims of child abuse are relatively unlikely to develop alter personalities. Dissociative identity disorder is now being diagnosed more frequently than in the past, but it is still rare, certainly much rarer than child abuse. Finally, only a subset of people with dissociative identity disorder report having had imaginary companions as children.[57]

Still, it is possible to learn something about the characteristics of imaginary companions invented as a response to abuse from people with dissociative identity disorder. Dr. Barbara Sanders of the University of Connecticut has recently conducted research in which she interviewed patients diagnosed with dissociative identity disorder about imaginary companions. She found that 14 of the 22 patients who participated in her study remembered having imaginary companions as children.[58] Most of these companions were described as being playmates of the same age and sex. Although the primary function served by these entities was companionship, the patients also mentioned a variety of functions that were related to the experience of abuse. For example, the imaginary companions kept secrets, held memories, endured sex, pain, and abuse, and felt sad for these children. One was described as an impish brat who answered back and was defiant; another was a tall male bodyguard.

One description was very similar to that of an imaginary companion in my own research. The one described by Sanders was an energetic girl who had long curls and cleaned the house a lot. The child we interviewed told us about a "ghost sister" named Olivia who was the same size and age as the little girl herself. Olivia was a very good girl who cleaned the kitchen, swept the floor, and dusted the house. The girl's parents reported that she started to talk about Olivia shortly after she was sexually abused by a neighbor. The similarity in the descriptions of Olivia and the imaginary companion in Sanders's report raises the question of whether systematic differences might be found if the imaginary companions created by abused children were compared with those of nonabused children. Perhaps certain themes such as being particularly good, putting things in order, or cleaning behaviors might be relatively more common for the imaginary companions of abused children.

Sanders speculates that the experience of having an imaginary companion is quite different for abused children who go on to develop dissociative identity disorder as adults than for other children. She suggests that in the former case, the imaginary companion might be more likely to engage in actions which run counter to the child's wishes or for which the child is amnesic. An alternative possibility is that the vividness and intensity of the fantasy experience could be at the root of this perceived uncontrollability of the imaginary companion's actions. Even in cases in which no abuse has occurred, children who are intensely involved with their imaginary companions may sometimes feel unable to control their actions. (This point will be discussed more fully in Chapters 7 and 8.)

One of the noteworthy aspects of our interview with the child who created Olivia was that she talked about her openly and with affection, despite the fact that the timing of Olivia's arrival in the family suggested that the ghost sister had been created in response to abuse. This point is important because some psychologists have suggested that a child will talk freely about an imaginary companion only if it serves the normal purposes of fun and companionship.[59] Fantasies created to fulfill other needs are believed to be guarded as secrets by young children. However, our research suggests that children talk openly about their imaginary companions, even when they seem to have been created for special needs.

A final point is that the elaborate and imaginative play of the children described in this section is not the type of play that clinicians point to when describing troubled children. In fact, the play of abused and neglected children is usually found to be strikingly less creative than that of their peers.[60] In addition, abused children tend to show none of the joy and delight that routinely accompany the everyday play of other children. Lenore Terr characterizes the play that follows trauma as "grim and monotonous."[61] Left to their own devices in a play therapy room, abused children engage in activities that lack coherence, spontaneity, and positive affect. Their pretense appears unimaginative and literal, such as "the child who sweeps the floor, washes the play dishes and play clothes, carefully arranges stray toys, and then quietly waits for his or her parent to arrive."[62] Thus, although some children create imaginary companions as a response to trauma, this in itself is not a bad sign. It is the children who *lack* the capacity to play freely, creatively, and happily who are more likely to elicit the concern of clinicians.

A method of processing interesting or significant events and people

Interactions with imaginary companions often include elements from the real lives of the children. It is as if play with an imaginary companion provides a forum for mulling over or thinking about things that catch their attention. Many of the topics listed in this chapter—issues of mastery or competence, fears, communication to parents, responses to trauma, and so on—are examples of this, but it is important to point out that the events addressed in play with an imaginary companion can be mundane. The child can enact with the imaginary companion any situation or event. This activity often helps children to reduce the anxiety associated with the event and to gain understanding of it. For example, when someone in the family has an injury such as a broken arm, the child might pretend that the imaginary companion has a broken arm, and act out a variety of hospital and home scenarios associated with the injury.

Wickes describes how the children in a family killed off an imaginary companion after they attended a funeral. One of the children, now grown up, said,

> Mrs. Comphret lived under the cellar stairs. She was short and plump and comfortable, and she was always smiling. She wore a little black bonnet tied in a neat bow under her chin. . . .
> One day a neighbor died. There was a funeral, A "finneral" we children called it. We were very much impressed with the solemnity and

hush. It was not very real to us except as an impressive bit of drama, but in that way it seemed very mysterious and important. Then one day Mrs. Comphret died and had a "finneral." It was strange to have her go but she never came back. I knew she never would.[63]

An imaginary companion can also provide a way of thinking about things that the child has heard about, but not experienced firsthand—cultural backgrounds or lifestyles that intrigue the child. Jalongo describes a case in which a 4-year-old white child invented an imaginary companion who was a large Native American man. The mother of this child first became aware of the imaginary companion when she observed her daughter becoming agitated while looking at a storybook. Finally, the little girl slammed the book shut and left the room. The mother followed her into the next room and asked what was wrong. The child replied, "If there's one thing I can't stand, it's an Indian looking over my shoulder."[64]

Imagining her Indian companion allowed this child to have a connection with a culture that was not accessible to her in real life. Play can do this and much more for children. It is a natural medium for self-expression, communication, release of feelings, and mentally digesting experiences and situations. The capacity of young children to use their imaginary companions for all these purposes is truly impressive. In particular, children have a wonderful ability to draw upon the power of their imaginations to help them survive life difficulties.

But does a dark side lurk in all this use of fantasy in early childhood? Does too much pretending muddle children's grasp of the difference between fantasy and reality? Do they sometimes lose track and perhaps believe their imaginary companions are real? These are the questions I'll address in the next chapter.

5

Do Children Think Their Imaginary Companions Are Real?

▼

Once upon a time, I, Chuang-tzu, dreamed I was a butterfly, fluttering hither and thither. . . . Suddenly I was awakened. . . . Now I do not know whether I was a man dreaming I was a butterfly, or whether I am a butterfly now dreaming I am a man.

—ancient Chinese sage

"Real isn't how you are made," said the Skin Horse. "It's a thing that happens to you. When a child loves you for a long, long time, not just to play with, but REALLY loves you, then you become Real."

—Margery Williams, *The Velveteen Rabbit*

A COLLEAGUE recently told me about an incident involving her 6-year-old son and his constant companion, a small stuffed dog. On the first leg of a family trip, the boy inadvertently left his toy dog behind at a picnic site. The family had traveled many miles before the absence was noted, so the parents vetoed the child's request to go back immediately to retrieve the toy. The little boy handled this decision pretty well, but over the course of the weekend, he was preoccupied with thoughts about what the dog might be doing to pass the time while waiting for the family's return. It was clear that the fate of his toy dog was weighing on his mind. Two days later, the family embarked on the return journey home. As they neared the location of the picnic, the boy's excitement and the parents' uneasiness mounted. They warned their son that the toy might be gone, but nothing they could say affected their son's anticipation. When they reached the site, the little dog was seated at the picnic table, looking none the worse for wear. The child was overjoyed and hugged him tightly the rest of the way home.

Although the parents were relieved, their son's reaction was worrisome to them. What did it mean that he was so sure the dog would be "waiting" for them at the picnic site? Wasn't his joy at reunion a little overblown for a child his age? Episodes like this fuel the concern that children's relationships with their pretend friends are not completely healthy. In many homes, families spend hours each week searching for a misplaced stuffed animal whose presence seems to be a prerequisite for the child's happiness and the parents' peace of mind. One child who participated in my research expected the whole family to wait when they went out to a restaurant until a table large enough to accommodate her imaginary companions, as well as the rest of the family, was available. Another child insisted that the TV be turned on whenever the family went out so that the imaginary friend wouldn't be lonely when nobody was home. For many parents, flickers of worry are associated with such demands, as well as with other evidence of the intense relationship between their child and an imaginary friend. At the base of their uneasiness is the concern that the child does not have a firm grasp of reality. Is the child fully aware that the imaginary companion belongs to the domain of fantasy?

The question of how well children understand the distinction between fantasy and reality crops up in other contexts as well as those associated with imaginary companions. Children are introduced to the world of make-believe from an early age. They are told fairy tales and are taken to movies portraying talking animals, mermaids, and space creatures; they participate in family rituals where such characters as the Tooth Fairy, Santa Claus, and the Easter Bunny figure prominently, and they are actively encouraged to engage in pretend play.[1] Given all these different kinds of fantasy contexts, keeping track of what is real and what is not is a substantial undertaking. How well do children do?

Sometimes they appear surprisingly sophisticated in their ability to negotiate the boundary between fantasy and reality. For example, 3- and 4-year-old children are impressive in their early understanding of the words "real" and "pretend" and their ability to answer questions about the differences between real and pretend entities, and their understanding that imagining is a private mental process occurring in a person's mind.[2] In addition, when asked to sort a variety of objects into real and not-real boxes, children as young as 3 were 75 percent correct. They put the ghosts, monsters, and witches in the "make-believe" box and the dogs, houses, and bears in the "real-life" box.[3] Other research has shown that 3-year-old children realize that knowledge reflects reality more accurately than imagination and that objects they have been asked to imagine do not really exist.[4] And in the domain of their own pretend play, young children are masters by 5 or 6 years of age. They easily step in and out of their fantasy roles in an ongoing game to give stage directions to other children ("No, you are supposed to be the baby") or to deal with the interruptions of everyday life.

But these same children who are so comfortable with the dual worlds of fantasy and reality in their pretend play might believe there really is a Santa Claus or wake up wondering if a dream was real. They might not understand the difference between animals that once existed, such as dinosaurs, and creatures that belong to the realm of fantasy, such as unicorns. They sometimes mistake the events portrayed in a television program as being real or misconstrue the fantastical stories read to them at bedtime as attempts to educate them about the real world. Even in their own play, children sometimes appear confused. For example, if an adult plays the role of a monster too well, the child might become truly frightened and start to cry.

Many authors are struck by the difficulty children experience with some types of fantasy/reality distinctions and summarize the research findings as indicating that children have a tenuous grasp of reality. In fact, the claim that young children cannot distinguish fantasy from reality crops up in myriad contexts, baldly stated as truth in newspaper columns, magazines for parents, as well as in developmental textbooks. For example, the all-time most respected adviser of parents, Dr. Benjamin Spock, writes:

> This is an appropriate time, while we are discussing imaginary companions, to think about how rudimentary small children's grasp of reality is. It is difficult for inexperienced parents to realize that children sense very little difference between something that they have imagined and something that has actually happened. Small children can't tell the difference at first between a dream and waking life. It isn't very clear to them that a movie or television program is only a performance on a screen or on a

tube. . . . What they enjoy, what they want, what they fear, are apt to seem most real. Their awareness of reality may be dim in comparison. One of the most important everyday jobs that parents have to take on as a matter of course is to teach their children—gradually over the months and years—to distinguish between fantasy and fact.[5]

The view that young children cannot tell the difference between fantasy and reality is consistent with claims that young children really believe in fairies, dwarfs, and giants, and that children's fantasies have the same status as reality in shaping their personalities.[6] Dr. Spock is not the only child expert who supports this position. Many developmental psychologists also belong to the ranks of those who believe children are incompetent when it comes to negotiating the boundary between fantasy and reality. For example, according to Newson and Newson:

> On the whole, the four-year-old is protected from real dangers in a way which will necessarily have to change once he starts school; but from the perils which are conjured up by his imagination there is little protection, and it is to these that he is most vulnerable. He is probably now at the peak of his imaginative powers, without the firm grasp on reality which can allow an older child to subdue its fears; and because of this, the adult's reasoned assurances are often quite ineffective in calming a panicky four-year-old.[7]

In contrast, other researchers (myself included) are more impressed by how well children understand fantasy.[8] Very young children are inundated with fantasy information, often mixed seamlessly with real-world content. Children interact with adults who talk to stuffed animals as if the toys could understand, act as if mud pie is something desirable to eat, and react to a child's gentle push by falling violently to the ground. Professor Alan Leslie of Rutgers University has pointed out how remarkable it is that even very young children are somehow able to understand such acts as pretense.[9] To use Leslie's example, when Mother speaks into a banana as if it were a telephone, the child does not become confused about either bananas or phones. Even though 2- and 3-year-olds are cognitively immature in many respects, they seem to grasp the idea that some statements and behaviors are not meant to be interpreted as pertaining to the real everyday world.

So where do imaginary companions belong in this assortment of contradictory findings and claims? To answer this question, I have first discussed a range of overlapping kinds of fantasy: cultural myths and rituals, storybooks and television programs, magic, joint pretend play with other people, and dreams. This discussion provides a general overview of children's understanding of the distinction between fantasy and reality, and the context for considering children's understanding of this distinction more specifically as it relates to their imaginary companions. My view is that there are many different kinds of fantasy/reality distinctions, each requiring different sorts of insights and having a different developmental trajectory.[10]

There are probably numerous dimensions on which these fantasy experiences vary, but one that I suspect is particularly relevant to children's ability to differentiate fantasy and reality is the extent that children have some creative control over the experience. For example, in cultural myths and stories, fantasy usually is presented ready-made to children, but in the case of imaginary companions, the children tend to make up most everything for themselves.[11] My reading of the literature suggests that confusions about fantasy and reality are most prevalent in contexts where other people present the fantasy to children. When the children are the ones in control of the fantasy, they more often know exactly what is going on. Thus, my answer to the question raised in the title of this chapter is no: Young children do not think their imaginary companions are real. This conclusion is based on the results of empirical research in which children were questioned about the reality of their imaginary companions, and it also follows from the results of research investigating the kinds of fantasy that elicit confusion and the kinds that are most readily understood.

Cultural myths and rituals

Cultural myths exemplify fantasies in which children have little control. For example, children raised in a Christian tradition are told an elaborate story about a bearded man in a red suit, and they participate in rituals associated with him. But do they actually believe that Santa Claus is real? In some surveys, results are based on the parents' perceptions of their children's beliefs, while others rely on interviews with the children themselves. Regardless of method, the results consistently show that the majority of young children whose cultural background includes the celebration of Christmas believe that Santa Claus is real. Of the 4-year-olds interviewed in a 1978 study, 85 percent strongly believed in Santa, 5 percent were nonbelievers, and 10 percent were categorized as transitional (i.e., the child was not sure and gave the interviewer evidence for both sides of the debate).[12] Belief in Santa declines markedly between 4 and 8 years of age. In the same survey, 25 percent of the 8-year-olds were believers, 20 percent were nonbelievers, and 55 percent were transitional. Many children also believe in the reality of other fantasy characters. More recently, Karl Rosengren at the University of Illinois and researchers at the University of Michigan asked parents about their children's (ages 4 to 6 years) beliefs in fantasy characters and found that 81 percent of the children believed in Santa.[13] These studies also show that substantial numbers of children believe in the reality of dragons, witches, ghosts, monsters, and fairies, as well as assorted characters from books and movies—Batman, the Little Mermaid, and Mickey Mouse, among others.

Should we interpret belief in Santa Claus as evidence that a child has a poor grasp of fantasy and reality? I don't think so. There are many reasons why children believe, perhaps the most important being that parents, other family members, and the community at large often go to great lengths to convince children and to provide concrete evidence that the characters are real. Although parents sometimes express concern that their children are "losing touch with reality" when they are caught up in a game of pretense, many of

Children's belief in imaginary characters

	Belief in Santa Claus			Belief in Easter Bunny			Belief in Tooth Fairy		
Age[a]	4	6	8	4	6	8	4	6	8
Level of Belief									
Believer	85%	65%	25%	75%	60%	35%	20%	60%	60%
Disbeliever	5	10	20	15	20	60	5	20	35
Transitional	10	25	55	10	20	5	5	5	0
No knowledge	-	-	-	-	-	-	70	15	5

[a] At each age, n=20 (males and females combined).
Reprinted with permission from Prentice, N. M., Manosevitz, M., Hubbs, L. (1978). Imaginary figures of early childhood, *American Journal of Orthopsychiatry*, 48, 618–628, 622.

these same parents work hard to perpetuate the cultural myths of childhood. As Michael Burkett, a reporter for the weekly *New Times* in Phoenix, Arizona, writes, "I have, on various occasions told my son that babies are delivered by storks . . . that the Easter Bunny does indeed lay his own eggs . . . that the Tooth Fairy pays cash for lost teeth . . . that Santa Claus would climb through our air-conditioning vent (we don't have a chimney) and shower him with merchandise if he were very very good . . . that Lothar the Brat-Eating Cyclops would swallow him whole if he were very very bad . . ."[14]

In some respects, the practice of inundating young children with fantasy information is a curious one. We might think the job of parents would be devoting themselves to teaching children about the real world. After all, there is so much for children to learn. Discovering the general characteristics and properties of objects in their environment, learning about themselves and others, and developing expectations about the structure of social interactions are critically important tasks of early childhood. Most parents do teach these things, but they also tend to mix in all sorts of potentially misleading information. Consider the advice given by syndicated columnist John Rosemond to a parent who asked how to handle her 2-year-old's unrelenting "why" questions:

> It is, first, a request for information. As such, you should give information, but it isn't necessary that the information be scientifically correct. In fact, your answer can be total fiction as long as it relates in some way to the original question. For example, if your son asks "why" the sun goes down, you can answer, "Because it's tired and needs to sleep," or "because it's playing peek-a-boo with you." One answer is really as good as the next. It's even all right to give a different answer every time he asks the same question![15]

Whether or not you agree with what Rosemond says, it is commonplace to provide children with all manner of factually incorrect information about the world, including convincing arguments for the reality of fantasy characters. In her recent book on contemporary children's myths, Cindy Dell Clark presents extensive information about the practices of parents who want their children to believe in Santa Claus, the Tooth Fairy, and other favorites. Her anecdotes demonstrate the lengths to which parents will go to support and encourage their children's beliefs. One parent described her practice of writing notes to her children in very tiny script signed by the Tooth Fairy. Another mother fabricated the following story when her child became upset about losing a tooth down a drain:

> He couldn't leave his tooth for the Tooth Fairy if he didn't have the tooth.
> . . . And I said, "It's OK, Jimmy, I'll call Uncle Joe . . . and maybe he could take the sink apart and get the tooth." I wasn't really going to ask him to take the sink apart, but he had to get to school. And then I told him that night "they couldn't get it apart. But it happened to a friend of ours, when they did take it apart, they couldn't find the tooth anyway. But maybe if you left a letter for the Tooth Fairy." So he did and taped it to the front door.[16]

As mentioned earlier, similar practices designed to blur the fantasy/reality distinction are common at Christmastime. Many families leave cookies and milk out for Santa Claus on Christmas Eve and perhaps some treats for the reindeer. One of the parents interviewed by Clark described her son's reaction after inspecting the bunch of carrots she bought for the reindeer: "He was awfully worried that there was six and not eight carrots [for the eight reindeer] [laughter]. I just bought a bunch, the kind with the green stuff at the end [laughter]. I didn't look at them. Well, [my son] was furious with me."[17]

Our efforts to make Santa Claus real to young children do not stop with the immediate family. The entire community pitches in to encourage children to believe in him. Across North America, children are taken to meet Santa in person at malls, hear him interviewed on TV or radio, and even have the chance to talk to him on the phone. On the front page of the December 24 issue of my local newspaper, a 900 phone number was provided for those who wanted to find out how Santa was progressing on his whirlwind trip. Parents' commitment to the Santa Claus myth was demonstrated in the reactions elicited by a gym teacher at an elementary school in Washington state who told his students there was no Santa. The entire community was outraged. One angry parent was quoted as saying, "I think the majority of this community wants their kids to believe in Santa. Nobody has the right to rape our kids of that belief."[18] In an attempt to undo some of the "damage," teachers read *The Polar Express* by Chris van Allsburg to the children. In the story a child who has been told by a friend that there is no Santa takes a trip on a train to the North Pole where he sees Santa and his elves for himself, and brings home a bell from Santa's sleigh.

Children also are given a strong negative message about nonbelievers. Christmas movies often have the theme of how a nonbeliever learns there really is a Santa—*Miracle on 34th Street* is the classic example, and *The Santa Clause* a more recent version. In children's stories as well, belief in imaginary characters is highly valued. Consider the power attributed to children's belief in fairies in the story of Peter Pan. When children affirmed their belief by clapping their hands, Tinkerbell was brought back from the brink of death. In the case of Santa Claus, there is another message about nonbelievers that is communicated to children, either explicitly or implicitly: If the child fails to believe, maybe Santa will fail to visit. The consequences of not believing in Santa or Peter Pan might be ones children do not want to risk.

Still, some logical impossibilities in cultural myths do not escape the notice of even quite young children. How does Santa get into homes without chimneys or manage to transport all the toys needed for his task on one sleigh in a single night to children all around the world? How does the Tooth Fairy know when a child has lost a tooth? The authors of some children's books have developed stories which present ways to deal with these difficulties. For example, *The Real Tooth Fairy* by Marilyn Kaye explains why a child who is pretending to be asleep might see her parent, instead of a fairy, exchange a quarter for the tooth under the pillow.[19] The child in the story is told that the Tooth Fairy changes her appearance to that of someone the child loves when she makes her visits. According to the story, the Tooth Fairy adopted this strategy because once a child woke during her visit and was frightened to see a stranger in the room.

What about the young children who never fully believe in fantasy characters? Have psychologists identified the characteristics that distinguish these young skeptics from children who are more accepting? Some psychologists have hypothesized that children who believe in cultural myths might be the ones who engaged in fantasy in other parts of their lives—children who have imaginary companions or in some way demonstrate an unusual absorption or interest in fantasy. However, children who spend a lot of time playing fantasy games, who have imaginary companions, or report having many dreams are no more likely to believe in fantasy characters than other children.[20] What research does indicate is that the extent to which parents promote these beliefs is a much better predictor of how fully the child believes than the child's overall interest in fantasy. The children of parents who support and encourage their children to think fantasy characters are real (e.g., take them to the mall to see Santa) are more likely to express belief than the children of parents who discourage or are ambivalent about their children's acceptance of cultural myths.[21] This finding underscores the importance of socialization in promoting children's beliefs.

Given all the efforts of parents and others, it is not surprising that most preschoolers truly do believe in Santa and may be quite convinced that a host of other imaginary beings exist as well. As Cindy Clark points out, parents perpetuate these cultural myths as much for themselves as for their children. Parents enjoy vicariously experiencing the excitement of a visit from Santa or the Tooth Fairy. Some parents associate belief in fantasy characters with the innocence of childhood and do not look forward to the time when their children no longer believe.

> I think I might, the day I have to explain about Santa and the Tooth Fairy, I think I'll be a little crushed. Because it's almost like a magic spell I've broken a part of, another sign of growing up, when this [ends,] the fairy tale, the imagination. 'Cause you want to cushion your kids. And you'd love to think you can cushion them all their life.[22]

Beliefs in cultural myths may do more than preserve childhood innocence. They support the development of children's imagination and may even contribute to the developing capacity to trust and have faith. This latter point was raised by some of the mothers in Clark's research who suggested that children's participation in rituals involving cultural myths and their beliefs in fantasy characters contribute to children's ability to accept something in the absence of concrete evidence, to believe in something they cannot see for themselves. This experience was believed to be related to the capacity for religious faith.[23]

But the point I want to make here is not that beliefs in fantasy characters are beneficial for young children (although I suspect that they are). My point is that children's belief in cultural myths should *not* be taken as evidence that they are generally confused about fantasy and have no ability to sort out what is real from what is not.

Children are not the originators of cultural myths; they are told about them in the same way as they are told about characters and events that are meant to be understood as real or to really have happened (e.g., the way they are told about dinosaurs or stories from the Bible). In addition, parents take concrete steps to blur the fantasy/reality boundary by leaving traces of the characters' actions.[24] Actually, it is quite impressive that by at least 8 years of age, the majority of children have figured out that Santa Claus and other fantasy characters are not real. They understand cultural myths for what they are.

Storybooks and television

> I know that Big Bird isn't real. That's just a costume. There's just a plain bird inside. —young child commenting on *Sesame Street* [25]

In addition to fantasies centering on special occasions or holidays, many young children encounter fantasy material on a daily basis in books, on television, and in movies. In most cases children's roles in these experiences are passive; they sit and listen to a story that has already been worked out from beginning to end.[26] How well can children distinguish between story content that is realistic and content that is fantasy?

The answer to this question is complicated,[27] but in general, 3- and 4-year-olds do not do particularly well. Across a variety of different kinds of research tasks and different storytelling mediums, young children exhibit considerable confusion about fantasy and reality. Some of children's difficulty reflects misunderstandings about the technology used to communicate the story. For example, preschool children sometimes question how characters get inside a television, speculating that somehow the characters become smaller and enter through the plug in the wall.[28] Another group of researchers showed children a televised image of a bowl of popcorn and found that some 3-year-olds reported that the popcorn would spill out if the top of the TV were taken off and the TV was turned upside down.[29] Similarly, a student told us that she recalled changing her clothes behind furniture when the television was on because she didn't want Bob Barker to see her naked. Even my editor at Oxford recalls thinking that people on TV could see her because she could see them.

Preschool children also show evidence of misconceptions about the content of what they see on television.[30] For example, young children fail to recognize the economic motives underlying the messages in commercials (i.e., products are portrayed in an overly positive way) and sometimes mistakenly believe that a person beaten or killed in a show has actually been hurt.[31] In research by John Wright and his colleagues at the University of Kansas, 5- and 7-year-old children were asked a variety of questions to assess their understanding of television reality.[32] Children in one study named their favorite TV show and then were asked a series of questions. For example, if the child named *Who's the Boss?*, she was asked if what happened on the show was in real life or just on TV, and if Tony Danza was a housekeeper when he was not on TV.

In responding to these questions, the younger children sometimes attributed too much reality to television and sometimes dismissed as fantasy the material meant to be educational. The 5-year-olds in the study mostly assumed that all televised events or stories were fiction. When questioned about the characters, though, these same children underestimated how much the actors were following scripts and seemed confused about the distinction between the actor's character on TV and his or her offscreen life. However, distinguishing actors from the roles they play on television can sometimes be difficult even for adults. For example, Robert Young, who played Marcus Welby, M.D., for many years on television, received thousands of letters each week from adults who wanted medical advice.[33] Avid soap opera fans reportedly behave in similar ways, suggesting a blending of fantasy and reality. An occupational hazard of playing a nasty character on television is that sometimes these actors are treated badly on the street by viewers of the program. This phenomenon is not unique to television. When Little Nell, (a character in Dickens's serialization of *The Old Curiousity Shop*) died, a sense of loss swept England. Dickens received so many letters from mourners that he felt he had committed a real murder.[34] Perhaps the most famous incident in which adults confused a fictional program for reality was Orson Welles's 1939 radio show *War of the Worlds*, which used a news format to tell the story of an invasion of Earth from outer space. Hundreds of adult listeners thought the report was real news, and mass hysteria ensued.

Young children also make errors when asked about the events described in storybooks. In one study, children were asked whether the events depicted in a series of pictures taken from storybooks, some fantasy (e.g., two rabbits, one sweeping the floor and one baking a cake) and some real life (e.g., a mother bird feeding its young), could really happen.[35] Three-year-old children were essentially unable to discriminate between the two types of pictures. Not until about 5 years of age did children consistently identify the pictures correctly as fantasy or real life. In a similar study, Adrienne Samuels and I showed fantasy and reality pictures to children and asked them if the event portrayed in the picture could happen in real life and if it could happen in a dream.[36] We found that by 5 years of age, children were very good at distinguishing fantasy from real-life events, but 3-year-olds had considerably more trouble. The younger children in this study were as likely to report that events such as a moose cooking in a kitchen could happen in real life as events such as a girl riding a horse. In addition, they were as likely to report that the fantasy events could happen in real life as to report that these events could happen in dreams. When the pictures showed scary real-life events, children tended to claim the events could not actually happen.[37]

Overall, the results of the storybook studies suggest that young children are not always able to identify events in children's books as fantasy or real life. When reading fantasy stories to children, adults should be aware that children might think the events could really happen. In addition, the opposite type of error sometimes occurs when children dismiss what is real as fantasy. When reading a story that is meant to be informative (e.g., promote wariness of strangers), adults may need to stress to a young child that scary situations, such as being treated badly by a stranger, can really happen.

Magic

In magic shows, we see demonstrations of events that defy the laws of nature. Before our very eyes, coins disappear, rabbits emerge from empty hats, blue scarves change into red ones, and assistants smile as they are sawed in half. The tricks are designed to suggest that a magician can make things happen simply by willing it so and can avoid the normal consequences of actions if he or she desires. To what extent do children understand demonstrations of magic as involving subterfuge and tricks, rather than real powers? Do children truly believe, for example, that thinking hard can bring about some event in the real world?

Some very interesting work on these questions has been conducted by Eugene Subbotsky of the University of Lancaster, England.[38] Subbotsky's procedures involved telling children stories about objects with magical qualities, presenting children with real-life props identical to the magical objects in the stories, and then observing the extent to which children treat the props as if they actually possess the qualities of their storybook counterparts. Thus, in this work, the content of the fantasy material is controlled by the researcher although the children are active in their exploration of the props. In addition, Subbotsky's procedures tend to include boundary crossing of the kind that occurs when parents provide children with concrete telltale signs that a fantasy character exists—the milk and cookies we leave out for Santa.

In one study, Subbotsky told 4- to 6-year-olds a story about a magic box that responded to the words "alpha beta gamma" by transforming a drawing inside the box into the object it depicted. At first, the child character in the story did not believe a drawing could come to life, but as the plot unfolded, she discovered that the magic box really had this power. A few days later, the child was invited back and was asked if he or she wanted to see the same magic box that had been described in the story. The researcher brought out a pretty box and some drawings (e.g., a ring, a brooch, a cigarette lighter, a fountain pen, a spider, and a wasp). Then he showed the child objects that he claimed had been produced by putting drawings in the box and saying the magic words. At this point, the researcher left the child alone, saying, "I'm going to do some things, and meanwhile you can play. If you want you can use the box—only don't forget that you have to say the magic words aloud; otherwise, the box can't hear them." Before leaving, the researcher repeated the magic words in case the child had forgotten them.

At the time of the first visit, all the 5- and 6-year-olds and 75 percent of the 4-year-olds denied the possibility of the direct action of thought on an object. Many of the older children explicitly stated their disbelief in magic—"objects in a picture cannot be transformed since they are not magical"; "there's no magic in real life." However, when they were briefly left alone with the box during the second visit, about 90 percent of the children at each age tried to transform the pictures by using the box. They picked the drawings of the more desirable objects to place in the box, avoiding the spider and wasp. Many of the children made gestures over the box as they said the words. When they opened the box and found the drawing unchanged, some of the children tried again and again, varying the way they said the words and the position of the drawing in the box. Later, when the researcher returned, the children expressed surprise and disappointment. Some asked for instructions about how to do it right. According to Subbotsky, the children's behavior, especially their disappointment when the box didn't work, suggests they thought it really might.

In other experiments, children were told a story about a magic table that could transform play animals into real ones. Later, they were brought into a room in which there was a table that resembled the one in the story illustration. The researcher left the child alone in the room with the table and several toy animals, and then observed the child through a one-way mirror. If the child placed an animal on the table, the researcher moved it by using a remote control that was rigged to a magnet hidden under the table. Most of the children gave the table a try and later in an interview attributed the movement of the animals to its magical powers. Half of these children selected the toy rabbit or squirrel to bring to life, keeping the lion away from the table. Subbotsky interpreted the children's pragmatic selections as additional evidence that they believed the table was magic.

Children do not attempt to try out the magical properties of an object if the outcome described in the story is one they do not find desirable. For example, in one story children learned about a magic potion that had the power of making the person who drank it younger—turning a child of 4 years into a 3-year-old.[39] The instructions of the researcher as he left the child alone with the potion were very suggestive: "If you drink a little bit, you will probably turn into a little boy (girl). Now you can try the water if you want. I want to see if it works. But if you do not want to try—it is up to you." Although the children had initially claimed that the action of the magic water was impossible (e.g., "Life does not go back," "Time only goes ahead," "It is difficult to grow downwards," etc.), most of the children refused to drink the water.[40]

What do we make of these results? Subbotsky interprets his research as exploring the conditions under which a magical reality is brought into one's reasoning about everyday life. His procedure was certainly successful in making children question or even abandon their earlier claims about what was possible and impossible. It is not clear, however, that these results indicate children are confused about the fantasy/reality distinction. When children are presented with fantasy material created by adults, they might consider the possibility that they are learning something new about the real world. When the contrast between her earlier statements and her behavior were pointed out, one child replied, "I didn't know; I'm still little." It's a telling comment. Children are still learning about physical reality, and the experimental procedures were very suggestive. In fact, I am surprised that some children did *not* get caught in Subbotsky's web. These young skeptics said things like, "I don't know what trick you used, but there is no magic here" and explicitly looked for wires, a motor, or something to explain the movements of the animals on the table.

The reactions of the child skeptics are like those of adults at a magic show. Adults understand that tricks are being played to make strange events occur, and they search for a logical natural explanation for what they've seen. Even when none is obvious, adults are reluctant to abandon the belief that there must be one. At some point though, even adults might start to wonder. In the foreword to Subbotsky's book, James Wertsch, a well-known psychologist who participated in one of Subbotsky's studies, writes, "I felt the solid ground of normal scientific rationality begin to slip away, and I found myself starting to entertain ideas about psychic forces and so forth—alternatives I would usually be loathe to consider in professional discussions with colleagues."[41]

Subbotsky would be the first to argue that children are not unique in their tendency to resort to magical thinking and to point to parallels in the behavior of adults. Although a scientific mode of explanation is dominant in Western culture, Subbotsky found that when presented with a problem that cannot be solved by natural means, 4 out of 23 adults acted on the researcher's suggestion to try a magical solution (e.g., telekinesis to move an object that could not be reached). In addition, children's refusal to drink the magic water in Subbotsky's experiment is reminiscent of the finding that many adults are reluctant to drink from a glass with the label "cyanide" on it, even though they themselves selected the glass to receive the label and they themselves poured sugar water into the glass.[42] Thus, I would argue that Subbotsky's research does not show that children are particularly gullible or have no understanding of the boundary between fantasy and reality. They might entertain the hypothesis that a magic box or table actually exists, but they have good reason to do so, and adults in some situations might be found to draw similar conclusions.

In other research, children have been shown events that appear to violate physical laws and their initial reactions and subsequent behavior have been observed. For example, in research by Michael Chandler and Chris Lalonde at the University of British Columbia, 3- and 4-year-old children watched one solid object appear to pass through the space occupied by a second solid object.[43] The procedures in this research were much less suggestive than Subbotsky's because the child did not hear a story and the researcher did not talk about magic or in any way suggest that he or she believed the objects had magical qualities. The children in these studies were astonished by the demonstrations, and most claimed that magic had occurred. However, they followed up their comments by investigating the apparatus to try to figure out the mechanism and by asking questions about tricks. Their use of the word *magic* did not indicate that these children actually had a belief in the supernatural. Instead, "magic" seemed to mean "something unusual" or "a trick."

Actually, children rarely resort to magical explanations for everyday events in their lives.[44] When they do, the explanations may not be magical from the point of view of the child. "From their own perspective, such children are simply doing their best at drawing upon what is typically a still imperfect understanding of how the world really works," Chandler and Lalonde write.[45] Distinguishing what is possible given the laws of physics and what is magical is an ongoing process. An appreciation for what is surprising, special, or magical depends on a solid knowledge base about the mundane—everyday causal principles and natural laws.[46] This point of view echoes Chukovsky's comments about the relation between learning about reality and understanding fantasy (see Chapter 3).

This idea is also captured in Chandler and Lalonde's comparison of children's "magical" explanations with medieval interpretations of physical events, the notion that "ontology recapitulates theology."[47] For example, young children might resort to magic to account for some illusion because they do not fully understand the natural laws that govern the world—just as adults in ancient times referred to magic in discussing the Northern Lights because they did not know how else to explain them.

Overall, the results of research on children's understanding of magic are consistent with the hypothesis that when children are presented with fantasy material created by adults, they sometimes entertain the possibility that they are learning something new and strange about the real world. However, their credulity in these situations does not necessarily reflect a general inability to distinguish fantasy and reality. In fact, when not presented with difficult-to-explain demonstrations of magic, young children are very good at distinguishing systematically between magical outcomes (e.g., a marble is moved from one box to another by a person thinking hard) and ordinary outcomes (e.g., a person uses his hands to move the marble).[48]

Social games of pretense

At first glance, the procedures used by the researchers we've considered might look as though they involve episodes of joint pretense—games of pretense that the children enter into with adults. Unlike most games of pretense, however, these experiments gave the children reason to think the researcher was not pretending when he told them about the magical objects, and the content of the fantasy was already worked out in advance. In social games of pretense, all participants have at least the possibility of contributing to the unfolding fantasy narrative, although a bossy play partner may sometimes call most of the shots.

Children frequently participate in pretend play with other people. Sometimes the invitation to pretend is implicit in the partner's actions—a father or mother may pick up a toy and make it talk to the child. Other times the context of pretense is made explicit—"Let's pretend that the rock is a bear." Young children's ability to understand pretend actions and statements and to act accordingly has been carefully documented in a series of experiments by Paul Harris at the University of Oxford and Robert Kavanaugh at Williams College.[49] These researchers initiated and directed games of pretense, then assessed children's ability to comprehend what was going on. In one study children watched a sequence in which a puppet tipped an empty milk carton over an empty bowl, picked up the bowl, and dumped its imaginary contents over the head of an unsuspecting stuffed monkey. Two-year-olds described the monkey as all soggy with milk, although in reality nothing came out of the milk carton and the monkey remained dry. This research shows that even very young children can comprehend a sequence of pretend actions performed by another person.

Once the game of pretense begins, children are pretty much expected to figure out for themselves which of the things their partner says and does are meant to be understood as pretense and which have to do with the real world. DiLalla and Watson wondered how children manage to keep track of an ongoing game of pretense while simultaneously coping with real-world demands.[50] They observed the reactions of children ages 2- to 6-years of age as they played a game of pretense with a researcher who interrupted the game in three different ways. The pretense involved superheros rescuing a doll, hiding from an alien monster, and either destroying the monster or playing with it. The three interruptions were (1) the adult's suggestion during the course of the game that a table being used as a tower be changed to a cave ("Hey, Batman, if only this tower were a cave, we could hide from the monster"), (2) the adult being called out of the room briefly, leaving the child alone, and (3) the adult suddenly pretending to be the monster instead of the child's partner in the search for the monster.

The older children could handle these changes and interruptions smoothly, incorporating them into the story line of the game. They had no difficulty operating simultaneously in fantasy and reality. For example, a child might pick up the story as soon as the researcher returned to the game after the brief absence ("Batgirl, while you were gone, I did [a behavior related to the game]"). In contrast, the 3-year-olds were confused and sometimes upset by the adult's behavior. They had difficulty coping with interruptions to their game (a knock on the door and subsequent departure of the adult) and tended to reject the proposed changes ("No, you're not the monster"). Their response to an interruption was often to stop playing and resist the researcher's attempt to resume where things had left off. What do we make of their reactions? The authors of the study suggest that very young children have difficulty seeing the boundary between fantasy and reality. But there are other possible explanations. Three-year-olds often simply do not like to be left alone, and they sometimes find monster games a little too scary. Children this age might be upset by unexpected interruptions in any ongoing activity, even ones that did not involve pretend play.

Taking another tack, psychologists Claire Golomb and Regina Kuersten at the University of Massachusetts at Boston wanted to know whether 3- and 4-year-olds could keep track of reality while engaged in fantasy play and not be confused by adult actions blurring the fantasy/reality boundary.[51] In this study, the adult playing with the child acted in ways that suggested she had lost track of reality. For example, at one point, the adult poured real water rather than pretend water out of a leaky "boat," soaking a blue blanket placed on the floor to represent the ocean. Later on, the adult who was having a pretend picnic with a young child actually bit into a Playdough cookie. Children were clearly shocked by these transgressions ("Oh, you took a real bite. Now your teeth are all pink. How does it taste? . . . Yuk, do you always eat that Playdough?")[52] Their surprise was clear evidence that, although they were engrossed in the game of pretense, they had not lost track of the fact that dumping water onto a blanket is bad behavior and that Playdough is not an edible substance.

Although these results indicate that young children can distinguish fantasy and reality while engaged in a game of pretense, preschool children don't always act that way. For example, children sometimes become genuinely afraid when engaged in scary pretend play.[53] Does their fear indicate they believe the pretend entity has somehow become real? Some authors have suggested that maintaining the boundary between what is real and what is pretend may just become too difficult when fantasy or pretend play arouses strong emotion in young children.

In a study by Paul Harris and his colleagues, children were asked to pretend a big scary monster was inside a box, a monster that liked to bite children's fingers.[54] Although they had previously seen that the box was empty, some children did not want to be left alone with it, and most of the children chose to poke a stick into a hole in the box rather than to use their fingers. Many of the children who agreed to be left alone in the room with the box looked inside it and later told the researcher that they had wondered if a monster really was in the box.

Note that in this procedure, the context of joint pretense was explicit. There was talk of *pretending* that a monster was in the box, and the researcher never acted as if he had any reason to believe that anything was in the empty box. Yet once children joined the researcher in the pretense they were apprehensive about the box's contents. According to Carl Johnson and Paul Harris, once children create an imaginary being in their minds, the vividness of the image and the ease in re-creating it make the possibility of the entity really existing seem more plausible, and the children check inside the box just to be sure.[55] Although the case of the monster is particularly striking, children act similarly even when the pretense involves non-scary pretend entities (e.g., a fairy).

Perhaps, as these psychologists suggest, children are not certain about the possibility of these characters somehow becoming real. Certainly, this is a common theme in stories read to young children, from *The Velveteen Rabbit* to *Pinocchio,* both of which describe how the love of a human can change a toy into a real animal or person. But can children's behavior be explained without resorting to a belief in magic? Claire Golomb and Lisa Galasso point out that the researchers in these studies did not explicitly end the pretense before leaving the room, and thus the children's explorations of the box could be understood as a continuation of the game of pretense. Children might also investigate the boxes because they have nothing else to do or are suspicious about the researcher's motives. To test these explanations, Golomb and Galasso tried a different procedure in which the pretense was explicitly ended before the child was given the opportunity to explore the box and the child was provided with something else to do to occupy the time (a box of toys). In this study, a small minority of the children inspected the boxes (11 out of 75 children).[56]

Jacqueline Woolley, a psychologist at the University of Texas at Austin, found similar results in a study in which children were asked to pretend a commonplace object such as a pencil was in a box and the question about reality was asked by someone who had not been involved in the pretense.[57] Once children assured the researcher that they were pretending a pencil was in the box, a second adult entered the room and asked the child if she or he knew where there was a pencil. Under these conditions, children did not refer the adult to the box containing the pretend pencil and showed few signs of confusion regarding what was real and what was pretend.

But what about children's emotional reactions to scary play? Are they an indication of confusion about whether the pretend entity has somehow become real? I think the best interpretation is that children (like adults) can be frightened by fantasy material. When this happens, children try to disengage from the play because it elicits uncomfortable emotions. The child who retreats from a scary game of monster may be akin to the adult who walks out of a movie that crosses the line of what the adult experiences as pleasurable arousal of fear.[58] Note that when watching the scary movie, the adult's emotional reaction in many respects indicates that he or she is really afraid.[59] The physiological reactions of people watching a scary movie, such as the heart pounding, adrenaline flowing, and muscles tensing, are those of real fear, but in no way do moviegoers act as if they feel endangered by what they are witnessing. They do not have any inclination to leave the theater to get away from a murderer or to intercede in the events taking place on the screen. Thus, an emotional response to a pretend entity is not an incontestable indication of confusion about whether the pretend entity has somehow become real.

Dreams

Dreams differ from the other kinds of fantasy I have been discussing in a number of ways.[60] First of all, there are no real-world props such as the toys and dress-up clothes that are thought to promote pretend play. In the case of dreams, the child has to imagine everything. In addition, although dreams are private fantasies created by the children themselves, children do not have conscious control over their dreams. Unlike pretend play, dreams come unbidden to the mind and seem real while they are unfolding. Walton makes this point about the unplanned nature of dreams when he notes that dreams, like real-world events, can surprise us.[61]

There is a lot of disagreement about dreams—what they are, what they mean, where they come from. Freud described dreams as the fulfillment of wishes, often forbidden ones.[62] According to Freud, dreams have strange sequences and odd juxtapositions of objects and people because the unacceptable kinds of themes dealt with in dreams must be disguised or transformed. For example, a dream about walking up a staircase might actually be about erotic desires. Other psychologists believe dreams reflect the special information-processing conditions that occur when a brain is active during REM sleep, but shut off from most external perceptual input. Memories from the day's events are particularly salient under these conditions, and these memories activate related past memories which are then strung together and interpreted in the disjointed way characteristic of dream narratives.[63] This point of view contrasts sharply with the Freudian hypothesis "of an internal dream playwright composing therapeutic dreamplays for the benefit of the ego and cunningly sneaking them past an internal censor by disguising their true meaning."[64] The psychological significance of dreams is not central to my argument, but I will assume dreams are privately created fantasies, because this is the dominant point of view in Western cultures.[65]

Whatever dreams are, there is no doubt that children have them. About 80 percent of 4-year-olds report having dreams at night. The results of an extensive study by Foulkes indicates that most dreams reported by young children involve very simple images, usually involving animals (e.g., a chicken pecking grain). Foulkes based this conclusion on an analysis of the dreams reported by children who slept in his lab for about 27 nights spread over a five-year period.[66] When their EEG patterns indicated they were dreaming, the children were awakened and asked to report the details of their dream. Other authors have asked children during the day to recall dreams they had at night. This daytime method seems to elicit more unusual dream contents. Jean Piaget's well-known book *Play, Dreams and Imitation* contains some interesting examples of children's dreams. Here is a sample:[67]

> I dreamt that mummy laid a lot of eggs and a little baby came out of them. (5 years, 8 months)

> I dreamt there was a tiny little man like that (four inches) with a very big head. He ran after me to hurt me. (5 years, 8 months; the previous day she had seen a picture of Humpty-Dumpty)

> I dreamt that Dr. M. fired a gun at a man who was high up in the air. The man was very ill and going to die so he killed him. He was very small, and then when he fell he was big: he got bigger and bigger; he had a fat tummy like you; he was just like you! (5 years, 9 months)

> Mummy made a big, green statue out of leaves. A fox came and knocked it over by pushing its head into the leaves. I was frightened of the fox and went back into mummy's inside to hide. Then he couldn't catch me. (5 years, 9 months)

> In the basin I saw a bean that was so big that it quite filled it. It got bigger and bigger all the time. I was standing by the door. I was frightened. I wanted to scream and run away, but I couldn't. I got more and more frightened, and it went on until I woke up. (6 years)

When children are interviewed about their dreams, their responses often suggest they do not completely appreciate that dreams belong to the realm of fantasy. Piaget described young children as believing their dreams were objective phenomena which originated from outside the dreamer, remained outside the dreamer, and could be shared with others in the room. He based this conclusion on interviews such as the following:

EXP: Do you ever have dreams?
CHILD (5 years, 6 months): Yes, I dreamed I had a hole in my hand.
EXP: Are dreams true?
CHILD: No, they are pictures we see.
EXP: Are your eyes open or shut when you sleep?
CHILD: Shut.
EXP: Could I see your dream?
CHILD: No, you would be too far away.
EXP: And your mother?
CHILD: Yes, but she lights the light.
EXP: Is the dream in you or inside you?
CHILD: It isn't in me or I shouldn't see it.

EXP: Where does the dream come from?
CHILD (5 years, 9 months): I think you sleep so well that you dream.
EXP: Does it come from us or from outside?
CHILD: From outside.
EXP: When you are in bed and you dream, where is the dream?
CHILD: In my bed, under the blanket. I don't know. If it was in my stomach, the bones would be in the way and I shouldn't see it.
EXP: Is the dream there when you sleep?
CHILD: Yes, it is in my bed beside me.
EXP: Is the dream in your head?
CHILD: It is me that is in the dream. It isn't in my head.[68]

Laurendeau and Pinard also asked young children questions such as: Do you know what a dream is? While you are dreaming, where is your dream? Many young children answered these questions by reporting that the dream was in the room and could be seen by others in the room.[69] Laurendeau and Pinard set the age at which children reach an adultlike understanding of dreams at about age 7, whereas Piaget claimed that it was only at about 9 or 10 years of age that children understand that dreams are internal and not caused by other people.

Woolley and Wellman have criticized this view of young children's conception of dreams, claiming that the kinds of questions asked elicit responses that underestimate children's understanding of the internal, private, and fantasy nature of dreams.[70] When children are asked strange questions like "Where are dreams made?" or "Where do dreams come from?" they may well be unsure what sort of answer is expected. Perhaps their on-the-spot answers should not be taken as literally as researchers have tended to do. Children might also misinterpret the questions. For example, when children are asked if a dream really happened, a "yes" response could reflect their recognition that some of the events they dreamed about were related to real events in their lives. Similarly, when children locate a dream somewhere other than in their own minds, they may be reporting the location of the events in the dreams, rather than expressing a misunderstanding of the mentalistic nature of dreaming.

Woolley and Wellman interviewed children to determine if they shared the beliefs about dreams that characterize Western thinking—namely, that dreams are nonphysical, private, and fictional. A researcher described short scenarios to 3- and 4-year-old children about people who were dreaming and then assessed their understanding of the scenario. For example, children were shown a simple line drawing of a child and told, "Here's Jimmy. His favorite toy is a ball. Right now Jimmy's asleep, and he's dreaming about a ball." Then children were asked (1) whether Jimmy could see the ball with his eyes, (2) if someone else in the room would be able to see the ball with their eyes, and (3) whether Jimmy could perform some action on the ball. Similar questions were asked about scenarios involving a child interacting with a real physical object (e.g., riding her bike), and a child looking at a photograph of a real object. Even the 3-year-olds in this study answered the dream questions very differently from the questions about real and photographed objects. They understood, for example, that the real and photographed objects could be seen by other people as well as by the child, but that only the child could see the objects in his or her dreams.

Three-year-olds are also quite accurate when asked about the kinds of things that can happen in dreams.[71] Even the youngest children understood that a person can have a dream about something that does not exist in the real world. For example, they knew that an ant crawling on the ground existed in real life, but an ant riding a bicycle could exist only in a dream. It seems young children also understand that dreams are not a reliable source of information about reality.[72] To demonstrate this, 3-year-olds were introduced to two puppets, one who claimed that he knew a cookie was in a can and another puppet who said he dreamed the cookie was in the box. Even the youngest children took the word of the first puppet and looked in the can for the cookie.

Children's answers to these questions indicate that by 3 years of age they share the beliefs about dreams that characterize Western adult thinking. (The only point of departure was that some 3-year-olds reported that two people sleeping in the same bed might share the same dream, a widely held belief of children from the Hausa tribe in Nigeria.)[73] This is not to say that children answer all questions about dreams in an adult way or that they never mistake dream events for real ones. Gleitman gives the example of a 3-year-old who "awakes and tells her parents how much she loved the elephants at the circus yesterday. The parents correct her; she has not been at the circus yesterday. But the child indignantly sticks to her story and appeals to her brother for corroboration, for 'he was there too.' When the brother shakes his head in denial, she begins to cry, angrily insisting that she told the truth."[74]

Parents of young children can probably recall similar anecdotes about their own children. Especially in the case of nightmares, children appear confused. If you have ever been awakened by the terrified cries of a child who has experienced a nightmare, you know how difficult calming the child can be. Keep in mind, however, that dreams can be confusing even for adults. Nightmares scare adults too, and sometimes dream events affect our waking behavior. For example, I have occasionally been startled when I suddenly realized that I was feeling annoyed with a friend because of his behavior in my dream the night before rather than anything he had said or done in real life. There are obviously gaps in our knowledge about dreams, but the overall picture that emerges is that children are not as naive or as different from adults in their concept of dreams as is commonly claimed. Overall, the evidence suggests that children arrive at an adult understanding of dreams by a surprisingly early age.

Imaginary companions

Imaginary companions can be based on a character the child hears about, sees in a movie (e.g., Batman, Wonder Woman), or knows in real life, but the idea of creating an imaginary version of the character to play with is probably almost always something children arrive at on their own. There are some exceptions to this claim—imaginary companions that are passed down from one child to the next in a family or ones suggested to the child by a therapist—but typically, an imaginary companion is an excellent example of a private act of fantasy controlled by the child him or herself.

By the time they are 3 or 4 years of age (the age at which many imaginary companions are created), children have been engaging in their own spontaneous pretense for a long time. Children start to pretend about the same time they start to talk. The first acts of pretense are pretty simple. The child might pick up an empty cup, act as if drinking (complete with sound effects) and smile at her caregiver. With children this young, it is difficult to be completely certain about their intentions, but there are signs that identify these acts as pretense. For example, if a child who tipped an empty cup to her lips mistakenly believed there was something to drink in the cup, one might expect the child to subsequently act surprised or to request a drink. Instead, the child smiles and makes no attempt to get an actual drink.[75] Even 18-month-olds appear to know what they are doing when they drink from empty cups, nibble on block "cookies," and pretend to fall asleep.

There also are signs that even quite young children never completely lose touch with the fantasy status of their imaginary friends—not that this is a particularly straightforward question, as I can attest from personal experience. However, Stephanie Carlson and I have found that children readily answer the question "Do you have a *pretend* friend?" by describing imaginary companions that are substantiated by the reports of their parents. They know what we are talking about. In fact, we have the distinct impression that after children spend a period of time answering detailed questions about a pretend friend for a researcher who listens carefully and even takes notes, they begin to wonder if the adult might be confused. So at some point during the interview, children are apt to help the interviewer by saying, "It's just pretend, you know" or "She isn't real."

Such attempts to keep the record straight are mentioned by other researchers as well. For example, Cohen and MacKeith describe an *incident involving* a 5-year-old boy named Dickie who created an imaginary farm populated with many imaginary animals which he had played with intensely since the age of 2 or 3. At a family get-together, a group of adult relatives had a prolonged discussion about Dickie's farm in his presence. After listening to their conversation for a while, Dickie quietly approached his father and whispered, "Tell them it isn't a real farm."[76]

There are several reasons why adults might sometimes wonder about the child's understanding of the imaginary companion. One reason has to do with the strong emotions elicited by these friends. Children often love their imaginary friends very much, sometimes even more than their real friends.[77] However, as discussed earlier in the context of scary pretense, strong emotion can be elicited by fantasy with no loss in the individual's grasp of the fantasy/reality distinction. In many ways our emotions sometimes seem strangely disconnected from what we know. We know Anne of Green Gables in the books by L. M. Montgomery is a made-up person, but we feel strong affection for her. We know the outcome of a scary movie we have seen before, yet we still feel suspense as the events unfold.[78] My point is that although children are often very absorbed and emotionally caught up in their play with imaginary companions, this is not good evidence that they are unclear about the friends' fantasy status.

The first research I did with children who had imaginary companions was designed to determine if children lost track of reality when they were actively playing with their pretend friends. Bridget Cartwright, Stephanie Carlson, and I interviewed 3- and 4-year-old children to determine if they had a pretend friend.[79] The children who told us they had one were asked a series of questions about the friend (name, age, gender, size, hair color, eye color, type of clothing, how often they played with the companion). The children who said they did not have an imaginary companion were asked the same questions about a real friend of their choice. After describing the friend, children were shown an attractive Snoopy play phone and asked to pretend to phone the friend (either imaginary companion or real friend) and invite him or her to the lab.

Children who had an imaginary companion did not hesitate to phone the friend and seemed comfortable pretending he or she was present. There were complications for some of the phone episodes, but these did not take the form of children not pretending. For example, one imaginary companion arrived with an imaginary father, creating a seating problem that was resolved by having the father sit in the chair and the imaginary companion on the child's lap. Another pretend friend had to travel from across town so we had to wait (in "real" time) for her while she made the trip. Two children had brought their imaginary companions along (unbeknownst to the researcher) and so the phone call was not required. In contrast, children who did not have imaginary companions were often very reluctant to pretend to phone the real friend and needed considerable prompting. Many initially reported that no one answered the phone or that the friend was too busy to come. Two children completely refused to pretend the friend was present.[80]

Once the children informed the researcher that the friend was in the lab sitting in the chair provided, they were prompted to interact with the friend and an attractive toy (e.g., "I have a really neat toy in this box and I bet you would really like to see it. Would you like to see it? Well, your friend has the box. Now if you want to see the toy, what would you say to her? Now show me how you and your friend would play with the toy."). The purpose of these questions was to get the child to interact with the friend. Then a series of questions designed to determine the extent to which the child was aware of the imaginary status of the friend was asked as follows:

- Can you see (friend's name)?
- Can you see (friend's name) the way you see me?
- Do you think I can see (friend's name) right now?
- Can you touch (friend's name)?
- Can you touch (friend's name) the way you touch me?
- Do you think I can touch (friend's name)?

We found that the majority of the children claimed both they and the researcher could see and touch their imaginary companions, but these responses did not seem to be the result of a confusion about the reality of the companions. First of all, children without imaginary companions answered the questions the same way. These children were clearly not confused about whether their friend was actually present. They required considerable prompting to pretend the friend was in the room. But once they reluctantly agreed to pretend their real friend was present, they most often reported that both they and the researcher could see and touch the friend. Thus, answering "yes" to questions about seeing and touching the friend probably is part of going along with the pretense, rather than an indication of fantasy/reality confusion. In addition, a third of the children explicitly told the researcher that the imaginary companion was not real when answering these questions (e.g., "She's not here for real"; "We're just pretending"). So, on the one hand, these children reported they could see their friend the same way they could see the researcher, but while they were being asked these questions, the same children cautioned the researcher in an aside that the friend was not real. As Golomb and Galasso point out, children and researchers are sometimes at cross purposes, with the researcher asking about the real state of affairs and children answering in the mode of pretense.

Overall, children appear to be clear about the fantasy status of their imaginary friends. But a final complexity is well worth some discussion. Although some children create companions or even worlds that they never share with others, in many cases, children's fantasies are given interpretations by those around them. These interpretations are influenced by the values and beliefs of individuals in the family as well as by the culture in which the children live. It is possible that part of children's understanding of their imaginary companions as fantasy is specific to Western culture.

My basis for this claim is a fascinating study by Antonia Mills on imaginary companions in India.[81] She began her research in India by conducting an informal survey in which she asked psychologists as well as other adults if they knew of any children who had imaginary companions. The answer was universally "no." At first, she attributed this result to the conditions in which children in India are raised. American children who have imaginary companions tend to have periods of time in which they are alone due to the circumstances of their place in the family (the youngest child who plays alone when the older children are at school) or where they live. In contrast, Indian children are rarely alone. They do not sleep, eat, or play alone. However, Mills realized that denial might also be based on the use of the word "imaginary." She began to wonder if children who were thought to have imaginary companions in the United States would be thought to be remembering previous lives if they lived in India, and vice versa.

Mills found that when Indian children talk to entities that adults cannot perceive, the entity is referred to as invisible rather than imaginary. The assumption is that the child is communicating with a very real being who exists on a spiritual realm or is part of the child's past life. Mills identified 49 cases in India of parents who claimed their children had memories for past identities. She found that the time frame that is typical for imaginary companions is similar for the phenomena of past lives and that most of the children who talked about past lives were the youngest or next to youngest in the family. At about age 7, children were taught not to remember the past life because adults feared the children would take on this past identity rather than pursuing their current one. Overall, memories for past lives are not as common in India as imaginary companions are in the United States (about 0.2 percent of children in northern India compared with at least 30 percent of North American children having imaginary companions). However, Mills's research suggests that the two phenomena are related and indicate that children are taught to understand and experience themselves and their perceptions in ways specific to their culture.

Overall, I think children's mastery of fantasy is impressive. They answer many questions about imaginary objects and events in the same way as adults, they understand the pretend actions of other people as pertaining to the domain of pretense, and explicitly label their imaginary friends as "just pretend." Especially when children are controlling the content of the fantasy, they seem to understand the fantasy/reality distinction. Even when parents and other adults present a convincing case for the existence of a fantasy character such as Santa Claus, children eventually figure out what is going on.

This is not to say that children's behavior in pretend play never suggests any confusion. When fantasy is emotionally charged, children sometimes appear confused. This can happen in the context of a scary pretend play scenario or when they wake up from a dream. However, an emotional response to fantasy is not an unambiguous sign of confusion about fantasy and reality. Adults often experience an uncomfortable level of fear for events they know are imaginary. I have argued that the fear elicited, for example, by movies should not be interpreted as evidence that the adult viewers have lost track of fantasy and reality. Perhaps we should also be cautious about attributing fantasy/reality confusion to young children on the basis of their emotional reactions to fantasy material.

In fact, an examination of the fantasy behavior of older children and adults provides many cautions in our interpretation of the behavior of preschool children. There is considerable continuity between early childhood fantasy and that of older persons, which is the topic to be discussed in Chapter 7. But first let's consider what happens to the imaginary companions created in early childhood.

6

What Happens to the Imaginary Companions Created in Early Childhood?

One gray night it happened, Jackie Paper came no more.
And Puff that mighty dragon,
    he ceased his fearless roar.
His head was bent in sorrow, green scales fell like rain.
Puff no longer went to play along the cherry lane.
Without his lifelong friend, Puff could not be brave
So Puff that mighty dragon,
    sadly slipped into his cave.

—From *Puff (the Magic Dragon)*

CHILDREN'S friendships with imaginary companions are often intense, emotional, and absorbing, but they don't last forever. One day, parents realize that the pretend friend they have been hearing about for months, or even years, is no longer mentioned. A once-cherished stuffed animal ends up in the back of the closet; invisible beings disappear without a trace. These endings are typically difficult to pinpoint and can be as perplexing as the initial appearances. When children are asked what happened to their imaginary companions, they usually report that they don't remember.[1] Curiously, they also express very little sadness or regret. Note that in Peter, Paul, and Mary's well-known song, it is Puff the Magic Dragon, not Jackie Paper, who mourns when their relationship is over. In real life most children, like the fictional Jackie, give up imaginary companions without fuss or fanfare. When they are finished with their pretend friends, they move on to something new and often forget about them completely.

Parents and other family members who have become accustomed to the invisible additions to their families are less cavalier, and sometimes become quite invested in keeping the memory alive. One woman we interviewed reported that her parents insisted on telling anyone she brought to their home about the invisible green gunkies she played with as a child. In an article published in the *Los Angeles Times*, Nancy Rivera Brooks described the feelings of loss that her family and friends experienced when her son stopped playing with Norey Porto, an imaginary boy with dark hair and green eyes who lived nearby with his family in a black house with blue trim.[2]

> Norey was Cord's imaginary playmate, and after spending a significant amount of time with us during the past three years, Norey has gone the way of baby bottles and potty chairs. But since this perfectly normal, age-appropriate milestone occurred, the strangest thing has happened: I've started to miss old Norey. My husband and 7-year-old daughter, when quizzed, have made similar reluctant confessions.
>
> Are we in mourning for Cord's lost toddler-hood? Is this one of those bittersweet passage of time things? Naw. I think we are pining for Norey himself and his odd family and their lavish lifestyle, all courtesy of the imaginings of our budding wordsmith.

Given the description Brooks provides of Norey, it is not surprising to me that the family misses him. Norey was pretty special. He had more birthday parties than any other kid, owned every imaginable toy (except Barbie), and had lots of pets, including buffalo, a hippo, a lion, and a hyena, as well as the more conventional ones. His family was also noteworthy. On Valentine's Day, Norey's mom (who was so tall she could touch the ceiling) found a dead snake and cooked it for Norey's dad. One sister died when someone stepped on her, and the other was a baby who drank out of Power Ranger bottles. Brooks compared the demise of Norey with the ending of a good movie or book. She missed hearing about all the strange events that occurred in Norey's life. In the end, though, she decided that his disappearance was for the best because, "you know you are in trouble when your kid's imaginary creations have a more interesting life than you do."

Christopher Milne, who inspired his father's (A. A. Milne) stories about Winnie the Pooh, experienced this nostalgic response of others to his childhood imaginary companions on a larger scale. He found that people were disappointed that he no longer possessed his collection of stuffed animals. Years ago, he had given them to the editor of the Pooh books, who in turn donated them to the New York City Public Library. They are currently on display in a climate-controlled case in Donnel Library Center on West 53rd (having recently weathered the attempt of a member of the British Parliament to bring them back to English soil). The readers of the *Winnie the Pooh* books somehow wanted and expected the real-life Christopher Robin to retain an attachment to Winnie the Pooh, Eeyore, Piglet, Kanga, Roo, and Tigger—the famous companions of his childhood. Thus, as an elderly man, Milne found it necessary to explain that he liked to surround himself with the things he currently enjoyed, rather than the things he had played with as a little boy.[3]

In any case, children do not seem to mourn the passing of imaginary companions. This point underlines the utilitarian nature of these friends. They tend to be abandoned when they have outlived their usefulness. This in no way indicates that the children's emotional attachment to their pretend friends was never real or important. As many of the descriptions in this book clearly show, children love their imaginary companions very much. And if the relationship ends prematurely, children are not so nonchalant. For example, sometimes a toy that has functioned as an imaginary companion is accidentally destroyed or lost. This sort of event can elicit strong emotional responses from young children.

A sad story from one of my graduate students illustrates this scenario. From early childhood, Lynn had a brown teddy bear named DeeZee who was her constant companion. The whole family was aware of Lynn's special relationship with her bear, and he is still mentioned in family stories. One day Lynn was playing with DeeZee in a huge sand pile that had been created in her parents' yard in preparation for a landscaping project. The game involved lots of tunneling in the sand. Things got a little out of control—"DeeZee dug too far"—and the bear disappeared in the sand pile. Lynn was upset, but hoped to find DeeZee as the project progressed. Unfortunately, insects located him before the landscapers did. When DeeZee finally surfaced, he was infested with bugs, and Lynn's parents threw him out. Lynn remembers picking him out of the garbage and hugging him, bugs and all, but her mother insisted that he had to go.

Clearly, having a stuffed animal as your imaginary companion has some hazards. They are subject to real-world dangers that do not trouble invisible friends, at least not without the collusion of the children. When children are finished with the invisible kind of pretend friend, these companions mostly just fade gradually away, but sometimes the children invent stories about their demise. One example of an abrupt ending was told to me by a colleague who played with three tiny invisible bears when she was a little girl. The bears lived on her hand. In some ways this was a convenient location because they were always nearby, but it also required keeping track of which hand they were in and switching the bears frequently from one hand to another with the demands of everyday life. Although she was usually very careful to keep the bears out of harm's way, one day she forgot to transfer the bears when her mother took her hand to cross the street. The bears were crushed, and that was the end of them.

In recalling the bear story, this woman wondered what it meant that she had been so calm and accepting of this brutal death. But her attitude is just another example of children's indifference about the old friends who are no longer part of their lives.[4] It is not unusual for imaginary companions to meet a violent end. There are many examples of children responding to questions about a missing imaginary companion by announcing that it is dead, was killed, or has drowned. One child reported that her imaginary dinosaur Gawkin was hit by a truck. She was holding his hand, but he lagged behind and the truck killed him. There were no tears or bad feelings—Gawkin was dead, and that was the end of the story. Children's accounts of their imaginary companions' fates are not always so dramatic. For example, children sometimes describe the companions as moving away to another city or state, retiring, or going on sabbatical.[5]

What makes children ready to give up an imaginary companion that was once so important to them? The purpose of this chapter is to present the little that is known about the circumstances associated with the final exits of imaginary companions created during the preschool years. I have pieced together a few empirical findings and case histories in an attempt to come up with something more substantive to say than simply recounting the speculations and assumptions of parents and psychologists. This makes for a short chapter, which belies the importance of the issue. If we knew more about when and how imaginary companions disappear, we might understand more fully the roles they play in the children's lives—why they were created in the first place.

Why do children give up their imaginary companions?

Loss of interest

Perhaps the disappearances of many imaginary companions are not that mysterious. Children simply lose interest in this type of play. In these cases, giving up an imaginary companion would not be much different from giving up play with blocks or finger paints. The activity becomes less absorbing or interesting over time, and the child moves on to other things. For example, one adult informant told me about the end of her relationship with an imaginary girl named Alice. For quite some time the child had enjoyed the imagined adventures of Alice, a brave girl who was nevertheless very afraid of her stepmother, a witchlike woman who beat her with a Gucci belt (she "was very evil, but also very elegant"). Alice hid under the table one day to escape her stepmother's notice and found that she liked living under the table. She still visited the little girl from time to time, but she no longer had much to say—after all, opportunities for adventure are limited when you live under a table. The little girl found she didn't enjoy Alice's visits as much as before. One day Alice, along with a pink rabbit, escaped from the stepmother's house altogether, stopping by the little girl's home to say goodbye before they hopped away to a place where they would be safe. The girl never saw them again.

Creation of a new imaginary companion

Sometimes the child loses interest in a particular imaginary companion, but not in the activity of making up pretend friends. As children's needs and interests change, their current imaginary companion might become outdated. Thus, the imaginary companions that are created early in childhood often drop out as the children dream up new ones. This revolving-door aspect of play with imaginary companions was described in a story by J. D. Salinger called "Uncle Wiggily in Connecticut," about a little girl who had an imaginary companion named Jimmy Jimmereeno. The mother was exasperated by Jimmy and his constant presence. "I get it all day long. Jimmy eats with her. Takes a bath with her. Sleeps with her. She sleeps way over to one side of the bed, so's not to roll over and hurt him."[6] One day the girl abruptly announced that Jimmy had been run over and killed. However, the mother later observed that the child was still sleeping so far to the edge of her bed that she was in danger of falling on the floor. She shook the child awake and demanded to know why she wasn't sleeping in the middle of the bed now that Jimmy was dead. The child replied that she didn't want to hurt Mickey Mickeranno. This was the last straw for the frazzled mother who apparently had enough trouble dealing with her real-life child and could not cope with the comings and goings of imaginary ones.

Like the girl in Salinger's story, many children routinely replace old imaginary companions with new ones. We first realized that imaginary companions have a high rate of turnover when we interviewed a group of 12 four-year-olds seven months after they had originally told us about their pretend friends.[7] Seven of the 12 children still played with these friends and were happy to provide updated descriptions, but the other children had new imaginary friends and were not interested in discussing the previous ones.

The following is part of an interview with one of these children, a boy who originally told us about two invisible pretend friends, a girl named Tippy and a boy named Tompy. They were described as being 5 years old, having blond hair and blue eyes, and being great playmates. At the time of the first interview, the child's mother confirmed the existence of Tippy and Tompy and reported that her son played with them regularly. Seven months later, it was difficult to engage the child in conversation about the pretend friends he had once discussed with great enthusiasm.

ADULT: Do you have a pretend friend named Tompy?

CHILD: Oh. Tompy, Tompy. They were dead. They got dead today. Oh . . . the day before the day. They just got dead, 'cause . . . (Stops and points to ceiling.) What's up there?

ADULT: I don't know. Can you tell me about Tompy before he died? Is that a boy or a girl?

CHILD: Oh, she was a girl.

ADULT: So how old is Tompy?

CHILD: Well, he's 7,200 years old.

ADULT: Is it a boy or a girl?

CHILD: Well . . . the other one's a girl. But Tompy's real defective. He has a sore knee. Sore leg though but . . . There's lots of times that Tompy . . . We're really good friends (nodding) . . . I can't . . .

ADULT: They're good friends?

CHILD: Yeah, they were.

ADULT: They were? So, are they still alive?

CHILD: Oh, they are still alive but . . . (makes sound effect and falls back as though hit) Have I told you to do that to my speeders! (speaking to someone other than the adult conducting the interview).

ADULT: Who did that?

CHILD: Oh, Gadget.

ADULT: Gadget?

CHILD: Gadget's a girl. Now go back to sleep! (says to pocket)

ADULT: Can you tell me about Gadget?

(Adult asks child several questions about Gadget, who is described as a small, frisky mouse. Then the adult tries to return to the topic of Tompy.)

ADULT: Do you play with Tompy sometimes?

CHILD: (in critical tone of voice) Did you forget about what I told you? Ouch! (reacting to some action of Gadget's)

This transcript gives some idea of how tricky it can be to extract information from preschoolers. The child seemed to be censoring some material, was inconsistent in some of his comments, and was distracted by the antics of a new imaginary companion who had come along to the interview uninvited. His comments about "the other one" being a girl make sense to someone who knows the history of Tippy and Tompy, but were bewildering to the person conducting the interview. She had been told only that the child used to have a pretend friend named Tompy and was instructed to try to elicit information about Tompy. (We did not want the second interviews in this study to be influenced by the adult's knowledge of what the children had previously said.) The interviewer was unsuccessful in learning much about Tompy, other than that he had been a good friend but was defective. The child's words and his tone of voice suggested that Tompy was remembered with some fondness, but no profound sense of loss. Gadget had clearly taken over.

Adults take control of the imaginary companion

One of the endearing things about imaginary companions is that children can boss them around, direct their activities, and dictate their communications with others. There are a few case studies suggesting that if children's sense of control over the imaginary companion is diminished, the pretend friend sometimes disappears. For example, Ronald Benson and David Pryor of the University of Michigan Medical Center described a disappearance of an imaginary companion that was associated with a concrete event not imagined by the child herself.[8] The imaginary companion in question was created by a 4-year-old girl who was the eldest of three children in the family (her mother was pregnant with the third child at the time Nosey, the pretend friend, joined the family). Nosey was a black and white dog, about five feet long, or rather, tall, because he always walked on his hind legs, who always wore a skirt, and held a mop or broom in his hands. The mother reported that Nosey was accepted by the other members of the family and was a regular participant in family events.

Nosey was abandoned suddenly after an incident that took place at the home of the child's grandparents. Unbeknownst to the child, the grandfather had installed a remote control for opening and closing his garage door. After coming home from a drive, the grandfather asked if Nosey could help by opening the garage door. After the child relayed this request to Nosey, the grandfather surreptitiously opened the door with the remote control. The child appeared to be very surprised by the opening of the door on cue by itself. A few weeks later the child's mother realized that Nosey had not been mentioned for some time and asked her daughter about him. The child reported that Nosey had stayed with her grandparents to help them with their garage door. She recalled that she had left him on the garage steps sweeping with his broom. An imaginary cat who also walked on her hind legs was with him. Although this ending was more abrupt that most, it did not seem to be associated with any upset feelings. At age 16, the girl recalled the incident as a pleasant memory about Nosey staying where he was needed.

Benson and Pryor interpret this case study as suggesting that interventions by others take the imaginary companion out of the realm of the imaginary and give the companion a meaning that differs from the child's needs, leading to the abandonment of the fantasy. The grandfather who operated the garage door took Nosey out of the domain of fantasy and made him part of the real world. From the child's point of view, Nosey appeared to have developed purposes and capabilities of his own that were independent of her needs. As additional evidence for this interpretation, Benson and Pryor report a second case of an imaginary companion who was given up as a consequence of outside intervention, but this time the child was emotionally disturbed and was being treated in a psychiatric hospital. The companion was described as an extraterrestrial creature named Ronzar. According to the boy who invented him, Ronzar gave him advice and helped him with his homework. Sometimes he felt that Ronzar transported him mentally to other planets. The boy was an A student who openly discussed Ronzar with his friends and teachers at school.

The boy's intense involvement with Ronzar contributed to his being admitted to a psychiatric hospital. The psychotherapist convinced him that Ronzar was a substitute for interactions with everyday people. The boy acknowledged that there might be some truth to this interpretation because he was aware that Ronzar helped him control angry feelings toward other people. He was disturbed by the thought of not having Ronzar ("I don't know what I'd do without Ronzar. I don't know how I would handle my hate"), but shortly after the psychotherapist proposed this view of Ronzar, the boy announced that Ronzar had been killed in a meteorite shower. According to Benson and Pryor, Ronzar had served caretaking and protective functions that were experienced by the child as an aspect of self that was under his complete control. "The psychiatrist, however, did not interpret that these were self-approving functions that Ronzar played for Simon, which protected his self-esteem and self-regard, but rather made an interpretation implying that Ronzar had a function in reference to Simon's object-directed drives."[9] This interpretation rendered Ronzar ineffective in the functions he had served, and thus he was abandoned.

Bruce Klein has described a case in which a girl gave up two imaginary companions after her grandfather became very involved in her play with them.[10] Her mother believed that losing control of the friends somehow made them less attractive to her as playmates. Similarly, Plinka and Planka, two pretend friends described as middle-age adults in tailored clothing, were immediately discarded the day the child's mother set two extra plates for lunch and began chatting to the imaginary women herself.[11] These last examples surprised me because I have found that many children enjoy the participation of others in their fantasy about an imaginary friend. Many parents report that when they pretend to see or hear the imaginary companion, their children react with delight.[12] The children may even insist upon the parent taking part in the fantasy by drying the imaginary companion after a bath or buckling the imaginary companion into the car with a seat belt.

Perhaps the key to the child's enjoyment of the parent's participation is that the child retains the role of director, and thus is in control of how the imaginary companion behaves, and exactly how the parent participates. Certainly we have found that children resist an adult's attempts to dictate the actions of imaginary companions. We tried unsuccessfully to do this in a study in which we were interested in the possibility that children might think of their imaginary companions as real when the play was emotionally charged. To create this type of play, we set up a situation in which the child and the imaginary companion were both present in the lab. The experimenter gave an attractive toy to the imaginary companion and then told the child that the imaginary companion refused to share the toy with the child. This study had to be discontinued because the procedure simply did not work. The children became annoyed with the researcher, not their companion. It was clear that these children were not about to relinquish their authority over the activities of the imaginary companion to someone else.

There is one caveat to the claim that children experience their imaginary companions as under their control. Research on the phenomenology of elaborate fantasy suggests that at least sometimes when people invent an imaginary other, they experience the imagined entity as having control of its own thoughts and actions.[13] This illusion of the locus of control residing within the imaginary entity is mostly documented with adults, but I suspect at least some children might experience it as well. This possibility will be discussed further in Chapter 7, where I take up the general question of the relation between fantasy experiences of adults and the early childhood phenomenon of imaginary companions.

Parental disapproval

When their children are preschoolers, some parents delight in their children's inventions, but parental enjoyment of a child's fantasy gives way to concern if the child continues in such play after the age that the parent believes it to be appropriate. Play with imaginary companions is no longer tolerated as readily when children enter middle childhood, and children become increasingly aware of the negative attitudes that imaginary companions sometimes elicit from onlookers. In the words of one mother, "she knows we're laughing at

her, sort of thing—you have to laugh at her, because it seems peculiar for her to answer herself back, sort of thing—and she'll stop playing. She goes all red, you know, blushy."[14]

Even adults who once had imaginary companions themselves
seem to believe there is something wrong with someone who continues to have an imaginary friend after the preschool years. I have
found that adults enjoy telling me about their childhood imaginary
companions until I ask how old they were when they stopped playing
with pretend friends. It's a question that elicits expressions of mild
dismay and comments like "I'd rather not say," "Well, that's the embarrassing part," or "How old can a person be before it isn't a good
thing anymore?" Their responses suggest that these adults believe
there is an appropriate age by which one should have given up an
imaginary companion, and that their own involvement had continued for entirely too long.

As a consequence of increasing disapproval from others, fantasy
play goes "underground" during middle childhood.[15] Parents know
less and less about their children's fantasy lives. In Newson and
Newson's research, children who retained their imaginary companions beyond the preschool years were described as playing with them
more privately and no longer making demands on other family
members to play along (e.g., to avoid sitting on the imaginary companion, carry the imaginary companion, etc.). The parents indicated
that they no longer actively participated in the fantasy games of
their children, and many expressed negative attitudes about such
play.[16]

As discussed in Chapter 4, parental disapproval does not wipe out
fantasy play, but children's increasing awareness of negative parental
attitudes does have an effect. They become more secretive about this
type of play, and in at least some cases, it is likely that social disapproval eventually brings about the disappearance of the imaginary
companion. As Newson and Newson point out, "Ridicule is the en-
emy of fantasy."[17] Older children might first be motivated to be more
private about their fantasy play than younger children, but eventually they stop engaging in this kind of play altogether. Hurlock and
Burnstein found that some children stop playing with their imaginary companions after being told they are too old to have one.[18]
Thus, one reason why at least some children might give up an imaginary companion is because as they get older this kind of play is no
longer tolerated by the people around them.

Child acquires more real friends

As discussed in Chapter 4, imaginary companions fulfill a variety of needs for young children. If the imaginary companion was created primarily to serve a particular need, then it makes sense that the imaginary companion would disappear when the need is satisfied.[19] This is true for any of the needs listed in Chapter 4, but here I have singled out companionship because it is one of the primary functions served by imaginary friends.

In children's stories, imaginary companions disappear when the child character finally acquires some real friends and the imaginary companion is no longer required for companionship. For example, the bear in Martha Alexander's *The Blackboard Bear* goes back to his original identity as a drawing inside a rectangle of slate.[20] Guy-guy, Bickerina, and Mr. Dobie are never heard from again when the little girl in *The Three Funny Friends* by Charlotte Zolotow makes friends with a child who lives next door.[21] The substitution of real friends for imaginary ones seems to be viewed by the authors of children's books as the most suitable or satisfying way to wrap things up.

This sort of ending also characterizes the reports of parents. When pressed for an explanation, parents link the fading of the imaginary companion with the beginning of school and its opportunities to socialize with real children.[22] And certainly there is a pronounced drop in the identification of imaginary companions when we compare parental reports for preschool children and children older than 6 years, the age when most children start school. In Newson and Newson's sample, only 3 percent of 700 7-year-olds were identified by their parents as having an imaginary companion (as compared with 22 percent of these children at age 4).

However, there is reason to question the tendency of parents to equate the disappearance of imaginary companions with the beginning of school. There are problems with the accuracy of parental reports, even for younger children, and these problems become worse as children get older. When researchers interview school children, they often discover that, unbeknownst to the parents, the pretend friends are still active in the children's fantasy lives.[23] The discrepancy between what children and parents report was particularly striking in Jennifer Mauro's study. Twenty-nine of the 38 parents in the sample reported that their children gave up their imaginary companions during the first year of the study, when the children were about 5 years of age. By the time the children were 7 years old, all the parents reported that their children no longer played with the imaginary companions. In contrast, most of the children claimed that either the imaginary companion was still around or that they had created a new one. Thus, many children continue to play with their imaginary companions into the school years, but parents do not know about it.[24] The tendency of older children to show less overt acting out of fantasy could account for the fact that parents underestimate the ages at which imaginary companions are abandoned.

Although I believe that some children very likely stop playing with imaginary friends when real ones become more available, for many others, imagining a pretend companion is not really the same sort of thing as playing with a real child. Interactions with pretend friends involve imaginative actvities that might differ from play with real children, and imaginary companions have special qualities as play partners that that are not necessarily found in real children. Thus, an imaginary companion is not always a pale substitute for the real thing. Children who enjoy using their imagination in this way are not necessarily going to give up fantasy friends when real ones come along.

Are they really gone?

In the fall of 1995, Bill Watterson rocked my world by announcing that he had decided to stop producing his comic strip. Along with countless others, I was going to have to adjust to life without a daily fix of *Calvin and Hobbes*. As the date for the final strip approached, my graduate students and I wondered how Watterson would choose to close this chapter of the *Calvin and Hobbes* saga. We were not the only ones engaged in such speculation—I saw one parody of the final panel that depicted Hobbes in a garbage can. I had confidence that Watterson would not be so harsh, but given the assumptions people have about imaginary companions, that sort of theme might have crossed his mind. However, on December 31, 1995, Calvin and Hobbes were excited to discover that everything outside was covered with a fresh layer of snow. The final panel shows them tobogganing away together down a hill, full of anticipation for the day ahead and their continued adventures.

Not much is known about the ultimate fate of real-life childhood imaginary companions, but this final drawing for *Calvin and Hobbes*

FIGURE 6. *Drawing of the Skateboard Guy next to the pocket where he lives.*

is probably more typical than most parents suspect. We have found that about half of the adults we have interviewed who report having had imaginary companions as children indicate that they stopped playing with their pretend friends sometime after they were 10 years of age.[25] Many schoolchildren report they still play with their imaginary companions, at home and sometimes at school. One 10-year-old boy described playing with his imaginary companion at recess break; a 7-year-old in our research told us about the Skateboard Guy, who waits in his shirt pocket during school, but then performs skateboarding tricks to entertain the child as he walks home from school.[26] Newson and Newson also include some descriptions of imaginary companions that lasted into the school years. One of the parents in their study reported that her son had an invisible friend named Lion who was a real comfort to him. One day when the mother was late coming home from work, her son was afraid that she had had an accident. He talked it over with Lion, who told him that she hadn't and that she wasn't dead. Another 7-year-old in this study still played with two friends named Robins and Jelly. They were 100 years old and knew everything. The parent reported that all the neighbors knew about Robins and Jelly because he talked to them frequently when he walked home from school.[27]

Professor Ronald Siegel of UCLA gives one detailed report of a 14-year-old girl whose mother was concerned because she was still playing with Chopsticks, the imaginary dragon who had been her friend since early childhood.[28] Chopsticks was quite a striking example of an imaginary companion. He was a royal blue color with pointed ears, green eyes, a poodlelike face, reptile feet, a little white beer belly, and the ability to shrink from his normal height of eight feet to fit any space. The mother described Chopsticks as being ferocious—"Watch out for Chopsticks. He'll rip your head off"—but otherwise didn't know much about him. When asked why, she replied, "That's because Nancy rarely talks about him, and I'm always afraid to ask."[29]

The girl had stopped playing publicly with Chopsticks since the age of 10, but carried on long conversations with him when she was alone in her room. Siegel met with the girl several times, and on one memorable occasion met with Chopsticks. Siegel ultimately had a benign view of Chopsticks—he didn't see much cause for concern. As it turned out, Chopsticks disappeared on his own without intervention from adults. Although Siegel and the mother had both overheard the girl discussing plans for her 16th birthday party with Chopsticks, he did not show up for the event and was never heard from again.

In some cases, traces of a childhood imaginary companion can be found in the lives of adults. Dovima, one of the top models of the 1950s who was described by Richard Avedon as the most remarkable and unconventional beauty of her time, was actually Dorothy Virginia Margaret Juba. When she became a model, she adopted the name of the imaginary companion she invented as a child when she was bedridden with rheumatic fever. Clearly, she still fondly remembered the invisible Dovima.[30] Similarly, the imaginary companion of Paul Taylor, the famous choreographer of the dance company that bears his name, still lingers in Taylor's imagination. The thin and elderly George Tacet, Ph.D. (Tacet is Latin for "he is silent"), who was blamed for Taylor's misdeeds as a child, is now given costume credit in the programs for some of the troupe's performances.[31]

The imaginary companion of Frida Kahlo, the famous Mexican artist, is described in her diary where it is linked to a large painting called "The Two Fridas" in which two likenesses of the artist are shown side by side holding hands. I was familiar with this painting, but did not make the connection with imaginary companions until a recent trip to Mexico City. During our visit to the Frida Kahlo Museum, my friend and colleague Deborah Legorreta translated for me the pages of Frida's diary that are on exhibit there beside a reproduction of "The Two Fridas." Here is what Frida wrote in her diary about her imaginary companion.

ORIGIN OF THE TWO FRIDAS
=Memory=
I must have been six years old when I had the intense experience of an imaginary friendship with a little girl . . . roughly my own age. On the window of my old bedroom facing Allende Street, I used to breathe on one of the top panes. And with my finger I would draw a "door". . . Through that "door," I would come out, in my imagination, and hurriedly, with immense happiness, I would cross all the field I could see until I reached a dairy store named PINZÓN . . . Through the "O" of PINZÓN I entered and descended impetuously to the entrails of the earth, where "my imaginary friend" always waited for me. I don't remember her appearance or her color. But I do remember her joyfulness—she laughed a lot. Soundlessly. She was agile and danced as if she were weightless. I followed her in every movement and while she danced, I told her my secret problems. Which ones? I can't remember. But from my voice she knew all about my affairs. When I went back to the window, I would enter through the same door I had drawn on the glass. When? How long had I been with her? I don't know. It could have been a second or thousands of years . . . I was happy. I would erase the "door" with my hand and it would "disappear." I ran with my secret and my joy to the furthest corner of the patio of my house, under a cedron tree; I would shout and laugh Amazed to be Alone with my great happiness and with the very vivid memory of the girl. It has been 34 years since I lived that magical friendship and every time I remember it, it comes alive and grows more and more inside my world.
PINZON 1950. Frida Kahlo[32]

Although many imaginary companions vanish without a trace or lingering thought, Kahlo's words speak for the adults who still cherish the memory of an invisible childhood friend. Another part of the story regarding the ultimate fate of imaginary companions created by preschool children is that, contrary to popular belief, at least some are maintained beyond the age of 6 or 7. In fact, they may continue in some form for years. What about the imaginary companions that are created later in life by older children or even adults? This is the topic of the next chapter.

7

Do Older Children and Adults Create Imaginary Companions?

▼
▼

I started to walk down the street when I heard a voice saying, "Good evening, Mr. Dowd." I turned, and there was this great white rabbit leaning against a lamp-post. Well, I thought nothing of that, because when you have lived in a town as long as I have lived in this one, you get used to the fact that everybody knows your name. Naturally, I went over to chat with him.

— Elwood Dowd explains how he first met his
imaginary companion in the movie *Harvey*

JIMMY Stewart's portrayal of a gentle adult who had an imaginary rabbit friend in the movie *Harvey* is the sort of example that comes to mind when we consider the possibility of adults having imaginary companions. But Elwood Dowd was not a run-of-the-mill adult. He would have been unusual even if he had refrained from talking to a giant invisible rabbit while walking down the main street of his town. Despite his age, Elwood's naive personality and sheltered existence (unmarried, unemployed, living with his sister) made him more like a child than a grownup. Harvey was a source of concern and embarrassment for Elwood's family and led others to gossip about him behind his back.

Adults with imaginary companions are also portrayed in works of fiction as mentally ill. For example, in *Who's Afraid of Virginia Woolf?* Edward Albee introduces us to George and Martha, an unhappily married couple who have collaborated for years on an elaborate fantasy about an imaginary son.[1] In Act Three ("The Exorcism"), the son is revealed as fantasy to the other characters in the play when Martha violently objects to George's decision to imagine that the son, now a 21-year-old college student, has been killed in a car accident. Their fantasy about an imaginary son is the basis for George and Martha being described in literary commentary as mentally ill. "Albee muffles, even camouflages madness. By act 2 we have a full sense of the characters' anger; but only in act 3 do we fully comprehend the extent of George and Martha's psychic dislocation."[2]

So what about real-life people who are psychologically healthy and have adult lifestyles with adult responsibilities? Do they ever have imaginary companions? The answer is yes. Although peak production of imaginary companions occurs during the preschool period, fantasies involving imaginary others are definitely not confined to early childhood. First of all, as discussed in Chapter 6, some children continue playing with their early childhood companions well beyond the preschool years. It also is true that some pretend friends, albeit a minority, arrive on the scene for the first time in late childhood or early adolescence and persist into adulthood. And yes, even adults sometimes describe fantasy experiences that bear a strong resemblance to the early childhood phenomenon that is the primary subject of this book.

Imaginary companions and worlds created by older children

Not much is known about the pretend friends created after the preschool period, but some cases have been recorded. Dr. Jerome Singer, whose work has been discussed extensively in this book, writes that as a 13-year-old boy he passed the time on subway rides to school by discussing twentieth-century life with an imaginary gentleman visiting from Ancient Rome.[3] Inge Seiffge-Krenke, a developmental psychologist at the University of Bonn in Germany, conducted a study in which she identified adolescents who kept diaries (94 of the 241 children in her study) and then analyzed the diary entries in search of references to imaginary companions. She found that 35 percent of the 11- to 13-year-olds, 55 percent of the 14- and 15-year-olds, and 28 percent of the 16- and 17-year-olds who had diaries mentioned imaginary companions.[4] Interestingly, the adolescents in this study who had imaginary companions did not differ from the other adolescents in the number or closeness of real friends, a finding that supports the claim that children with imaginary companions are not individuals who have difficulty making real friends (see Chapter 3).

Although the available descriptions are somewhat limited, these later-appearing pretend friends seem to be just as varied as the preschool variety, and they mirror some of the same themes. Sometimes children create them for companionship, such as one 12-year-old who created an imaginary dog to keep her company on her early morning paper route.[5] Harriman has documented several case studies of teenagers who created imaginary companions that embodied characteristics that the creators wished to have themselves.[6] One boy, upon starting school, created an imaginary companion named Bill, who never made a mistake and received the highest grades in the class. After four years, Bill was replaced by Joe, who was a great athlete. This boy also had a female imaginary friend named Helen, who had a great personality, was a good student, and was involved in many extracurricular activities at school. The boy gave up all these imaginary companions at age 18.

Occasionally the fantasies of older childhood go well beyond the invention of a pretend friend. In fact, some children, typically at about 9 or 10 years of age, create "paracosms"—entire societies or worlds for the imaginary people to inhabit. An example of a paracosm is described in the movie *Heavenly Creatures,* a true story about two adolescent girls in New Zealand who developed a close friendship based, in part, on their shared imaginary world. The girls spent countless hours together discussing the interpersonal intrigues of an imaginary royal family and making clay figurines of their favorite characters. Their preoccupation with this invented world and with each other reached a fever pitch, making a coming separation so unthinkable that the girls committed an actual murder to prevent it.

How common is it for children to create such elaborate fantasies, and what does the invention of a paracosm say about its creator? The bulk of what is known about paracosms comes from the comprehensive account of imaginary worlds in the work of Robert Silvey and Stephen MacKeith, which is most fully described in a book by David Cohen and MacKeith.[7] Robert Silvey was the head of the BBC's Audience Research from 1932 until 1968. After he retired from this position, he published a paper about an imaginary world he had created as a child which he called the Hentian States. In this article, he indicated that he would welcome communications from any of his readers who had also created imaginary worlds. From this beginning, Silvey and MacKeith collected 64 case studies, including paracosms created by 61 adults and three children with about equal numbers of males and females. These authors were primarily interested in private worlds that: (1) were clearly recognized by the child as being imaginary, (2) held the child's interest for an extended period of time, and (3) were considered to be very important to the child.

The paracosms described in this report were extremely varied; 17 of the 64 were magical kinds of places, 45 were naturalistic, and 2 combined both magical and naturalistic features. Some of the worlds were based on toy or object props, and some were entirely in the minds of the creators. They also varied tremendously in the amount of structure and artifacts associated with them. Some of the paracosms were equipped with government systems, documents, maps, cultures, religions, histories, public transportation systems, currency, national anthems, magazines, and languages specified by the child. One child had created a special script for his imaginary world that was based on a Tamil primer brought back from India by his father. One of the paracosms was a world known as Branmail inhabited entirely by cats ("Access could only be obtained by scaling a height called Bumpety Banks").[8] In another, two sisters shared "Mrses," an imaginary world in which hot-water bottles were used as husbands and a variety of toys were the children. Friskyland, a paracosm shared by an 8-year-old girl and a 10-year-old boy, was populated by children called Friskies, good-natured hedgehog-like animals called Big Dears and Little Dears, and horrible creatures called Naughts. Friskyland was described as "a pleasant land, somehow not far away, but out of sight until you were there, and then you were amongst its green and pleasant fields and undulating hills. . . there were no houses in Friskyland, but very many Friskies."[9] Other paracosms included an imaginary village with a list of 282 residents that the child used as the setting for a series of stories she told herself about the people who lived there, and Coneland, a place with hollowed-out giant cones in which you could live and fly. The trees in Coneland were the tallest in the world, and their soft insides were tinned as "good Conish food." There was also Possumbul (two male cousins shared the throne of this kingdom), whose inhabitants spoke Possumbulese. The heir to the throne was a teddy bear. One 8-year-old girl and her brother created a world inhabited by a tiny race of people called the Minaturians. World 2 was a Utopian domain where the child "was very happy, did nothing in particular but just enjoyed being there. It was a happy, enjoyable un-evil place."[10]

Although these descriptions were collected in a relatively unsystematic way—primarily by asking friends and acquaintances and by advertising in journals and newspapers for individuals who remembered having a paracosm when they were younger—they are valuable for the rich detail and insight they provide about the fantasy lives of school-aged children. The peak age for creation of a paracosm was identified as 9 (74 percent were created between the ages of 7 and 12, 19 percent between 3 and 6 years, and 7 percent between 13 and 16). Some of the paracosms invented by these individuals had been freely shared with family and friends at the time of their creation, while others had been kept private until the participants decided to report the information to Silvey and MacKeith. Some of the creators received support from their parents, some kept their paracosms private, and others had parents who knew about the paracosms and actively discouraged the children's involvement. For example, one participant recalled that his father found a list of the radio and television programs available in the paracosm and wrote "rubbish" across it. In many cases involving the creation of imaginary companions, children have some time to be alone or they are in situations in which other people are not readily available for play. However, very few of the participants in this study were only children. In fact, one boy lived with seven family members in a four-and-a-half-room apartment. He described the outhouse as the only place where a person could be alone. The imaginary world he created was private and invisible rather than based on toys as props.

Descriptions of paracosms are also plentiful in historical accounts and autobiographies when these include details about the subject's childhood. Silvey and MacKeith list several such examples, including a fairy world based on toy soldiers, porcelain figures, and miniature paintings created by Friedrich Wilhelm Nietzsche, and the rival kingdoms of Nosingtonia and Encyclopedia created by Robert Louis Stevenson at the age of six in collaboration with his cousin Robert Alan Mowbray Stevenson. The four Brontë children, Charlotte, Branwell, Emily, and Anne, created two imaginary worlds that lasted into their adult years and may well have contributed to their development as novelists. Charlotte and Branwell invented the country of Angria, including descriptions of the geography, politics, community leaders, writers, and ordinary citizens. They wrote a literature of poems, stories, and history for Angria and worked out the personalities of its leaders. Anne and Emily created Gondal, which was a simpler, more emotional sort of place than Angria.[11]

One of the most elaborate literary cases I have come across is described in a biography of Barbara Follett, a writer who achieved early fame as a novelist, but tragically and mysteriously disappeared while still a young adult. According to her biographer, she was engrossed for several years as a young girl and teenager in the creation of an imaginary world called Farksolia.[12] This book includes her detailed accounts of the plants, animals, people, and history of Farksolia and excerpts from a dictionary of its language, Farksoo (e.g., "Ar peen maiburs barge craik coo" means "As the mayflowers begin to come").

Is the invention of an imaginary world associated with mental illness or an inability to deal with a community of real people? For the most part the participants in Silvey and MacKeith's research seemed to have enjoyed happy family lives—their paracosms were not escapes from hostile environments. The inventors of imaginary worlds also did not appear to suffer from isolation or an inability to get along with others. In fact, many of the worlds were shared among several children who played together happily. In most cases the paracosms were abandoned by 18 years of age, although some of the informants reported having some participation in fantasy worlds even as adults. Like imaginary companions, most of the paracosms were described as eventually fading away, as the child lost interest and began to spend more time participating in other activities.

Even more than with imaginary companions, it is tempting to assume that paracosms are rare, but I have found that once you start looking for them, accounts of paracosms are surprisingly easy to come by. Among my own acquaintances I know of several, including a preschooler who regularly told his mother about "the planet Geranium" and a 10-year-old who created an imaginary institute complete with an invisible train to take him there and back. Another child I know began to talk about Martians at an early age and over the years developed an increasingly elaborate fantasy about Mars. The child's parents initially interpreted his fantasy as reflecting a special interest in learning about Mars; however, when they supplied him with factual information about the planet, he responded as if they were attempting to challenge him. He would listen patiently to what they had to say, then inform them that things operated differently on *his* Mars.

The fact that locating a child who has a paracosm is not difficult and that there are many accounts of paracosms created by children who became famous as adults does not tell us anything about how common paracosms are in the general population. As far as I know, no one has questioned a large random sample of adults about whether they created imaginary worlds as children. However, the results of a small pilot study conducted by Stephanie Carlson and myself were interesting and suggestive, although preliminary. We gave a questionnaire about imaginary worlds to 22 students (12 females, 10 males, ranging in age from 17 to 28 years) who were registered for a summer class in psychology. Eleven of the 22 students claimed to have had an imaginary world, defined in the questionnaire as "a spontaneously created, fictional private world that is maintained and elaborated, sometimes for a number of years." We excluded six of these fantasies from the paracosm category, one because the student simply described her enjoyment of being under a table or in a closet, and five because they did not go beyond simple daydreams (i.e., a fantasy about using magic words, daydreams about the people in her life doing the things she wanted them to do, a fantasy about a bedroom being an apartment that was separate from her parents' house, a fantasy about being a hero in a variety of war-type situations, and a daydream about relaxing on a tropical island).

The other five descriptions were clear examples of the phenomenon: (1) a tropical rain forest inhabited by talking animals, (2) a Utopian planet in outer space where there was no war or sadness, (3) a magical place where you could fly, heal yourself, communicate by telepathy, and influence the outcomes of events, (4) a forest by the ocean inhabited by many animals, and (5) a place called Rho Tichris. The last one, a paracosm the male subject created at age 9 and abandoned at age 12, was described in meticulous detail. Here are some excerpts:

> While Rho Tichris was a vast world of various ecosystems, I had only been able to visit arid regions, with rolling dunes and an incarnadine sky; yet the heat normally associated with such an environment was not there.

> The planet I labeled Rho Tichris was situated a million miles from Earth, yet I could be transported there with but a thought; apparently my con-

sciousness was catapulted into the body of a being I know not (but he had blue skin); there may have been a reciprocal transference of his consciousness into my body, but I never gave it much thought.

The most important character was Marc Namor, another earthling who had arrived prior to myself and was technically the ruler of the planet. (He appeared as human; either he had arrived in body or was using magic to alter his appearance.) Other beings included dune dogs (gigantic hounds that bore riders through the desert), the Blue (blue-skinned humanoids such as myself) and the Dire Grim, our hated race with sinister features such as telescoping eyes, seven rows of teeth, and the protrusion of a third arm from the groin.

Marc Namor was able to manipulate the forces of nature as well as atomic particles themselves so as to perform a number of tasks that were impressive, but not very useful. (He was especially adept at fashioning windows out of sand.) He was also capable of levitation and flight (as was I, but to a lesser degree).

It (Rho Tichris) used pictograms to describe events. I was the sole chronicler of history and was forced to write in a style comprehensible to others, as the Blue could not fathom a phonetic alphabet.

Cohen and MacKeith took care to distinguish imaginary worlds from the creation of pretend friends, pointing out that paracosms are much more elaborate, tend to be the property of children older than is typical for imaginary companions, and, unlike imaginary companions, are remembered very well for decades. However, I see the two phenomena as quite closely related. Perhaps the more private nature of play with imaginary companions by older children lends itself to the creation of an imaginary world for the pretend friends to inhabit. After all, the imaginary companions of older children are less welcome in the real world than those of preschoolers. Like Cohen and MacKeith, we found that paracosms are largely a phenomenon of middle and late childhood. What about adults? Do they ever have imaginary companions? More generally, is there any continuity between the pretend play of children and adult fantasy activities?

Do adults have imaginary companions?

Consider this anecdote provided by a flight attendant working on a trip from New York to Miami. When she asked one of the passengers

FIGURE 7. *B. Hickerson,
Copyright 1993. Distributed
by the Los Angeles Times
Syndicate. Reprinted
with permission.*

**"Oh NO! My WIFE . . . and my IMAGINARY
FRIEND!"**

if she wanted a drink, the woman answered, "I'll have a scotch and soda, and he'll (gesturing to the empty seat beside her) have a scotch and soda." The attendant placed two drinks in front of the woman who complained, "Well, aren't you going to let his tray down and give him a napkin?" The attendant let down the tray and placed one of the drinks in front of the empty seat and then said, "That will be $5 please." The woman gestured to her invisible companion and said, "He'll pay for it."[13]

Our response to someone like this woman would probably be similiar to the reactions elicited by the fictional portrayals of Elwood Dowd *(Harvey)* and Martha and George *(Who's Afraid of Virginia Woolf?)*. To put it bluntly, she comes across as a little crazy. Even more so than with children, adults who create and interact with invisible friends are assumed to be disturbed. Margaret Svendsen, who was relatively positive about the imaginary companions of children, spoke for many when she wrote that when the phenomenon was encountered in adults, it was a sign of psychopathology.[14] But is this necessarily true? I think there is an erroneous assumption here that having an imaginary companion is like having a delusion or hallucination—the creator, whether a child or an adult, believes the friend to be real. This sort of behavior might be tolerated to some extent in children because of the widespread belief that childhood is a stage of life in which it is normal to lack a firm grasp on reality. But in adults, the expression of delusional beliefs and hallucinations is not normative, and often is central to the identification of mental illness.

I have argued, against this view (see Chapter 5), that the imaginary companions of young children are quite different from delusions. There is at least some evidence that even young children understand that their imaginary friends are pretend. Thus, if we want to identify an adult version of the phenomenon, we need to identify imaginary companions that the adults know are not real. We should stay away from the residents of psychiatric wards who talk to Napoleon and look for something closer to the child model of a pretend friend.

These restrictions—that (1) the companion be imaginary and (2) the adult know the companion is imaginary—rule out lots of entities that bear at least a passing resemblance to imaginary companions. For example, I am often asked if guardian angels are imaginary companions. Actually, guardian angels are only one of many candidates that have been suggested to me as constituting the imaginary companions of adults. What about fairies, ghosts, creatures from outer space, or even God? Should any of these be considered imaginary companions? I think not. In these cases, both the actual and the perceived realities are debatable. This point is most clear in the domain of religion. Many adults around the world strongly believe that God, angels, and spirits of various sorts are absolutely real. Faith, the capacity to believe without doubt, is prayed for and highly valued. An atheist observing the practices of someone who believes in God might refer to the person as having an imaginary companion, but the experience of the believer is quite different from that of a child interacting with a pretend friend. The term "imaginary companion" in this context would be considered insulting.[15]

The case for ghosts, creatures from outer space, and similar beings is less clear. For one thing, considerable disagreement exists about whether these beings are real or imaginary. Although there is currently no accepted scientific evidence for the paranormal, a 1990 Gallup Poll of 1,236 American adults indicated that 25 percent believe in ghosts, 17 percent report they have been in touch with someone who has died, 10 percent believe they have been in the presence of a ghost, more than 50 percent believe in the devil (10 percent reported having talked with the devil), and 14 percent say they have seen an unidentified flying object.[16]

Belief in the paranormal is not limited to a particular social class or education level. Sir Arthur Conan Doyle, who is famous for his stories about Sherlock Holmes (ironically, a detective who found natural explanations for events that struck others as supernatural), had an intense interest in the occult in his private life. In his book *The Coming of Fairies,* he documented his efforts to determine if a series of photographs taken by two young girls showing small winged people were veridical.[17] Doyle concluded that fairies, gnomes, and other small humanlike beings exist, and speculated that some of them might have evolved from insects.[18] He was not alone in these ideas. Debate continues over the status of many such creatures, with skeptics dismissing believers as mentally deranged or, at best, unintelligent, and believers criticizing skeptics as narrow-minded.

If we broaden our view to take a cross-cultural perspective, the magnitude of the problem of how to decide what is real and what is fantasy becomes even more staggering. There is not one objective truth about the boundary between fantasy and reality. Essentially, the same belief can be judged as a delusion or a nondelusion depending on the culture of the believer.[19] For example, one of the most basic differences in world views concerns the distinction based on reality as perceived by the senses and reality that cannot be apprehended with our senses because it is masked by material reality.[20] In any case, my point is that in order to qualify as an imaginary companion, the entity in question has to be imaginary. According to many people, one cannot categorically rule out the possibility that the entities mentioned above have some basis in reality.

Fortunately it is not necessary for me to decide whether a particular invisible entity is real. All that matters to me is the belief of the person who communes with it. In order to be similar to the childhood phenomenon of imaginary companions, the adult who claims to interact with a ghost, for example, would have to conceptualize the ghost as a figment of his or her imagination. In many cases, however, adults who claim to interact with things like ghosts are individuals who believe these entities are real. Are there any experiences of adults that are more like children's imaginary companions?

A few adults do seem to have relationships with pretend friends that closely resemble the phenomenon observed in childhood. The incidence of imaginary companions among adults is not known, in part because questionnaires given to adults have been biased by researchers who assumed imaginary companions were the domain of childhood. Unfortunately, I have been guilty of this bias myself.

In one study with adults, we asked, "How old were you when you stopped thinking about the imaginary companion?"—a question that suggests the imaginary companions are no longer around. Despite being asked in this way, a few adults reported that they continued to interact with their imaginary companions as adults. One woman wrote that when she was "debating something in my mind somehow they are the other voices of reasoning which help me come to a conclusion." A couple of respondents reported that they still interacted with stuffed animals who had been with them since childhood ("I still tell my bunny my problems"). One professional woman told me that she used a stuffed animal as a go-between when discussing difficult issues with her husband. A couple described the personalities and adventures of the stuffed animals in their extensive collection. The husband, an award-winning writer of fiction, also reported that he had relationships with story characters long after he had finished writing about them. Together, he and his wife recounted some of the past exploits of these characters, in and out of their respective novels.

For a week in 1995 (12/7 to 12/13), the "Cool Site of the Day" on the World Wide Web was *Fred's Place,* a home page for imaginary companions. The page was started by the creator of Fred, an imaginary companion described in the following way:

> Fred is my friend and I love him dearly. Nonetheless he does not exist. This fact would surely be hard to live with, so I do not bug him with it. (Does he know he does not exist? I really do not know. I don't really want to ask. Massless people have feelings too, you know.) Until now he has had absolutely no representation in reality and has begged to be acknowledged as an entity even though he is without volume or mass. Though for some time I could think of no solution to his problem I have felt that it is my duty to bring him into YOUR reality. Now, with the advent of the information highway, he is able to enter that realm by means of the Internet!

Probably not many adults have a friend like Fred, but this should not be interpreted as evidence for a wholesale abandonment of pretense. Kendall Walton, professor of philosophy at the University of Michigan, makes a strong case for the relation between fantasy behavior in childhood and common adult activities such as going to movies, reading novels, and enjoying the visual arts. Walton goes so far as to describe representational works of art such as Michelangelo's *David* as props in adult games of make-believe just as dolls and trucks are props in children's pretend play. "I take seriously the association with children's games—with playing house and school, cops and robbers, cowboys and Indians, with fantasies built around dolls, teddy bears, and toy trucks. We can learn a lot about novels, paintings, theater, and film by pursuing analogies with make-believe activities like these."[21]

Most adults enjoy some sort of fantasy consumption, whether movies or novels, but the more interesting comparison with childhood imaginary companions centers on adult *production* of fantasy material. Role-playing games like "Dungeons and Dragons" and groups like the "Society for Creative Anachronism" provide opportunities for many adults, as well as adolescents, to engage in fantasy. There are also a variety of experiences reported by adults that share some of the features of having an imaginary companion. These kinds of experiences vary from intellectual exercises such as Hillary Clinton's imagined conversations with Eleanor Roosevelt to much more fully developed and maintained fantasies. Some adults have such active imaginations that psychologists refer to them as fantasy-prone.[22] This relatively small segment of the population (about 3 percent to 4 percent) spend half or more of their waking hours absorbed in fantasies involving elaborate scenarios, much like real-life Walter Mittys. A variety of developmental antecedents have been identified for this select group including being encouraged to pretend by a significant adult, early engagement in activities such as ballet, piano, or drama, and their enjoyment of imaginative games, such as having an imaginary companion.[23] Here is a narrative taken from an excellent chapter on fantasy-proneness by Stephen Jay Lynn, Judith Pintar, and Judith Rhue.

My imagination is my best friend. Ever since I was a child, I lived in a special world. I could manipulate it and keep it private. It was for no one else. I talked to dolls, stuffed animal, and toys. Each had a separate personality. I had an imaginary companion, Alexis. I would ask Alexis for advice, have extensive discussions with her, and play games with her. My parents knew about her and even talked with her as I was growing up, addressing her by name. We would set a place at the table for her, and my mother and I would play games like tea party with her. I would draw her in different clothes. I have many drawings of me and Alexis. My parents told me to trust my fantasy life, it was sacred and as real as I wanted it to be. Even when I grew older, and stopped talking to rocks and trees and the sky, I had Alexis; she was part of me, always in the background, a benevolent presence. To me, she played many parts. I never had a sister. She was a sister to me in some ways, and in other ways a sort of parent figure who was always available. As I grew older, she seemed to grow with me, age with me. When I am afraid, I sometimes talk to her, and she is a source of comfort. When I have writer's block, she is my muse. We are separate yet together. It is the separateness that is still enriching, now she is less a sister, less a parent, more a sort of guardian angel.[24]

My reading of the literature suggests that, for the majority of fantasy-prone adults, extensive fantasy activities are just one aspect of their interesting and productive lives. For some fantasy-prone individuals, however, engagement in fantasy seems to have developed as a strategy for dealing with chaotic and difficult life situations. In this minority group, there is often a reported history of physical or sexual abuse and psychological problems. Clearly there are multiple paths to fantasy-proneness, and this aspect of personality interacts with life experiences to result in a variety of outcomes.[25]

Beyond this restricted group of fantasy-prone individuals, many adults in the general population enjoy the production of fantasy. In a fascinating book, *Imaginary Social Worlds,* cultural anthropologist John Caughey of the University of Maryland at College Park claims that the social worlds of most people include a large number of individuals whom they know only through television, books, movies, and other forms of media, as well as the people they interact with face-to-face in their everyday lives.[26] According to Caughey, the experience of having a personal social relationship with a famous individual one has never actually encountered in real life is quite common. These fantasy relationships often go beyond intense interest and admiration and actually involve imagined conversations, meetings, and extended interactions.

When we think of fantasy relationships with well-known people, pathological examples come to mind—John Hinkley Jr.'s fantasy relationship with Jody Foster, Mark Chapman's obsession with John Lennon. Caughey argues that these extreme cases tend to make us overlook how common imagined relationships are in the population. Often the focus of these relationships is love and/or sexual attraction, such as imagined romantic attachments to Paul McCartney, Kurt Cobain, or Madonna. However, imaginary social relationships can also be a source of comfort, advice, companionship, or an avenue for intellectual debate. For example, Machiavelli is said to have

had imaginary dinner conversations with ancient poets and historical figures such as Moses, Romulus, and Theseus.[27] Caughey ex-
haustively describes the many forms such relationships take and the
important role he believes they play in people's lives.

Novelists, playwrights, and screenwriters also provide interesting
examples of adults who are preoccupied with the production of fantasy. For fiction writers, creating an imaginary character or an invented world is all in a day's work. Actually, there is some evidence
that literary creativity, in particular, is related to having had an imaginary companion in childhood.[28] C. S. Lewis explicitly pointed out
the relation between his childhood creation of a paracosm named
Animal-Land and his later career.

> At the age of six, seven, and eight—I was living almost entirely in my
> imagination; or at least the imaginative experience of those years now
> seems to me more important than anything else. Thus, I pass over a hol-
> iday in Normany (of which, nevertheless, I retain very clear memories) as
> a thing of no account; if it could be cut out of my past I should still be al-
> most exactly the man I am. But imagination is a vague word and I must
> make some distinctions. It may mean that world of reverie, daydream,
> wish fulfilling fantasy. Of that I knew more than enough. I often pictured
> myself cutting a fine figure. But I must insist that this was a totally dif-
> ferent activity from the invention of Animal-Land. Animal-Land was not
> (in that sense) a fantasy at all. I was not one of the characters it con-
> tained. I was its creator, not a candidate for admission to it. Invention
> is essentially different from reverie; if some fail to recognize the differ-
> ence that is because they have not experienced both. Anyone who has will
> understand me. In my daydreams I was training myself to be a fool;
> in mapping and chronicling Animal-Land I was training myself to be
> a novelist.[29]

The reflections of fiction writers about the creation of imaginary
characters contain insights and observations that are fascinating and
instructive. In particular, I am intrigued by the commonly reported
experience that the characters become almost real and seem to have
minds of their own. Some writers experience the illusion that their
novel is being dictated to them, or that the characters are the ones
who are working out the plot. This adult experience of having an
imaginary collaborator or being essentially the secretary for an invis-
ible entity who takes the major role in determining what is written
dates to the time of the Greeks, who described the role of Muses in
the creative process.

There are also plenty of more recent examples. In her fascinating book *Invisible Guests,* Mary Watkins describes in careful detail how some creative activities in adulthood seem to promote the presence of imaginal others who are experienced as having an autonomous existence.[30] She makes a distinction between deliberate daydreams and more spontaneous imaginings in which the imaginer feels like a spectator, with imagined events and people surprising her just as events in the real world can surprise. Watkins's most striking examples were taken from the autobiographies and biographies of famous writers. Their accounts document the common experience of having the characters narrate the story to the author, as described by Enid Blyton:

> I shut my eyes for a few moments, with my portable typewriter on my knee—I make my mind blank and wait—and then, as clearly as I would see real children, my characters stand before me in my mind's eye. I see them in detail—hair, eyes, feet, clothes, expression—and I always know their Christian names, but never their surnames. . . . I don't know what anyone is going to say or do. I don't know what is going to happen. I am in the happy position of being able to write a story and read it for the first time, at one and the same moment. . . . Sometimes a character makes a joke, a really funny one, that makes me laugh as I type it on the paper— and I think, "Well, I couldn't have thought of that myself in a hundred years!" And then I think, "Well, who did think of it, then?"[31]

In another example, Watkins quotes Henry James's description of himself in relation to the novel in progress:

> These things continued to fall together, as by the neat action of their own weight and form even while their commentator James himself scratched his head about them; he easily sees now that they were always well in advance of him. As the case completed itself he had in fact, from a good way behind, to catch up with them; breathless and a little flurried, as he best could.[32]

The experiences reported in these quotes do not seem to be unique to these authors. Writers from Jean-Paul Sartre to Quentin Tarantino have described how their writing often seems to take the form of surrendering control of the content to the characters they have created. Alice Walker lived with the presences of Celie and Shug for a year while writing the novel *The Color Purple,* characters who not only advised Walker about events in the world of the novel, but also about matters concerning her real life.[33] Sue Grafton, the author of a best-selling mystery series, reports, "To this day every book I do is a surprise to me." She believes her best work comes "when I am able to get out of my own way. The object, as far as I'm concerned, is to let what I call my 'shadow side' write the book."[34] Grafton is working her way through the alphabet with her books (e.g., *A is for Alibi, B is for Burglar,* etc.). In referring to the actions of the female character in her books, Grafton says that when she finally gets to her 24th book, "I honestly don't know what she'll do. I'm going to give her the last book. Its all hers. It may not even be a mystery. All I know is that when we get to Z, she gets to do anything she wants."

In a move that was discomfiting to some readers but provided tremendous grist for the mills of literary commentators, John Fowles stepped completely out of the narrative in his novel *The French Lieutenant's Woman* to comment on the fact that he had lost control of the story and had no idea what was coming next. In Chapter 7 of the novel, Fowles writes:

> You may think novelists always have fixed plans to which they work, so that the future predicted by Chapter One is always inexorably the actuality of Chapter Thirteen. . . . We (novelists) know a world is an organism, not a machine. We also know that a genuinely created world must be independent of its creator; a planned world (a world that fully reveals its planning) is a dead world. It is only when our characters and events begin to disobey us that they begin to live. When Charles left Sarah on her cliff edge, I ordered him to walk straight back to Lyme Regis. But he did not; he gratuitously turned and went down to the Dairy.
>
> Oh, but you say, come on—what I really mean is that the idea crossed my mind as I wrote that it might be more clever to have him stop and drink milk . . . and meet Sarah again. That is certainly one explanation of what happened; but I can only report—and I am the most reliable witness—that the idea seemed to me to come clearly from Charles, not myself.[35]

Ventriloquist Edgar Bergen reported having a similar experience of his wooden dummy, Charlie McCarthy. Siegel describes this anecdote in his book *Fire in the Brain* in which he discusses the phenomenon as a kind of channeling:

> One day, a visitor came into Bergen's room and found him talking—not rehearsing—with Charlie. Bergen was asking Charlie a number of philosophical questions about the nature of life, virtue, and love. Charlie was

responding with brilliant Socratic answers. When Bergen noticed that he had a visitor, he turned red and said that he was talking with Charlie, the wisest person he knew. The visitor pointed out that it was Bergen's own mind and voice coming through the wooden dummy. Bergen replied, "Well, I guess ultimately it is, but I ask Charlie these questions and he answers, and I haven't the faintest idea of what he's going to say and I'm astonished by his brilliance—so much more than I know."[36]

Mystery writer John D. McDonald helped Dr. Raymond Fowler, professor emeritus at the University of Alabama, attempt to understand the relationship between the personalities of characters in works of fiction and the personality of their creators—how novelists live through the characters they create.[37] Fowler administered the Minnesota Multiphasic Personality Inventory (MMPI) to McDonald three times. McDonald took the test as himself; as Travis McGee, the main character in most of McDonald's books; and as Meyer, another character in McDonald's novels, McGee's close friend and confidant. The idea was to analyze the similarity of the two characters' personalities to each other and to that of John McDonald. The results showed that McDonald and McGee were radically different in personality, but that McDonald and Meyer were virtually indistinguishable. Fowler interpreted his results as suggesting that by creating a character like Meyer to inhabit the whole of his books, he was able "to enter McGee's life, to talk with him, advise him, and react to him."[38]

Perhaps this is what Kurt Vonnegut had in mind when he showed up at a bar in the middle of *Breakfast of Champions* in order to observe an interaction that was about to take place in the novel.

> "Give me a Black and White and water," he [Wayne Hobbler, one of the book's characters] heard the waitress say, and Wayne should have pricked up his ears at that. That particular drink wasn't for any ordinary person. That drink was for the person who had created all Wayne's misery to date, who could kill him or make him a millionaire or send him back to prison or do whatever he damn pleased with Wayne. That drink was for me.
>
> I had come to the Arts Festival incognito. I was there to watch a confrontation between two human beings I had created: Dwayne Hoover and Kilgore Trout. I was not eager to be recognized.[39]

At what point does an author's loss of control over a character occur, and what does it mean? There aren't many answers here, but lots of interesting questions and speculations. Our understanding of

how this illusion is possible might be informed by a new line of inquiry in cognitive psychology concerning automatisms in daily life,
instances in which people produce actions, but do not experience
the actions as voluntary, that is, they have no "feeling of doing." Professor Daniel Wegner of the University of Virginia believes that our
sense of having consciously intended our voluntary actions is something of an illusion.[40] According to Wegner, knowing what we are doing at the time of the action prompts the belief that we are causal
agents who made the act occur. However, he makes a strong case
that the conscious intention to move and the actual sequence of
events that gives rise to the movement are separable components.
His argument is based partly on a variety of examples in which the
performance of voluntary actions is clearly distinguishable from the
conscious intention to act (e.g., phantom limbs, dissociative experiences such as driving a car while thinking about something else,
etc.). Although Wegner focuses primarily on our impression of having caused our voluntary actions, he alludes to the same principles
being at work in actions that are entirely mental. The point here is
that the possibility of experiencing an imagined being as acting in
dependently is entirely consistent within the larger framework proposed by Wegner. Given the comments of adult authors, it seems
likely that this process takes some time to develop. In other words, I
suspect that imagined entities become unruly only after the fantasies
involving them are well established. This hunch fits with work by
Hubert Dreyfus and Stuart Dreyfus showing that performance becomes automatized with increasing expertise.[41]

What about children and their imaginary companions? Perhaps
the experience of imaginary others as having a somewhat autonomous existence that is not completely under the creator's control is
common to master pretenders of all ages. A particularly compelling
example of an uncontrollable pretend friend was described to me by
an adult who, between the ages of 3 and 5, enjoyed the company of
two invisible boys, Bing and Hood. Hood functioned as a regular
playmate, and was similar in most respects to the boy himself. Bing,
on the other hand, was smarter and generally superior to both Hood
and the boy. Bing had a better sense of humor, more impressive
things to say, and more interesting things to do. In fact, he was often
too busy to play; Bing had places to go and people to see. He was experienced by the boy as having a mind and life of his own. A large
part of what the adult recalled about having imaginary companions

was his conversations with Hood about Bing—wondering what he was doing that day and if he would show up to play—and his feelings of longing for him.

Difficulties in controlling the actions of imaginary companions have come up in several of the interviews we have conducted for our research. For example, a parent in one study described a trying situation that arose one afternoon when she took her 3-year-old daughter to a horse show. The child loved horses, but the outing was ruined because the child's imaginary pony was not there. The child was sure he would be with all the other horses, but a thorough search of the grounds indicated that the invisible pony must have had other plans for the day. The child's frustration seemed entirely genuine—the episode did not seem to be a manipulative ploy on the child's part to spend the afternoon some other way. The situation was exasperating for the mother who saw a seemingly obvious solution to the problem. Why couldn't her daughter just pretend the pony was there? For some reason, this didn't seem to be an option.

Other children have complained to us about imaginary friends who would not share, talked too loud, or would not do as they were told. There are a variety of ways to account for these sorts of complaints, but adults have sometimes taken them as evidence that the child thinks the pretend friend is real. However, the observation that adults also tend to experience imagined characters as having a mind of their own makes this interpretation troublesome. Do we want to claim that adult novelists believe their characters are real? Writers certainly become immersed in the fantasy worlds they create and, as they work, may lose track of their real-world surroundings. In fact, even *consumers* of fiction experience this disengagement with the real world when they become absorbed in a fantasy. But do novelists ever begin to think the fantasy characters or events belong to the real world? This would constitute a much stronger breakdown of the boundary between fantasy and reality, and I don't think it is going to turn out to be an accurate account of adult fantasy experience. Yet on the occasions that an imagined character is experienced as thinking and acting independently, he or she must seem eerily real.

The work of Marcia Johnson, professor of psychology at Princeton University, is relevant here. Johnson believes that "reality is not given by experience, but by judgment processes,"[42] and she has identified the characteristics of mental experience that allow one to determine that an event is real or imagined. For example, imagined events tend to have less sensory detail than actual perceptions of the real world, and they are more under conscious control. To the extent that imagined events become more detailed and less under control they are more difficult to distinguish from real perceptions. According to Johnson, one of the reasons that dreams, hallucinations, and delusions seem real is that they do not come and go as directed by the individual; instead they have an "unbidden quality" that makes them similar to real perception. Johnson writes:

> Most of the time, we have a sense of control over our imagination. One way, for example, of differentiating a present perception from a present imagination is to attempt to change the appearance of the object. Perceptions are more stable, whereas imaginations can be changed at will (e.g., Casey, 1976). Loss of control makes a self-generated event seem like a perceptual event.[43]

Maybe the loss of perceived control is a normal part of the phenomenology of elaborate sustained fantasy—a development that actually has the effect of making the fantasy more like real life.[44] This possibility adds an interesting caveat to the conclusion of Chapter 5 where I have argued that young children are relatively adept at distinguishing fantasy from reality. What about cases in which the pretend friend is imagined in great detail for sustained periods, possibly resulting in the illusion of independent agency? These conditions break down some of the differences between what is perceived and what is imagined, making the distinction harder to draw. Perhaps young children are not so sure about a fantasy friend if they begin to experience the companion as not completely under their control. This illusion might even have the effect of making the imaginary companion a less desirable playmate (see Chapter 6).

Unfortunately, these possibilities will need to await future investigations because the experience and process of fantasy creation either in adults or children is currently not well understood. Maybe opportunities for learning more will increase as more adults spend time pretending. Actually, as a consequence of access to computers and to the Internet, many adults now have expanded opportunities for flexing their imaginations. Every night thousands of people interact in hundreds of electronic chatrooms. The topics discussed are diverse, but a cursory glance at the names of rooms available on services such as America Online show that a majority involve sexual exploration. The fascinating part is that no one knows exactly what their partner in online sex is actually like. On the computer, people can present themselves in any number of fictitious ways. The joys of creating alter egos are being discovered by many people who wander into chatrooms and pretend to be 30 years younger, a different gender, a different sexual orientation, or in some other way take on an identity that is markedly different from their own. Thus, a man might fall in love and leave his wife for a beautiful young woman he met online, and then find out she is actually the imagined persona of a 75-year-old man.

In her research, Sherry Turkle, professor of sociology of sciences at Massachusetts Institute of Technology, explores how interactive computer environments, known as MUDs (multiuser domains), are transforming people's views of relationships and of reality.[45] MUDs provide a virtual reality that people share with many other people. When you begin, you create a description of your character that is totally up to you. The social interactions and ongoing events in MUDs can be thought of as a form of collaboratively written literature. Sherry Turkle describes the process in the following way:

> On some of these MUDs, players are invited to help build the computer world itself. Using relatively simple programming languages, they can make a "room" in the game space where they are able to set the stage and define the rules. That is, they make objects in the "second nature" and specify how they work. An eleven-year-old player builds a room she calls "the condo." It is beautifully furnished; she has created magical jewelry and makeup for her dressing table. When she visits the condo, she invites her friends, she chats, orders pizza, and flirts. Other players have more varied social lives: They create characters who have casual and romantic sex, hold jobs, attend rituals and celebrations, fall in love, and get married. To say the least, such goings-on are gripping: "This is more real than my real life," says a character who turns out to be a man playing a woman who is pretending to be a man.[46]

I am not sure what this person meant by "more real than real life." It could have been a way of expressing boredom with his mundane everyday existence and his engagement in the more exciting activities of his virtual character. However, his claim clearly speaks to the ability of adults, like children, to become engrossed in their fantasy creations.

8

Fantasy in the Lives of Children and Adults

▼

Even when the bird is walking we know that it has wings.

—Victor Hugo

NORMALLY developing children start to show clear evidence of their growing imaginations when they begin to pretend in the second year of life. For some, pretend play quickly becomes one of the dominant activities of their waking hours. How wonderful that this capacity is available so early on to help children process life events, achieve mastery of their emotions, enrich their social understanding, and develop their communication abilities.

Imaginary companions are only one of many forms that fantasy production takes during these early years, but I think they are quite special. First of all, the breathtaking diversity of imaginary companions bears witness to the richness of children's fantasy lives. Imaginary friends come in all shapes and sizes, all ages, genders, and species. They also have many different nationalities. In our work, we have identified cases of imaginary companions created by children in the United States, Canada, England, New Zealand, Italy, Israel, Hong Kong, and Japan. In ongoing research, Deborah Legorreta is finding many cases of imaginary companions created by children in Mexico City. Large scale studies investigating cross-cultural differences and similarities have yet to be done, but it is safe to say that imaginary companions circle the globe.

The variety of forms taken by imaginary companions defies the attempts of researchers to make generalizations about what imaginary companions are like and what it means to have one. The phenomenon is also rife with interesting contradictions. Imaginary companions strike adults as unusual and exotic, but it is common for children to have them. They seem to be the products of special minds, but researchers have struggled to identify any substantial differences between children who have them and children who do not. Parents are pushed to extremes of pride and concern by their children's friendships with imaginary beings, applauding the creativity evidenced by their child's inventiveness until some line is crossed and they begin to wonder about their child's mental health. The children themselves love their imaginary companions dearly, but many don't miss or even remember them after they are gone. Parents often feel nostalgic for ones that have disappeared, but become worried if they stay around too long. Lots of grist for the psychologist mill.

What are parents supposed to make of all of this? One recurrent theme in this book is that the invention of an imaginary companion should not be interpreted as a symptom of emotional or interpersonal problems. In fact, children who create imaginary companions tend to be particularly sociable individuals who enjoy the company of others and are somewhat advanced in social understanding. I have included clinical case studies in this book because they demonstrate the beneficial role of fantasy in helping children cope with traumatic events, but it is important to keep in mind that the creation of an imaginary companion is best interpreted as a positive sign of mental health.

Is there ever legitimate cause for concern? Parents often say that it is fine to be reassured that imaginary companions are *usually* a healthy, relatively common variation of the normal play behavior of young children. However, they don't really care about the general phenomenon; they are focused on the specific case of their own child. Maybe your child's behavior seems more extreme than the examples I have discussed, or the characteristics of your child's imaginary companion are more peculiar than any of the ones I have described. The phenomenon of having an imaginary companion is so varied that many parents are not going to find the counterpart of his or her child's pretend friend in the pages of this book. It may seem that, at some point, it makes sense to worry about a child's absorption in play with a fantasy friend.

I believe that imaginary companions, *themselves*, should not be a source of concern. However, an imaginary companion is sometimes created as a response to psychological distress, so I would want to know some other information about the child: Does he or she have any real friends? Does he or she have trouble sleeping, show nervous habits, or seem depressed? The answers to these questions would help determine if there was a problem. But note—a parent would be worried about a child who had no friends or was unhappy, whether or not he or she was involved in play with an imaginary companion. Actually, I would be more concerned about a lonely, unpopular child who did *not* have an imaginary companion or a child whose play showed the kind of grimness and monotony that raises red flags for child therapists. The presence of the imaginary companion may indicate that the child is at least trying to cope with his or her un-happiness. In the absence of any signs of distress, an imaginary companion, in and of itself, does not warrant concern. Quite the contrary. Relax and enjoy this positive sign of your child's active imagination.

Parents also ask about their own influence on their child's pre-tend play. Did they do anything that contributed to the appearance of an imaginary companion in the family? There is substantial varia-tion in the support and encouragement of fantasy behavior, as well as in family structure and socialization, that affects the probability of children having imaginary companions. For example, children whose lives are fully scheduled or who have very little time by them-selves are less likely to invent pretend friends. Conditions that are conducive for imaginary companions include having supportive adults, some props, time, and space. Parents who provide this sort of environment are promoting the development of their children's imaginations. Christopher Milne points out the importance of the conditions that nurtured his own childhood fantasies: "If we wanted to go to the Forest we went on foot. And so did others: only those who could walk to the Forest went there. This meant that when we got there we had the Forest almost entirely to ourselves. And this, in turn, made us feel that it was our Forest and so made it possible for an imaginary world—Pooh's world—to be born within the real world. Pooh could never have stumped a Forest that was littered with picnic parties playing their transistor radios."[1]

How much should a parent enter into play with imaginary com-panions? Some participation seems to be positive for both the parent and the child. Children enjoy sharing their imaginary companions with others, and parents can gain insight about their children by monitoring the ongoing events in the lives of the imaginary companions. Ask about the pretend friend and pay attention to parallels between imaginary events involving the friend and the child's real-life concerns. Think of the imaginary companion as providing a window on your child's thoughts and feelings. One note of caution however—it may be crucial to take a supporting role in this play, rather than trying in any way to direct the activities of the imaginary companion. Some of children's pleasure is in their mastery of their friend. Relinquishing control to the parent strips the fantasy of its most important appeal, at least for some children. In this type of play, follow your child's lead and enjoy where it takes you.

In addition to all the practical questions that parents have about how to interpret and deal with the imaginary companions in their own households, the phenomenon raises a variety of more general questions about child development. Anyone who has observed a child playing and laughing with a pretend friend might become interested in issues such as children's grasp of the fantasy/reality distinction, the relation between emotion and fantasy, the similarities and differences between child and adult forms of fantasy behavior, and the phenomenology of elaborate extended fantasy production. In what follows, I have reiterated a few of the points made elsewhere in this book and added some final thoughts.

The fantasy/reality distinction

My point of view is that children's understanding depends upon the way the distinction is instantiated, but overall they are surprisingly able in this domain. Children answer many questions about imaginary objects and events in the same way as adults, they understand the pretend actions of other people as pertaining to the domain of pretense, they explicitly label their imaginary friends as "just pretend," and they distinguish systematically between magical and ordinary events. I consider children's ability to integrate the activities of imaginary beings into their everyday lives as additional evidence that young children are skilled negotiators of the boundary between fantasy and reality.

My point of view is controversial because the prevailing notion is that young children do not understand the fantasy/reality distinction.[2] I have described much of the evidence for this negative view of children's understanding as problematic. For example, some of children's apparent confusion might actually reflect a breakdown in communication between the adult asking the questions and the child who is answering. Children might interpret "Is it a real monster?" as "Is it a real pretend monster?" or "Are you pretending it is a real monster?" Maybe the child is still pretending when the researcher starts to ask "serious" test questions. A child in one study responded to a question about whether or not a monster was pretend by opening the empty box in which the child and adult had been pretending there was a monster, looking inside and replying, "a real monster."[3] This child was clearly continuing to pretend although the question was meant to pertain to the real state of affairs. This sort of miscommunication problem is not unique to the study of fantasy. The possibility that children might be interpreting test questions in ways not intended by the researcher is faced by developmental psychologists in all areas of inquiry.

Sometimes, however, children seem genuinely confused about what is real and what is fantasy. They might believe that the events portrayed in a television show actually occurred, or that the unicorns, fairies, and ghosts in storybooks are real. Young children place lost teeth under their pillows for the Tooth Fairy to exchange for money, hang up their stockings on Christmas Eve for Santa Claus to fill, and look forward to eating the chocolate eggs left by the Easter Bunny. However, all these examples involve fantasy material that is not under children's creative control. Perhaps children are particularly prone to confusion when they are presented with fantasy made up by other people and are given little or even misleading information about whether or not it is true.[4] Children's errors in judging fantasy and reality in these cases should not be taken as evidence that they are completely at a loss in understanding what fantasy is about. A focus on children's mistaken beliefs about Santa Claus and his kind can result in adults seriously underestimating children's understanding of fantasy.

Emotion and fantasy

There is no question that young children have strong emotional responses to fantasy material. They become terrified while engaging in a game of pretense involving monsters. They love their imaginary companions very deeply. They feel bad when the other elephants make fun of Dumbo for having big ears. Sometimes when children react emotionally to fantasy, their behavior is taken as evidence that they have not clearly grasped the reality of the situation. The fact that they are afraid of the imaginary monster suggests that they think there really is one.

This line of reasoning is compromised by adult reactions to fantasy. For both children and adults, fantasy is often emotionally charged. Maybe this is a crucial point about the function of fantasy in our lives. We fantasize about emotional, often taboo, topics, and as a consequence develop some understanding of them. Through fantasy we can confront dangerous thoughts. But my main point is that children are not the only ones who respond emotionally to fantasy. Even adults feel sad when Old Yeller gets sick. When an adult cries at a movie, however, no one accuses him or her of believing the events to be real. Walton has systematically analyzed the emotion elicited by movies and concluded that although the emotion itself is quite real, adults do not act in any way to suggest they have lost their grasp of the distinction between fantasy and reality in this context.[5] If adults can respond to fantasy emotionally while simultaneously understanding that the situation is not real, we must be cautious in our interpretation of the behaviors of children. Perhaps the child's fear of the pretend monster is akin to the adult's fear in a scary movie.[6] On the other hand, it is possible that children and adults differ in how they interpret the experience of fear elicited by fantasy material. The experience of a strong emotional response to the fantasy might confuse children and result in their being less sure about what is real. In any case, the emotional response itself should not be taken as clear evidence that children have a problem distinguishing fantasy from reality.

This brings up an important practical point. If children's grasp of reality is not faulty, then trying to calm a panicky child by assuring her that a scary pretend entity is not real is likely to be ineffective. Children might be well aware that ghosts and monsters don't exist, but when they think about them, they feel frightened anyway. Sometimes it may help if parents are able to work within the pretense context and change the nature of how the entity is conceptualized—help children imagine the entity as having characteristics that make it less scary. For example, Golomb and Galasso found that some children were able to manage the fear elicited by a scary game of pretense involving a monster when they changed the nature of the game. Children who appeared genuinely afraid when engaged in the game of pretense involving a monster changed the emotional tone of the play by describing the monster as "a little beast" (that was subsequently destroyed in a play oven), as having no mouth or teeth, or as being friendly.[7]

Child and adult forms of fantasy

As the discussion of emotional responses to fantasy demonstrates, it can be very instructive to compare adult and child fantasy behaviors. I think there is more continuity between children and adults in this domain than is often believed to be the case.[8] The capacity to enjoy and be absorbed in fantasy continues throughout life. For example, adults often become very attached to imaginary entities, both the pretend friends of their children and the fictional characters they meet in novels and films. By the end of the film *Harvey,* the audience has a powerful awareness of the rabbit. His presense seems almost palpable. Just as it is hard to imagine anyone but Jimmy Stewart in the role of Elwood Dowd, it is inconceivable to imagine a giant penguin or a 250-pound canary in the role of Harvey, two of the possibilities the playwright Mary Chase actually considered for the character.[9]

The importance of fictional characters in adult lives was underscored for me recently when I learned that Anne of Green Gables, the protagonist in L.M. Montgomery's novels, and Evangeline, the heroine in Henry Wadsworth Longfellow's famous poem, were included in a list of the 100 most important Canadians in history, side by side with real people such as Alexander Graham Bell, Wayne Gretsky, and Pierre Trudeau. These two fictional characters were considered more important by *Maclean's* Magazine's prestigious panel of judges than many accomplished real-life Canadians who did not make the list (e.g., Margaret Atwood). Clearly adults respond to and are influenced by fantasy. In addition, adults engage in a variety of fantasy activities, ranging from common daydreaming to reenactments of the Civil War. According to Singer and Singer, "our impulse for make-believe and fantasy, for role-enactment and fantasy, scarcely fades at all."[10]

Adult descriptions of their fantasy experiences raise fascinating questions about those of young children. For example, as discussed in Chapter 7, adult novelists often struggle with invented characters who seem to have their own agendas for what is going to happen in the novel. They sometimes find it difficult to control the imaginary characters they have invented. I have speculated that perceived loss of control might characterize a particularly intense involvement in fantasy, whether the pretender is an adult or a child. The imaginary companions of some children come and go as they please and don't always behave as the children wish. How common are these observations and what do they mean? We tend to assume that because we are the authors of our fantasies, we can anticipate the insights and/or benefits they might provide. But although we might set up the parameters and steer the contents, once set in motion, fantasies unfold in a dynamic fashion. Maybe part of becoming an expert pretender is learning to relinquish control of an fantasy and allow ourselves to be surprised by it.

The bottom line is that, as we study the early developing capacity to pretend, we are likely to learn as much about ourselves as about our children. Although children are the ones who come to mind when we think of pretenders, the imagination is a powerful tool that is available to all of us throughout life. Even having an imaginary companion—a form of pretend play strongly associated with the preschool years—has analogs in adult behavior, both cognitively and emotionally.

Finally, although individual differences in fantasy behavior are fascinating, it is important to remember that imaginative thought is an integral part of everyday cognition and human experience.[11] Fantasy is not just a form of entertainment or a means of escape. With our imaginations, we can relive (even improve) the past, process, and come to terms with issues in our present, and anticipate the future. As Jean-Paul Sartre said, freedom to act in the world is a function of the ability to perceive things not only as they are, but as they are not.[12]

Notes

Chapter 1: Introduction

1. King, S., *The Shining*. 1977, New York: Doubleday & Company, Inc.

2. Watterson, B., *The Calvin and Hobbes tenth anniversary book*. 1995, Kansas City: Andrews and McMeel.

3. Ames, L. B., & Learned, J., Imaginary companions and related phenomena. *Journal of Genetic Psychology*, 1946. 69: 147–167; Breckenridge, M. E., & Vincent, E. L., *Child Development: Physical and psychological growth through adolescence*. 1965, Philadelphia: W. B. Saunders Co.; Myers, W. A., Imaginary companions, fantasy twins, mirror dreams and depersonalization. *Psychoanalytic Quarterly*, 1976. 45: 503–524; Vostrovsky, C., A study of imaginary companions. *Education*, 1895. 15: 383–398.

4. Bretherton, I., Pretense: The form and function of make-believe play. *Developmental Review*, 1989. 9: 383–401.

5. Singer, D. G., & Singer, J. L., *The house of make-believe: Children's play and developing imagination*. 1990, Cambridge, MA: Harvard University Press.

Chapter 2: What are imaginary companions like?

1. Wickes, F. G., *The inner world of childhood*. 1927, New York: D. Appleton & Company.

2. Anderson, S., personal communication, 1997.

3. Mauro, J., *The friend that only I can see: A longitudinal investigation of children's imaginary companions*. 1991, unpublished doctoral dissertation, University of Oregon.

4. Svendsen, M., Children's imaginary companions. *Archives of Neurology and Psychiatry*, 1934. 2: 985–999, 988.

5. Ibid., 988–989.

6. Walton, K. L., *Mimesis as make-believe.* 1990, Cambridge, MA: Harvard University Press.

7. Benson, R. M., & Pryor, D. B., When friends fall out: Developmental interference with the function of some imaginary companions. *Journal of the American Psychoanalytic Association,* 1973. 21: 457–468.

8. Winnicott, D. W., Transitional objects and transitional phenomena. *International Journal of Psychoanalysis,* 1953. 34: 89–97.

9. Singer, D. G., & Singer, J. L., *The house of make-believe: Children's play and developing imagination.* 1990, Cambridge, MA: Harvard University Press, p. 100.

10. Mauro, J., *The friend that only I can see.*

11. Newson, J., & Newson, E., *Four years old in an urban community.* 1968, London: George Allen & Unwin.

12. Tracy Gleason and her colleagues at the University of Minnesota have some preliminary evidence for at least some differences between these two types of imaginative play (Gleason, Sebane, McGinley, & Hartup, 1997). For example, she found that invisible friends are more likely to be people (as opposed to animals) and less likely to be known beyond family members. Invisible friends also tend to be played with when the children are alone. The toys that serve as imaginary companions are more often animals who are known to children and adults outside the family, and who are likely to be included in daily routines. Also the children who personify a toy are more likely to participate in other kinds of pretend play than are children with invisible friends or children who do not have any kind of imaginary companion.

13. The impersonation of imagined characters, like play involving a stuffed-animal companion, is sometimes not easily distinguished from play involving invisible friends. In our research, we found that some children engaged in both kinds of play simultaneously or in a developmental sequence. For example, one child in our sample pretended to be a pony named Kirby for some months before Kirby evolved into a separate invisible entity who functioned as a close companion. According to Newson and Newson, cases in which children take on another identity and insist on being called by the name of the imaginary character should be considered a special version of the imaginary companion phenomenon. Personally, I think the impersonation of a character is distinct from having an invisible friend, but should be included in research investigating the forms of elaborate pretense in young children.

14. Ames, L. B., & Learned, J., Imaginary companions and related phenomena. *Journal of Genetic Psychology,* 1946. 69: 147–167.

15. Ibid., 156.

16. Ibid., 154.

17. Ibid., 157.

18. Ibid., 154. I don't know how many children actually urinate like an animal when pretending to be one, but I have observed children pretending to do so. In fact, a colleague recently told me that, as a 6-year-old, his daughter had the unseemly habit of pretending to urinate like a male dog on their living room furniture, a practice which elicited some interesting reactions from visitors to the household.

19. Ustinov, P., *Dear me*. 1977, Middlesex, England: Penguin, p. 72.

20. Ibid., p. 74.

21. Singer, D. G., & Singer, J. L., *The house of make-believe*.

22. Harriman, P. L., Some imaginary companions of older subjects. *The American Journal of Orthopsychiatry*, 1937. 7, 368–370.

23. Subbotsky, E. V., *Foundations of the mind*. 1993, Cambridge, MA: Harvard University Press.

24. Newson, J., & Newson, E., *Fours years old in an urban community*, p. 184.

25. Wickes, F. G., *The inner world of childhood*, p. 206.

26. Fraiberg, S. M., *The magic years*. 1959, New York: Simon & Schuster.

27. Nordlinger, J., The life of a lonely determined golfer, in *The Weekly Standard*. August 11, 1997, 35.

28. Mauro, J., *The friend that only I can see*; and Taylor, M., Cartwright, B. S., & Carlson, S. M., A developmental investigation of children's imaginary companions. *Developmental Psychology*, 1993. 29(2): 276–285.

29. Manosevitz, M., Prentice, N. M., & Wilson, F., Individual and family correlates of imaginary companions in preschool children. *Developmental Psychology*, 1973. 8: 72–79. The definition used in this study was "a very vivid imaginary character (person, animal, or object) with which their child interacts during his play and daily activities" (p. 74). It is quite possible that some parents interpreted this definition as including stuffed animals.

30. Jersild, A. T., Markey, F. V., & Jersild, C. L., Children's fears, dreams, wishes, daydreams, likes, dislikes, pleasant and unpleasant memories. *Child Development Monographs*. Vol. 12. 1933, New York: Teachers College, Columbia University.

31. Ibid., p. 103.

32. In fact, a new theme is emerging in the field of cognitive development which emphasizes the dynamic nature of children's thinking. Continuous change and variability in the child's thinking are beginning to be considered the rule rather than the exception or something that occurs in a circumscribed period of transition (Siegler, 1996).

33. Piaget, J., *Play, dreams, and imitation in childhood*. 1962, New York: Norton, p. 103.

34. Schaefer, C. E., Imaginary companions and creative adolescents. *Developmental Psychology*, 1969. 1: 747–749, 748.

35. Taylor, M., & Carlson, S. M., The relation between individual differences in fantasy and theory of mind. *Child Development*, 1997. 68: 436–455.

Chapter 3: The characteristics of children who create imaginary companions

1. Vostrovsky, C., A study of imaginary companions. *Education*, 1895. 15: 383–398.

2. Svendsen, M., Children's imaginary companions. *Archives of Neurology and Psychiatry*, 1934. 2: 985–999, 991.

3. Ames, L. B., & Learned, J., Imaginary companions and related phenomena. *Journal of Genetic Psychology*, 1946. 69: 147–167, 162.

4. Bender, L., & Vogel, B. F., Imaginary companions of children. *American Journal of Orthopsychiatry*, 1941. 11: 56–65.

5. Manosevitz, M., Prentice, N. M., & Wilson, F., Individual and family correlates of imaginary companions in preschool children. *Developmental Psychology*, 1973. 8: 72–79; Singer, D.G., & Singer, J. L., *The house of make-believe: Children's play and developing imagination.* 1990, Cambridge, MA: Harvard University Press.

6. Mauro, J., *The friend that only I can see: A longitudinal investigation of children's imaginary companions.* 1991 unpublished doctoral dissertation, University of Oregon.

7. Mauro's definition of imaginary companion included stuffed animals or dolls, as well as invisible imaginary companions. She collected information from both parents and children, but relied most heavily on child report when identifying children as having an imaginary companion.

8. Derryberry, D., & Rothbart, M. K., Emotion, attention and temperament, in *Emotion, cognition and behavior*, C. E. Izard, J. Kagan, & R. Zajonc, editors. 1984, New York: Cambridge University Press, pp. 132–166.

9. More specifically, there were no differences on the following dimensions: activity (rate and extent of locomotion), anger (amount of negative affect related to the interruption of ongoing tasks or goal blocking), approach (amount of excitement and positive anticipation for expected pleasurable activities), discomfort, (amount of negative affect related to sensory qualities of stimulation), soothability (rate of recovery from peak distress, excitement, or general arousal), fear (amount of negative affect related to anticipated pain or distress and/or potentially threatening situations), high intensity pleasure (amount of pleasure or enjoyment related to situations involving high stimulus intensity, rate, complexity, novelty and incongruity), impulsivity (speed of response initiation), inhibition (the capacity to plan and to suppress inappropriate approach responses under instructions or in novel

or uncertain situations), low intensity pleasure (amount of pleasure or enjoyment related to situations involving low stimulus intensity, rate, complexity, novelty, and incongruity), perceptual sensitivity (amount of detection of slight, low intensity stimuli from the external environment), sadness (amount of negative affect and lowered mood and energy related to exposure to suffering, disappointment, and object loss), and smile/laughter (amount of positive affect in response to changes in stimulus intensity, rate, complexity, and incongruity).

10. Singer, J. L., & Singer, D. G., *Television, imagination, and aggression: A study of preschoolers.* 1981, Hillsdale, NJ: Lawrence Erlbaum.

11. Wingfield, R. C., Bernreuter personality ratings of college students who recall having had imaginary companions during childhood. *Journal of Child Psychiatry,* 1948. 1: 190–194.

12. Manosevitz, M., Prentice, N. M., & Wilson, F., Individual and family correlates of imaginary companions in preschool children.

13. Singer, J. L., Imagination and waiting ability in young children. *Journal of Personality,* 1961. 29: 396–413.

14. Singer, D. G., & Singer, J. L., *The house of make-believe,* p. 148.

15. Manosevitz, M., Fling, S., & Prentice, N. M., Imaginary companions in young children: Relationships with intelligence, creativity and waiting ability. *Journal of Child Psychology and Psychiatry,* 1977. 18: 73–78.

16. This difference failed to reach significance because children were extremely variable in their waiting times. The standard deviation in waiting time for the children with imaginary companions was 247.4 seconds and 198.0 seconds for the children without imaginary companions.

17. Ames, L. B., & Learned, J., Imaginary companions and related phenomena; Harvey, N. A., *Imaginary playmates and other mental phenomena of children.* 1918, Ypsilanti: Michigan State Normal College; Svendsen, M., Children's imaginary companions.

18. Jersild, A. T., Markey, F. V., & Jersild, C. L., Children's fears, dreams, wishes, daydreams, likes, dislikes, pleasant and unpleasant memories. *Child Development Monographs.* Vol. 12. 1933, New York: Teachers College, Columbia University.

19. See Bairdain, E. F., Psychological characteristics of adolescents who have had imaginary companions. *Dissertation Abstracts International,* 1959. 29: 747; and Singer, D. G., & Singer, J. L., *The house of make-believe.*

20. Gardner, H., *Multiple intelligences: The theory in practice.* 1993, New York: Basic Books.

21. Mauro, J., *The friend that only I can see.*

22. Taylor, M., & Carlson, S. M., The relation between individual differences in fantasy and theory of mind. *Child Development,* 1997. 68: 436–455.

23. See Kalyan Masih, V., Imaginary companions of children, in *Piaget-*

ian theory and its implications for the helping professions, R. B. R. Weizmann, P. J. Levinson, & P. A. Taylor, editors. 1978, Los Angeles: University of Southern California; and Manosevitz, M., Fling, S., & Prentice, N. M., Imaginary companions in young children.

24. Mauro, J., *The friend that only I can see;* Manosevitz, M., Fling, S., & Prentice, N. M., Imaginary companions in young children.

25. Kalyan Masih, V., Imaginary companions of children.

26. Singer, J. L., Imagination and waiting ability in young children; Singer, J. L., & Singer, D. G., *Television, imagination, and aggression.*

27. Schaefer, C. E., Imaginary companions and creative adolescents. *Developmental Psychology,* 1969. 1: 747–749.

28. For the effects of family size, see Hurlock, E. B., & Burnstein, M., The imaginary playmate: A questionnaire study. *Journal of Genetic Psychology,* 1932. 41: 380–391.

29. Manosevitz, M., Prentice, N. M., & Wilson, F., Individual and family correlates of imaginary companions in preschool children.

30. Kalyan Masih, V., Imaginary companions of children; Singer, D. G., & Singer, J. L., *The house of make-believe.*

31. Yawkey, T. D., & Yawkey, M. L., *Assessing young children for imaginativeness through oral reporting: Preliminary results.* Paper presented at International Conference on Play and Play Environments: Research and its Application to Play Settings. 1983, Austin, Texas.

32. Singer, D. G., & Singer, J. L., *The house of make-believe.*

33. Taylor, M., & Carlson, S. M., The relation between individual differences in fantasy and theory of mind.

34. Singer, D. G., & Singer, J. L., *The house of make-believe.*

35. Astington, J. W., *The child's discovery of mind.* 1995, Cambridge, MA: Harvard University Press.

36. Perner, J., Leekam, S. R., & Wimmer, H., Three-year-olds' difficulty understanding false beliefs: Representational limitation, lack of knowledge or pragmatic misunderstanding. *British Journal of Developmental Psychology,* 1987. 5: 125–137; Wimmer, H., & Perner, J., Beliefs about beliefs: Representation and constraining function of wrong beliefs in young children's understanding of deception. *Cognition,* 1983. 13: 103–128.

37. Chandler, M. J., & Helm, D., Developmental changes in the contributions of shared experience to social role-taking competence. *International Journal of Behavioral Development,* 1984. 7: 145–156; Taylor, M., Conceptual perspective taking: Children's ability to distinguish what they know from what they see. *Child Development,* 1988. 59: 703–718.

38. Flavell, J. H., Flavell, E. R., & Green, F. L., Development of the appearance-reality distinction. *Cognitive Psychology,* 1983. 15: 95–120.

39. Taylor, M., & Carlson, S. M., The relation between individual dif-

ferences in fantasy and theory of mind. Another way to test the hypothesis might be to identify children who rarely engage in pretense and then assess their performance on theory of mind tasks. A deficit in pretend play is characteristic of children with autism. Autism is a neurological disorder marked by disturbances in affect, social understanding, language, and pretend play (for a general discussion of autism see Frith 1989). Autistic children might be fascinated with blocks or other toys and spend hours interacting with them, but they do not use them as props in games of make-believe in the way that is so common in normally developing children. Instead, they might organize a set of toy trucks in lines or arrange them to make organized designs. The trucks are manipulated as if they were a set of blocks.

Exactly what constitutes the core deficit in autism is a matter of debate, but a growing number of researchers believe that autistic children have a specific impairment in their understanding of mind (Baron-Cohen, 1995). These children not only fail to pretend, they also have great difficulty with theory of mind tasks, such as the ones described in this chapter. The fact that difficulty with theory of mind and pretend play co-occur in autism strengthens the case for a conceptual link between the two.

40. The results of this study provide evidence that there is a relation between theory of mind development and pretend play in 4-year-old children. However, the nature of the relation cannot be determined from our correlational data, and inferences about causality are not warranted. It is possible that extensive fantasy experience promotes an understanding of mind, but it is also possible that children who have an early developing understanding of mind are more interested in fantasy play or that some third factor underlies development in both areas.

41. See Dunn, J., Brown, J., Slomkowski, C., Tesla, C., & Youngblade, L., Young children's understanding of other people's feelings and beliefs: Individual differences and their antecedents. *Child Development*, 1991. 62: 1352–1366; and Perner, J., Ruffman, T., & Leekam, S. R., Theory of mind is contagious: You catch it from your sibs. *Child Development*, 1994. 65: 1228–1238.

42. Vostrovsky reported 39 cases of girls and only 7 of boys. (A Study of Imaginary Companions). Hurlock and Burnstein found that 31 percent of females and 23 percent of males in their sample of 701 adults recalled having had an imaginary companion in childhood. Svendsen's sample of imaginary companion children was 75 percent female, Mauro's was 64 percent female, Jersild, Markey, and Jersild's was 57 percent female, and Taylor and Carlson's was 64 percent female. Singer and Singer report no gender difference in the incidence of imaginary companions, but I have not seen a single study in which the number of boys was greater than the number of girls.

43. Jersild, A. T., Markey, F. V., & Jersild, C. L., Children's fears, dreams, wishes, daydreams, likes, dislikes, pleasant and unpleasant memories.

44. Taylor, M., & Carlson, S. M., The relation between individual differences in fantasy and theory of mind.

45. In this task, children are asked to pretend to act out a series of actions such as brushing their teeth or combing their hair. Most 4-year-old children use parts of their bodies to represent the objects they were pretending to use in the actions (e.g., when asked to pretend to brush their teeth, they use their finger as a toothbrush). By 6 years of age, children tend to imagine the absent object rather than to substitute a body part (e.g., they pretend to hold an imaginary toothbrush). This sequence has been interpreted as reflecting the developing ability to distance the representation of imagined objects from the gestures used when pretending to use the imagined objects (Overton & Jackson, 1973). In past research (Taylor et al., 1993), we found that children with imaginary companions are develop mentally advanced on the pretend action task. Four-year-old children with imaginary companions used imaginary objects when performing pretend actions significantly more often than 4-year-olds without imaginary companions (58 percent versus 26 percent). In our most recent work we have found that children who impersonate imaginary characters also tend to hold imaginary objects when performing pretend actions.

46. Hurlock, E. B., & Burnstein, M., *The imaginary playmate.*

47. Copple, C., Fantastic voyages. *Sesame Street Magazine,* October 1991.

48. The parents in this family were completely mystified about the origins of the name "Rainbow Cutter." Then one day they were watching a *Sesame Street* tape that they hadn't played for some time. During one of the songs, the little girl became very excited and said, "That's where I got it from!" It was Elmo singing, "a rainbow of beautiful colors. . . ." After rehearing the song, she changed the name of her character to "Rainbow Color," which pleased her parents because "Rainbow Cutter" has an unpleasant sound to it. As far as I know, however, the father is still just a piece of string.

49. Newson, J., & Newson, E., *Four years old in an urban community.* 1968, London: George Allen & Unwin, p. 176.

50. However, when Mauro asked the mothers of children in her sample if they would encourage, discourage, or ignore an imaginary companion and if they thought an imaginary companion would be good for their child, harmful to their child, or would have no effect, she found no differences in the responses of mothers whose children had imaginary companions and mothers of children who did not have imaginary companions. Most of these

mothers were positive about the companions, indicating that they would encourage their child to play with the imaginary companion (70 percent), and that the companion would have a positive effect on their child (65 percent).

51. Farver, J. M., & Howes, C. Cultural differences in American and Mexican mother-child pretend play, *Merrill-Palmer Quarterly,* 1993. 39: 344–358.

52. Brooks, M., & Knowles, D., Parents' views of children's imaginary companions. *Child Welfare,* 1982. 61: 25–33. Brooks and Knowles assessed the parents' views on imaginary companions by asking 60 mothers and fathers of preschoolers and found that the parents, especially the fathers, did not hold very positive attitudes about imaginary companions. The results of this study might be somewhat biased because some of the questions were ones that would clearly elicit negative responses. For example, parents were asked how they would feel about a child insisting that a place be set at a crowded table on Thanksgiving for the imaginary companion. Most parents would probably be annoyed by this sort of situation, but the parents in this study were also somewhat negative when asked about their reactions to more neutral situations. For example, when asked about a situation in which a child's response to being asked to play quietly was to go outside and play with her imaginary companion, only 31 percent of the parents said they would encourage this behavior. There was a tendency for the parents of daughters to be more encouraging of imaginary companion behavior than the parents of sons.

53. Newson, J., & Newson, E., *Seven years old in an urban environment.* 1976, London: George Allen & Unwin, p. 189.

54. Ibid., p. 161.

55. Gross, R., & Gross, B. Let the child teach himself. *New York Times Magazine,* 1965 May 16, pp. 34, 42.

56. Chukovsky, K., *From two to five.* 1925/1963, Berkeley: University of California Press, p. 90.

57. Ibid.

58. Newson, J., & Newson, E., *Seven years old in an urban environment.*

59. Brooks, M., & Knowles, D., Parents' views of children's imaginary companions, p. 31.

60. Heath, S. B., *Ways with words: Language, life, and work in communities and classrooms.* 1983, Cambridge: Cambridge University Press, p. 158.

61. Ibid., p. 160.

62. Ibid.

63. Clark, C. D., *Flights of fancy, leaps of faith: Children's myths in contemporary America.* 1995, Chicago: University of Chicago Press.

64. Allport, G. W., *The individual and his religion*. 1950, New York: The Macmillan Co.

65. Scheibe, C., Developmental differences in children's reasoning about Santa Claus and other fantasy characters, 1987. Unpublished doctoral dissertation, Cornell University. Cited in C. D. Clark, *Flights of fancy, leaps of faith*.

66. Ibid., p. 56.

67. Anderson, N. T., Vanderhook, P., & Vanderhook, S., *Spiritual protection for your children*. 1996, Ventura, CA: Regal, pp. 195–196.

68. The Mennonite faith is a form of fundamentalist Christianity, but Mennonites (and their Amish subgroups) are much less preoccupied with issues related to spiritual warfare. Instead, they are concerned with leading a simple, truthful life of devotion to God. To accomplish this goal, they live separately from modern mainstream American culture without some of the conveniences of modern technology and avoid worldly influences. They espouse agricultural living because it promotes the Puritan values of hard work, thrift, and mutual aid as opposed to the "restlessness, rootlessness, and anxiety" associated with urban mobility (Hostetler & Huntington, 1971, p. 9).

In order to gain access for research purposes, Carlson visited one school for six months and assisted the teachers by reading to the children, leading recitation exercises, and correcting workbooks. During these visits, she took great care in her dress, wearing clothing that was very plain and traditional: long black skirt, high-collared blouse or sweater, black stockings, and flat shoes. She kept her hair in a bun and did not wear any make-up, nail polish, perfume, or jewelry. Although the teachers and children were very positive about her visits, ultimately she had to initiate contact in a different school because the parents in this Old Order community did not approve of her presence. The teacher was reprimanded by the elders of the community at a church meeting, and it was decided that one of their own young people would act as a helper to the teacher. Although the Mennonite community represents an extreme case because Mennonites have chosen to separate from mainstream society, it is possible that other fundamentalist groups would not be overly welcoming to researchers who do not share their beliefs. Even when asking questions in Christian bookstores, we have encountered some suspicion about our motives and some understandable concern about being misrepresented or misunderstood.

69. Redekop, C., *Mennonite society*. 1989, Baltimore, MD: Johns Hopkins University Press; for a different view, see D.B. Kraybill, *The riddle of Amish culture*. 1989, Johns Hopkins University Press.

70. Hostetler, J. A., & Huntington, G. E., *Children in Amish society: Socialization and community education*. 1971, New York: Holt, Rinehart & Winston, Inc., p. 46.

71. Carlson, S. M., Taylor, M., & Levin, G. R., The influence of culture on pretend play: The case of Mennonite children. *Merrill-Palmer Quarterly*, in press.

72. Weaver, L. H., Forbidden fancies: A child's vision of Mennonite plainness. *Journal of Ethnic Studies*, 1982. 11: 51–59.

Chapter 4: Why do children create imaginary companions?

1. Seuss, Dr., *The cat in the hat.* 1957, New York: Random House.

2. Singer, D. G., & Singer, J. L., *The house of make-believe: Children's play and developing imagination.* 1990, Cambridge, MA: Harvard University Press.

3. McCurdy, H. G., & Follett, H., *Barbara: The unconscious autobiography of a child genius.* 1966, Chapel Hill: The University of North Carolina Press, p. 27.

4. Newson, J., & Newson, E., *Four years old in an urban community.* 1968, London: George Allen & Unwin.

5. Acredolo, L. P., Goodwyn, S. W., & Fulmer, A. H. *Why some children create imaginary companions: Clues from infant and toddler play preferences.* Paper presented at the biennial meeting of the Society for Research in Child Development, 1995, Indianapolis, IN. Although their mothers did not differ from the other mothers in their choice of toys, the infants who would later go on to create imaginary companions showed greater interest in the kinds of toys that elicit fantasy play than in toys that are used in nonfantasy activities. For example, the infants who would later develop imaginary companions enjoyed playing with toy phones and dolls, which are props in pretend conversations and play, but were less interested in toys such as a shapersorter and busy box, which focus the child's attention on the real properties of objects and are less likely to elicit pretense.

6. Bender, L., & Vogel, B. F., Imaginary companions of children. *American Journal of Orthopsychiatry*, 1941. 11: 56–65, 59.

7. Lindsey, R., Promises to keep. *New York Times Magazine.* 1988 July 24, pp. 23–24.

8. Nagera, H., The imaginary companion: Its significance for ego development and conflict resolution. *The Psychoanalytic Study of the Child*, 1969. 24: 165–196.

9. Ames, L., & Learned, J., Imaginary companions and related phenomena. *Journal of Genetic Psychology*, 1946. 69: 147–167; Manosevitz, M., Prentice, N. M., & Wilson, F., Individual and family correlates of imaginary companions in preschool children. *Developmental Psychology*, 1973. 8: 72–79; Svendsen, M., Children's imaginary companions. *Archives of Neurology and Psychiatry*, 1934. 2: 985–999.

10. Nagera, H., The imaginary companion, p. 183.

11. Ibid, p. 186.

12. Harter, S., & Chao, C., The role of competence in children's creation of imaginary friends. *Merrill-Palmer Quarterly*, 1992. 38: 350–363.

13. Ibid., p. 357.

14. Ibid., p. 358.

15. Ibid., p. 359.

16. Piaget, J., *Play, dreams, and imitation in childhood.* 1962, New York: Norton, p. 132.

17. Singer, J. L., & Streiner, B. F., Imaginative content in the dreams and fantasy play of blind and sighted children. *Perceptual and Motor Skills*, 1966. 22: 475–482.

18. Warfield, F., *Cotton in my ears.* 1948, New York: The Viking Press, pp. 7–9.

19. Singer, D. G., *Playing for their lives: Helping troubled children through play therapy.* 1993, New York: The Free Press, pp. 135–136.

20. Wickes, F. G., *The inner world of childhood.* 1927, New York: D. Appleton & Company.

21. Bender, L., & Vogel, B. F., Imaginary companions of children, p. 62.

22. Ibid., p. 64.

23. Wickes, F. G., *The inner world of childhood.*

24. Burlingham, D., & Freud, A., *Infants without families.* 1944, London: George Allen & Unwin.

25. Machtlinger, V. J., Psychoanalytic theory: Pre-oedipal and oedipal phases with special reference to the father, in *The role of the father in child development*, M. E. Lamb, editor. 1976, New York: Wiley, pp. 277–305, p. 298.

26. Newson, J., & Newson, E., *Four years old in an urban community*, p. 183.

27. Sakol, J. L., *The Royals.* 1987, New York: Congdon & Weed, p. 67.

28. Nagera, H., The imaginary companion, p. 182.

29. Newson, J., & Newson, E., *Four years old in an urban community*, p. 204.

30. Singer, D. G., & Singer, J. L., *The house of make-believe.*

31. Fraiberg, S. H., *The magic years.* 1959, New York: Charles Scribner's Sons, p. 141.

32. Ibid., p. 107.

33. Wickes, F. G., *The inner world of childhood*, pp. 162–163.

34. The children at her day care took turns one day taking the box into the bathroom, turning out the light, and letting the ghost out of the box. In the pitch dark of the windowless bathroom, all the children were able to enjoy playing with the baby ghost.

35. Lazurus, A., *In the mind's eye: The power of imagery for personal enrichment.* 1984, New York: Guilford Press, p. 103.

36. Nagera, H., The imaginary companion, p. 170.

37. Gottman, J. M., & Parker, J. G. (eds.), *Conversations of friends: Speculations on affective development.* 1986, Cambridge, UK: Cambridge University Press.

38. Bender, L., & Vogel, B. F., Imaginary companions of children.

39. Singer, D. G., & Singer, J. L., *The house of make-believe.* p. 89.

40. Freud, A., *The ego and the mechanisms of defense.* 1936/1966, New York: International Universities Press.

41. Fraiberg, S. H., *The magic years,* pp. 19–20.

42. Newson, J., & Newson, E., *Four years old in an urban community,* p. 183.

43. Piaget, J., *Play, dreams, and imitation in childhood.* 1962, New York: Norton, p. 132.

44. Imperiale, N., Imaginary pals say lots about kids, *Orlando Sentinel Tribune.* 1992 September 30, p. e1.

45. In this book, I am primarily focused on a very special type of pretend play—the spontaneous creation of an imaginary other. However, pretend play is a very powerful tool used by child therapists. Actually, therapy with adults also often involves the imagination, such as Jung's use of "active imagination" (see *Jung on Active Imagination* edited by Joan Chodorow). The use of play in therapy originated with Sigmund Freud in 1909 and was written about extensively by Anna Freud and Melanie Klein.

Therapists view the role of play differently and do not agree on the extent that the play should be structured or directed. Some describe play as a way to build a strong relationship with the therapist. For others, play is a direct substitute for verbalizations, a method for uncovering the child's unconscious conflicts and desires, a way of free-association, a window for the adult trying to understand the child's perspective of his or her life, and/or a way to provide corrective and reparative experiences for the child. The use of play in therapy with children is a tremendously interesting topic that is beyond the scope of this book. There are many excellent volumes on play therapy including *The healing power of play* by Eliana Gil, *The therapeutic use of child's play* edited by Charles Schaefer, *Play therapy* by Virginia Axline, and *Playing for their lives* by Dorothy Singer.

46. Imperiale, N., Imaginary pals say lots about kids.

47. Opie, I., & Opie, P., *The lore and language of school children.* 1959, Oxford: Oxford University Press.

48. Bender, L., & Vogel, B. F., Imaginary companions of children, p. 60.

49. Nagera, H., The imaginary companion.

50. Ibid., pp. 187–188.

51. Ibid., p. 189.

52. Terr, L., *Too scared to cry: Psychic trauma in childhood.* 1990, New York: Basic Books, pp. 202-203.

53. Murphy, L. B., *The widening world of childhood: Paths toward mastery.* 1962, New York: Basic Books, p. 125.

54. Putnam, F. W., *Diagnosis and treatment of multiple personality disorder.* 1989, New York: Guilford Press.

55. Kluft, R. P., An update on multiple personality disorder. *Hospital and Community Psychiatry,* 1987. 38: 363–373.

56. Putnam, F. W., *Diagnosis and treatment of multuple personality disorder.*

57. Kluft, R. P., Treatment of multiple personality disorder: A study of 33 cases. *Psychiatric Clinics of North America,* 1984. 7: 9–29.

58. Sanders, B., The imaginary companion experience in multiple personality disorder. *Dissociation,* 1992. 5: 159–162.

59. Nagera, H., The imaginary companion.

60. White, J., & Allers, C. T., Play therapy with abused children: A review of the literature. *Journal of Counseling and Development,* 1994. 72: 390–394.

61. Terr, L., *Too scared to cry,* p. 238.

62. White, J., & Allers, C. T., Play therapy, p. 392.

63. Wickes, F. G., *The inner world of childhood,* pp. 162–163.

64. Jalongo, M. R., Imaginary companions in children's lives and literature. *Childhood Education,* 1984. 60: 166–171.

Chapter 5: Do children think their imaginary companions are real?

1. Kavanaugh, R. D., Whittington, S., & Cerbone, M. J., Mothers' use of fantasy in speech to young children. *Journal of Child Language,* 1983. 10: 45–55.

2. Bretherton, I., & Beeghley, M., Talking about internal states: The acquisition of an explicit theory of mind. *Developmental Psychology,* 1982. 18: 906–921; Flavell, J. H., Flavell, E. R., & Green, F. L., Young children's knowledge about the apparent-real and pretend-real distinctions. *Developmental Psychology,* 1987. 23: 816–822; Wellman, H. M., & Estes, D., Early understanding of mental entities: A reexamination of childhood realism. *Child Development,* 1986. 57: 910–923. When shown a boy described as pretending to have a cookie and a boy described as really having a cookie, children as young as 3 years are very accurate in their judgments about which boy could eat the cookie, touch the cookie, save the cookie for tomorrow, and share the cookie with friends; Winner, E., Gardner, H., & Silverstein, L., Creating a world with words, in *The development of language and language researchers: Essays in honor of Roger Brown,* F. Kessel, editor. 1988, Hillsdale, NJ: Lawrence Erlbaum, pp. 353–371.

3. Harris, P. L., Brown, E., Marriott, C., Whittall, S., & Harmer, S., Monsters, ghosts and witches: Testing the limits of the fantasy-reality distinction in young children. *British Journal of Developmental Psychology,* 1991. 9: 105–123.

4. Woolley, J. D., & Wellman, H. M., Origin and truth: Young children's understanding of imaginary mental representations. *Child Development,* 1993. 64: 1–17.

5. Spock, B., *Bringing up children in a difficult time.* 1974, Boston: The Bodley Head, p. 50.

6. Freud, A., The ego and the mechanisms of defense. 1936/1966 New York: International Universities Press.

7. Newson, J., & Newson, E., *Four years old in an urban community.* 1968, London: George Allen & Unwin, p. 193.

8. Woolley, J., Thinking about fantasy: Are children fundamentally different thinkers and believers from adults? *Child Development,* 1997. 68: 991–1011.

9. Leslie, A. M., Pretense and representation: The origins of "theory of mind." *Psychological Review,* 1987. 94: 412–426.

10. Taylor, M., The role of creative control and culture in children's fantasy/reality judgments. *Child Development,* 1997. 68: 1015–1017.

11. I do not mean to suggest that fantasy activities fall neatly into categories with children either as passive recipients of fantasy created entirely by others or as isolated fantasy masterminds untouched by the influences of environment and culture. Actually, the child's role is probably very rarely all or nothing. Still, fantasy experiences vary considerably in how much control is exercised by children.

12. Prentice, N. M., Manosevitz, M., & Hubbs, L., Imaginary figures of early childhood: Santa Claus, Easter Bunny and the Tooth Fairy. *American Journal of Orthopsychiatry,* 1978. 48: 618–628.

13. Rosengren, K. S., Kalish, C. W., Hickling, A. K., & Gelman, S. A, Exploring the relation between preschool children's magical beliefs and causal thinking. *British Journal of Developmental Psychology,* 1994. 12: 69–82.

14. Burkett, M., Double standard for double talk. *The Register-Guard,* 1993, Eugene, OR.

15. Rosemond, J., Boy, 2, continually asks, "Why?": His mother wants to know why. *Corvallis Times,* 1991 OR.

16. Clark, C. D., *Flights of fancy, leaps of faith: Children's myths in contemporary America.* 1995, Chicago: University of Chicago Press, p. 6.

17. Ibid., p. 48.

18. Teacher says there's no Santa; parents outraged. *Oregon Daily Emerald,* 1994 January 7, p. 14.

19. Kaye, M., *The real tooth fairy.* 1990, New York: Harcourt Brace & Co.

20. Prentice, N. M., Manosevitz, M., & Hubbs, L., Imaginary figures.

21. Taylor, M., Cartwright, B. S., & Carlson, S. M., A developmental investigation of children's imaginary companions. *Developmental Psychology,* 1993. 29(2): 276–285.

22. Clark, C. D., *Flights of fancy,* pp. 17–18.

23. Ibid.

24. Of course, in many families children create their own variations to rituals associated with cultural myths, and parents accept them. I do not mean to say that children make *no* contributions. Yet, even in these cases, children are following the leads of others in their participation.

25. Morison, P., & Gardner, H., Dragons and dinosaurs: The child's capacity to differentiate fantasy from reality. *Child Development*, 1978. 49: 642–684, p. 643.

26. There is also a large and interesting literature on children's own narratives (e.g., Sperry & Sperry), including studies in which young children create stories themselves that interweave the real world with the fictional one—the children interact directly with the imagined characters (e.g., Miller, Hengst, Alexander, & Sperry, in press).

27. Bruno Bettelheim has written about the meaning and impact of fairy tales for young children. According to Bettelheim (1977) "fairy tales teach children that "a struggle against severe difficulties in life is unavoidable; is an intrinsic part of human existence—but that if one does not shy away, but steadfastly meets unexpected and often unjust hardships, one masters all obstacles and at the end emerges victorious" (p. 8). The interested reader is also directed to the works of Joseph Campbell on the importance and meaning of myths and legends.

28. Quarforth, J. M., Children's understanding of the nature of television characters. *Journal of Communication*, 1979. 29: 210–218.

29. Flavell, J. H., Flavell, E. R., Green, F. L., & Korfmacher, J. E., Do young children think of television images as pictures or real objects? *Journal of Broadcasting and Electronic Media*, 1990. 34: 399–419. But the same children answered questions about photographs in a similar way, indicating that their answers could be a result of their difficulty conceptualizing images as different from their referents.

30. A full discussion of the many levels of fantasy/reality distinctions on television (e.g., cartoons versus live action; documentaries versus fictionalized events; commercials; actors and the roles they portray) is beyond the scope of this book. For more complete treatments of children's understanding of fantasy on television see Bryant and Anderson (1983), Davies (1997), and Singer and Singer (1981, 1990).

31. Dorr, A., No shortcuts to judging reality, in *Children's understanding of television: Research on attention and comprehension*, J. Bryant and D. R. Anderson, editors. 1983, San Diego CA: Academic Press, pp. 199–220.

32. Wright, J. C., Huston, A. C., Reitz, A. L., & Piemyat, S., Young children's perceptions of television reality: Determinants and developmental differences. *Developmental Psychology*, 1994. 30: 229–239.

33. Proctor, J. T., Children's reactions to Christmas. *Journal of the Oklahoma State Medical Association*, 1967. 60: 653–659.

34. Wullschläger, J., *Inventing Wonderland: Lewis Carroll, Edward Lear, J. M. Barrie, Kenneth Grahame, and A. A. Milne.* 1995, New York: The Free Press.

35. Taylor, B., & Howell, R. J., The ability of three-, four-, and five-year-old children to distinguish fantasy from reality. *Journal of Genetic Psychology,* 1973. 122: 315–318.

36. Samuels, A., & Taylor, M., Children's ability to distinguish fantasy events from real-life events. *British Journal of Developmental Psychology,* 1994. 12: 417–427; Also see Dierker, L. C., and Sanders, B., Developmental and individual differences in children's ability to distinguish reality from fantasy. *Imagination, cognition, and personality,* 1996. 16: 25–49.

37. Also see Morison, P., & Gardner, H., Dragons and dinosaurs: The child's capacity to differentiate fantasy from reality. *Child Development,* 1978. 49: 642–648. Perhaps when children feel afraid of something, they think of it as fantasy as a defense against the fear.

38. Subbotsky, E. V., *Foundations of the mind.* 1993, Cambridge, MA: Harvard University Press.

39. Subbotsky, E., Early rationality and magical thinking in preschoolers: Space and time. *British Journal of Developmental Psychology,* 1994. 12: 97–108.

40. Ibid., p. 103.

41. Subbotsky, E.V., *Foundations of the mind,* p. viii.

42. Rozin, P., Markwith, M., & Ross, B., The sympathetic magical law of similarity, nominal realism, and neglect of negatives in response to negative labels. *Psychological Science,* 1990. 1: 383–384.

43. Chandler, M. J., & Lalonde, C. E., Surprising, magical and miraculous turns of events: Children's reactions to violations of their early theories of mind and matter. *British Journal of Developmental Psychology,* 1994. 12: 83–96.

44. This is true even in cultures in which adults commonly consider divine intervention or sorcery when accounting for the events of their day (Mead, 1932).

45. Chandler, M. J., & Lalonde, C. E., Surprising, magical and miraculous turns, p. 85.

46. Harris, P. L., Unexpected, impossible and magical events: Children's reactions to causal violations. *British Journal of Developmental Psychology,* 1994. 12: 1–8.

47. Chandler, M. J., & Lalonde, C. E., Surprising, magical and miraculous turns, p. 85.

48. Johnson, C., & Harris, P. L., Magic: Special but not excluded. *British Journal of Developmental Psychology,* 1994. 12: 35–51.

49. Harris, P. L., Kavanaugh, R. D., & Meredith, M. C., Young children's comprehension of pretend episodes: The integration of successive

actions. *Child Development*, 1994. 65: 16-30; Harris, P. L., & Kavanaugh, R. D., Young children's understanding of pretense. *Monographs of the Society for Research in Child Development*, 1993. 58 (1).

    50. DiLalla, L. F., & Watson, M. W., Differentiation of fantasy and reality: Preschoolers' reactions to interruptions in their play. *Developmental Psychology*, 1988. 24: 286–291.

    51. Golomb, C., & Kuersten, R., On the transition from pretense play to reality: What are the rules of the game? *British Journal of Developmental Psychology*, 1996. 14: 203–217.

    52. Ibid., p. 208.

    53. See DiLalla, L. F., & Watson, M. W., Differentiation of fantasy and reality; Garvey, C., *Play*. 1977, Cambridge, MA: Harvard University Press; and Scarlett, W. G., & Wolf, D., When it's only make-believe: The construction of a boundary between fantasy and reality in storytelling," in *New directions for child development: Fact, fiction and fantasy in childhood*, E. Winner & H. Gardner, editors. 1979, San Francisco: Jossey-Bass, pp. 29–40.

    54. Harris, P. L., Brown, E., Marriott, C., Whittall, S., & Harmer, S., Monsters, ghosts and witches.

    55. Johnson, C., & Harris, P. L., Magic: Special but not excluded.

    56. Golomb, C., & Galasso, L., Make believe and reality: Explorations of the imaginary realm. *Developmental Psychology*, 1995. 31: 800–810.

    57. Woolley, J. D., & Phelps, K. E., Young children's practical reasoning about imagination. *British Journal of Developmental Psychology*, 1994. 12: 53–67.

    58. Lillard, A., Making sense of pretenses, in *Children's early understanding of mind*, C. Lewis and P. Mitchell, editors. 1994, Hillsdale, NJ: Lawrence Erlbaum, pp. 211–234.

    59. Walton, K. L., *Mimesis as make-believe*. 1990, Cambridge, MA: Harvard University Press.

    60. Woolley, J. D., The fictional mind: Young children's understanding of imagination, pretense, and dreams. *Developmental Review*, 1995. 15: 172–211.

    61. Walton, K. L., *Mimesis as make-believe*.

    62. Freud, S., *The interpretation of dreams*. 1900/1965, New York: Avon Books.

    63. Dennett, D. C., *Consciousness explained*. 1991, Boston: Little, Brown & Company.

    64. Ibid., p. 14.

    65. Dreams are written off by many adults in Western cultures as meaningless bits of fantasy, but in some cultures dreams are taken much more seriously. For example, they are sometimes believed to contain important messages from the spiritual world. The Senoi people of Malaysia discuss their dreams each morning over breakfast.

66. Foulkes, D., *Children's dreams.* 1982, New York: Wiley.

67. Piaget, J., *Play, dreams, and imitation in childhood.* 1962, New York: Norton, pp. 178–179.

68. Piaget, J., *The child's conception of the world.* 1929, London: Routledge and Kegan Paul, p. 94.

69. Laurendeau, M., & Pinard, A., *Causal thinking in the child.* 1962, New York: International University Press.

70. Woolley, J. D., & Wellman, H. M., Children's conception of dreams. *Cognitive Development,* 1992. 7: 365–380.

71. Ibid.

72. Wilcox, S. A., & Woolley, J. D. *Children's evaluation of statements of belief as sources of information.* Paper presented at the biennial meeting of the Society for Research in Child Development, 1989, Kansas City, MO.

73. Shweder, R. A., & Levine, R. A., Dream concepts of Hausa children. *Ethos,* 1975. 3: 209–230.

74. Gleitman, H., *Psychology.* Third ed. 1991, New York: W. W. Norton, p. 11.

75. Nicolich, L. M., Beyond sensorimotor intelligence: Assessment of symbolic maturity though analysis of pretend play. *Merrill-Palmer Quarterly,* 1977. 23: 88–99.

76. Cohen, D., & MacKeith, S. A., *The development of imagination: The private worlds of childhood.* 1991, London: Routledge, p. 51.

77. Mauro, J., *The friend that only I can see: A longitudinal investigation of children's imaginary companions.* 1991, unpublished doctoral dissertation, University of Oregon.

78. Gerrig, R. J., *Experiencing narrative worlds: On the psychological activities of reading.* 1993, New Haven, CT: Yale University Press.

79. Taylor, M., Cartwright, B. S., & Carlson, S. M., A developmental investigation of children's imaginary companions.

80. One interpretation of this result is that children with imaginary companions are more willing or able to participate in pretense than children who do not have imaginary companions. An alternative explanation is that children with imaginary companions are used to pretending someone is present and interacting with the pretend person in the presence of others. Thus, these children would have had experience interacting with a friend in a way similar to the type of interaction required in the study. In contrast, children who were pretending to interact with a real friend probably had very little experience interacting with the friend in this way. The difference between children's willingness to pretend their friend was present could have been due to the nature of the friend (imaginary or real) rather than the nature of the child. We ruled out this alternative possibility by asking another group of children with imaginary companions to pretend to phone one of their real friends. They had no difficulty with this request.

81. Mills, A. *Are children with imaginary playmates and children said to*

remember previous lives cross-culturally comparable categories? Paper presented at annual meeting of the American Anthropological Association, 1992, San Francisco.

Chapter 6: What happens to the imaginary companions created in early childhood?

1. Taylor, M., Gerow, L., & Charlie, C., A longitudinal follow-up of children with imaginary companions. 1998. Unpublished data.

2. Brooks, N. R., Goodbye to an imaginary friend, *Los Angeles Times*. 1997 January 19.

3. Milne, C., *The enchanted places*. 1974, London: Eyre Methuen Ltd.

4. Newson, J., & Newson, E., *Four years old in an urban community*. 1968, London: George Allen & Unwin.

5. Mauro, J., *The friend that only I can see: A longitudinal investigation of children's imaginary companions*. 1991 unpublished doctoral dissertation, University of Oregon; Taylor, M., Cartwright, B. S., & Carlson, S. M., A developmental investigation of children's imaginary companions. *Developmental Psychology*, 1993. 29 (2): 276–285.

6. Salinger, J. D., *Nine stories*. 1953, Boston, MA: Little, Brown & Co., p. 27.

7. Taylor, M., Cartwright, B. S., & Carlson, S. M., A developmental investigation of children's imaginary companions.

8. Benson, R. M., & Pryor, D. B., When friends fall out: Developmental interference with the function of some imaginary companions. *Journal of the American Psychoanalytic Association*, 1973. 21: 457–468.

9. Ibid., pp. 470–471.

10. Klein, B. R., A child's imaginary companion: A transitional self. *Clinical Social Work Journal*, 1985. 40: 272–282.

11. Imperiale, N., Imaginary pals say lots about kids, *Orlando Sentinel Tribune*. 1992 September 30, p. e1.

12. Taylor, M., Cartwright, B. S., & Carlson, S. M., A developmental investigation of children's imaginary companions.

13. Casey, E. S., *Imagining: A phenomenological study*. 1976, Bloomington: Indiana University Press; Watkins, M., *Invisible guests: The development of imaginal dialogues*. 1990, Boston: Siego Press.

14. Newson, J., & Newson, E., *Seven years old in an urban environment*. 1976, London: George Allen & Unwin, p. 158.

15. Singer, D. G., & Singer, J. L., *The house of make-believe: Children's play and developing imagination*. 1990, Cambridge, MA: Harvard University Press.

16. Newson, J., & Newson, E., *Seven years old in an urban environment*.

17. Ibid., p. 149.

18. Hurlock, E. B., & Burnstein, M., The imaginary playmate: A questionnaire study. *Journal of Genetic Psychology,* 1932. 41: 380–391.

19. Bender, L., & Vogel, B. F., Imaginary companions of children. *American Journal of Orthopsychiatry,* 1941. 11: 56–65.

20. Alexander, M., *The blackboard bear.* 1988, Dial books for young readers.

21. Zolotow, C., *The three funny friends.* 1961, New York: Harper & Row.

22. Manosevitz, M., Prentice, N. M., & Wilson, F., Individual and family correlates of imaginary companions in preschool children. *Developmental Psychology,* 1973. 8: 72–79.

23. Mauro, J., *The friend that only I can see.*

24. Also see Taylor, M., Gerow, L., & Charlie, C., A longitudinal follow-up of children with imaginary companions. When asked about the circumstances of the disappearance, parents reported that their children did not seem to be bothered by the loss of the imaginary companion—the imaginary companion simply disappeared or the child gradually lost interest. The children who reported that they no longer played with an imaginary companion also had little explanation for its disappearance, although a few children gave reasons such as there being a fight between the imaginary companion and child or the imaginary companion moving away.

25. Taylor, M., Kavanaugh, R., & Carlson, S. M. Adult memories of childhood imaginary companions. 1998. Unpublished data.

26. Taylor, M., Gerow, L., & Charlie, C., A longitudinal follow-up of children with imaginary companions.

27. Newson, J., & Newson, E., *Seven years old in an urban environment.*

28. Siegel, R. K., *Fire in the brain: Clinical tales of hallucination.* 1992, New York: Penguin Books.

29. Ibid., p. 141.

30. Dovima, a Regal Model of the 50s is dead at 63, *New York Times.* 1990, p. 31.

31. Kriegsman, A. M., Paul Taylor: The long shadow of a master, *Washington Post,* 1988 November 13, p. G1.

32. Kahlo, F. (Introduction by Carlos Fuentes, essay by Sarah M. Lowe), *The diary of Frida Kahlo: An intimate self-portrait.* 1995, New York: Harry N. Abrams, Inc.

Chapter 7: Do older children and adults create imaginary companions?

1. Albee, E., *Who's afraid of Virginia Woolf?* 1962, New York: Atheneum.

2. Roudane, M. C., *Who's afraid of Virginia Woolf?: Necessary fictions, terrifying realities.* 1990, Boston: Twayne Publishers.

3. Singer, D. G., & Singer, J. L., *The house of make-believe: Children's play and developing imagination.* 1990, Cambridge, MA: Harvard University Press.

4. Seiffge-Krenke, I., Close friendship and imaginary companions in adolescence. In *Close friendships in adolescence*, B. Laursen, editor. 1993, San Francisco: Jossey-Bass, pp. 73–87; Seiffge-Krenke, I., Imaginary companions in adolescence: Sign of a deficient or positive development? 1997. 20: 137–154.

5. Taylor, M., Kavanaugh, R., & Carlson, S. M., Adult memories of childhood imaginary companions. 1998. Unpublished data.

6. Harriman, P. L., Some imaginary companions of older subjects. *The American Journal of Orthopsychiatry,* 1937. 7: 368–370.

7. Cohen, D., & MacKeith, S. A., *The development of imagination: The private worlds of childhood.* 1991, London: Routledge.

8. Ibid., p. 27.

9. Ibid., p. 31.

10. Ibid., p. 97.

11. Ibid.

12. McCurdy, H. G., & Follett, H., *Barbara: The unconscious autobiography of a child genius.* 1966, Chapel Hill: The University of North Carolina Press.

13. Arnold, J., High jinks: O'Hare may handle more flights but none as crazy as the New York-to-Miami run. *Chicago Tribune.* 1986 March 11, p. 1.

14. Svendsen, M., Children's imaginary companions. *Archives of Neurology and Psychiatry,* 1934. 2: 985–999.

15. Although some children mention Jesus when asked if they have an imaginary friend, I think this is due to confusion about exactly what is being asked. Sometimes children simply don't know what you are talking about when you ask if they have a pretend friend, so they answer the question by describing someone in the ball park of what might be an acceptable answer, usually a friend who is real rather than imaginary. Children might consider Jesus an acceptable response because he is invisible, but they are taught and most likely believe that he is anything but imaginary.

16. Gallup, G. H., & Newport, F., Belief in paranormal phenomena among adult Americans. *Skeptical Inquirer,* 1991. 15: 137–146.

17. Doyle, A. C., *The coming of fairies.* 1921/1872, New York: Samuel Weiser.

18. Although the case that Doyle was particularly concerned with in his book, the photographs taken by the Cottingley cousins Elsie, 16, and Frances, 10, has been considered the strongest evidence for the existence of fairies and was recently the basis for a movie titled *Fairies: A True Story,* in

the 1980s it was shown to be a hoax, and the cousins confessed that they had faked the photographs (Kottmeyer, 1996).

19. Heise, D. R., *Delusions and the construction of reality,* in *Delusional beliefs,* T. F. Oltmanns and B. A. Maher, editors. 1988, New York: Wiley, ,pp. 259–272.

20. Sorokin, P., *Social and cultural dynamics.* 1957, Boston: Porter Sargent.

21. Walton, K. L., *Mimesis as make-believe.* 1990, Cambridge, MA: Harvard University Press, p. 4.

22. Wilson, S. C., & Barber, T. X., Vivid fantasy and hallucinatory abilities in the life histories of excellent hypnotic subjects ("somnambules"): Preliminary report with female subjects. In E. Klinger (ed.), *Imagery, Vol. 2: Concepts, results, and applications.* 1981, New York: Plenum Press, pp. 341–387.

23. Rhue, J. W., & Lynn, S. J., Fantasy: Developmental antecedents. *Journal of Personality,* 1987. 55: 121–137.

24. Lynn, S. J., Pintar, J., & Rhue, J. W., *Fantasy proneness, dissociation, and narrative construction,* in S. Krippner & S. M. Powers (eds.), *Broken images, broken selves: Dissociative narratives in clinical practice.* Washington, DC: Brunner/Mazel, Inc. pp. 274–275.

25. Ibid.

26. Caughey, J. L., *Imaginary social worlds.* 1984, Lincoln: University of Nebraska Press.

27. Hillman, J., *Re-visioning psychology.* 1975, New York: Harper & Row.

28. Schaefer, C. E., Imaginary companions and creative adolescents. *Developmental Psychology* 1969, 1: 747–749.

29. Lewis, C. S., *Surprised by joy: The shape of my early life.* 1955, New York: Harcourt Brace & Co., p. 15.

30. This description has some superficial similarity to the ideas of Julian Jaynes (1977). However, in contrast to Watkins, Jaynes associates the experience of imagined autonomous others with an early stage in the evolution of consciousness in human beings. "Volition, planning, initiative is organized with no consciousness whatever and then 'told' to the individual in his familiar language, sometimes with the visual aura of a familiar friend or authority figure or 'god,' or sometimes as a voice alone. The individual obeyed these hallucinated voices because he could not 'see' what to do by himself" (p. 75).

31. Stoney, B., *Enid Blyton: A biography.* 1974, London: Hodder, pp. 206–207.

32. Watkins, M., *Invisible guests: The development of imaginal dialogues.* 1990, Boston: Sigo Press, p. 315.

33. Ibid.

34. Basbanes, N., 'L' is for latest mystery bestseller, in *Register-Guard,* Eugene, OR, p. 3e 1995 October 1.

35. Fowles, J., *The French Lieutenant's Woman.* 1969, Boston: Little, Brown & Company, pp. 96–97.

36. Siegel, R. K., *Fire in the brain: Clinical tales of hallucination.* 1992, New York: Penguin Books, p. 163.

37. Fowler, R. D., The case of the multicolored personality. *Psychology Today,* November 1986, pp. 38–49.

38. Ibid., p. 49.

39. Vonnegut, K., *Breakfast of champions.* 1973, New York: Dell Publishing, p. 192.

40. Wegner, D. M., *On purpose: The illusion of conscious agency.* In preparation.

41. Dreyfus, H. L., & Dreyfus, S. E., *Mind over machine.* 1986, New York: The Free Press.

42. Johnson, M., Discriminating the origin of information, in T. F. Oltmanns & B. A. Maher (eds.), *Delusional Beliefs.* 1988, New York: John Wiley & Sons, p. 57. For a review of this literature, see Johnson, Hashtroudi, and Lindsay (1993).

43. Ibid., p. 53.

44. Casey, E. S., *Imagining: A phenomenological study.* 1976, Bloomington: Indiana University Press.

45. Turkle, S., *Life on the screen: Identity in the age of the Internet.* 1995, New York: Simon & Schuster, pp. 224–225.

46. Turkle, S., *Identity in the Internet,* in J. Brockman & K. Matson (eds.), *How things are: A science tool-kit for the mind.* 1995, New York: William Morrow & Co, pp. 224–225.

Chapter 8: Fantasy in the lives of children and adults

1. Milne, C., *The enchanted places.* 1974, London: Eyre Methuen Ltd., p. 61.

2. For a review of this controversy, see Woolley, J., Thinking about fantasy: Are children fundamentally different thinkers and believers from adults? *Child Development,* 1997. 68: 991–1011.

3. Golomb, C., & Galasso, L., Make believe and reality: Explorations of the imaginary realm. *Developmental Psychology,* 1995. 31: 800–810.

4. Taylor, M., The role of creative control and culture in children's fantasy/reality judgments. *Child Development,* 1997. 68: 1015–1017.

5. Walton, K. L., *Mimesis as make-believe.* 1990, Cambridge, MA: Harvard University Press.

6. Lillard, A., Making sense of pretense. In C. Lewis & P. Mitchell (eds.), *Children's early understanding of mind.* 1994, Hillsdale, NJ: Lawrence Erlbaum. pp. 211–234.

7. Golomb, C., & Galasso, L., Make believe and reality.

8. Chandler, M., Rescuing magical thinking from the jaws of social determinism. *Child Development,* 1997. 68: 1021–1023.

9. Died, in *Newsweek.* 1981, November 2, p. 70.

10. Singer, D.G., & Singer, J. L., *The house of make-believe: Children's play and developing imagination.* 1990, Cambridge, MA: Harvard University Press, p. 232.

11. Vandenberg, B., The realities of play, in *Organizing early experience: Imagination and cognition in childhood,* D. C. Morrison (editor). 1988, Amityville, NY: Baywood Publishing Co. pp. 198–209, p. 205.

12. Sartre, J.-P., *The psychology of the imagination.* 1940, London: Methuen & Co. Ltd.

References

Acredolo, L. P., Goodwyn, S. W., & Fulmer, A. H. (1995). *Why some children create imaginary companions: Clues from infant and toddler play preferences.* Paper presented at the biennial meeting of the Society for Research in Child Development, Indianapolis, IN.

Albee, E. (1962). *Who's afraid of Virginia Woolf?* New York: Atheneum.

Alexander, M. (1988). *The blackboard bear.* Dial books for young readers.

Allport, G. W. (1950). *The individual and his religion.* New York: The Macmillan Co.

Ames, L. B., & Learned, J. (1946). Imaginary companions and related phenomena. *Journal of Genetic Psychology, 69,* 147–167.

Anderson, N. T., Vanderhook, P., & Vanderhook, S. (1996). *Spiritual protection for your children.* Ventura, CA: Regal.

Arnold, J. (1986 March 11). High jinks: O'Hare may handle more flights but none as crazy as the New York-to-Miami run. *Chicago Tribune,* p. 1.

Astington, J. W., & Gopnik, A. (1988). Knowing you've changed your mind: Children's understanding of representational change. In A. W. Astington, P. L. Harris, & D. R. Olson (eds.), *Developing theories of mind* (pp. 193–206). New York: Cambridge University Press.

Axline, V. M. (1969). *Play Therapy.* New York: Ballantine Books.

Bairdain, E. F. (1959). Psychological characteristics of adolescents who have had imaginary companions. *Dissertation Abstracts International, 29,* 747.

Baron-Cohen, S. (1995). *Mindblindness: An essay on autism and theory of mind.* Cambridge, MA: MIT Press.

Basbanes, N. (1995 October 1). 'L' is for latest mystery best seller. *Register-Guard.* Eugene OR, p. 3e.

Bender, L., & Vogel, B. F. (1941). Imaginary companions of children. *American Journal of Orthopsychiatry, 11,* 56–65.

Benson, R. M., & Pryor, D. B. (1973). When friends fall out: Developmental interference with the function of some imaginary companions. *Journal of the American Psychoanalytic Association, 21,* 457–468.

Bettelheim, B. (1977). *The uses of enchantment: The meaning and importance of fairy tales.* New York: Vintage Books.

Breckenridge, M. E., & Vincent, E. L. (1965). *Child Development: Physical and psychological growth through adolescence.* Philadelphia: W. B. Saunders Co.

Bretherton, I. (1989). Pretense: The form and function of make-believe play. *Developmental Review, 9,* 383–401.

Bretherton, I., & Beeghley, M. (1982). Talking about internal states: The acquisition of an explicit theory of mind. *Developmental Psychology, 18,* 906–921.

Brooks, M., & Knowles, D. (1982). Parents' views of children's imaginary companions. *Child Welfare, 61,* 25–33.

Brooks, N. R. (1997 January 19). Goodbye to an imaginary friend. *Los Angeles Times.*

Bryant, J., & Anderson, D. R. (eds.) (1983). *Children's understanding of television: Research on attention and comprehension.* New York: Academic Press.

Burkett, M. (1993). Double standard for double talk. *The Register-Guard.*

Burlingham, D., & Freud, A. (1944). *Infants without families.* London: George Allen & Unwin.

Carlson, S. M., Taylor, M., Levin, G. R. (in press). The influence of culture on pretend play: The case of Mennonite children. *Merrill-Palmer Quarterly.*

Casey, E. S. (1976). *Imagining: A phenomenological study.* Bloomington: Indiana University Press.

Caughey, J. L. (1984). Imaginary social worlds: A cultural approach. Lincoln, NE: University of Nebraska Press.

Chandler, M. (1997). Rescuing magical thinking from the jaws of social determinism. *Child Development, 68,* 1021–1023.

Chandler, M. J., & Helm, D. (1984). Developmental changes in the contributions of shared experience to social role-taking competence. *International Journal of Behavioral Development, 7,* 145–156.

Chandler, M. J., & Lalonde, C. E. (1994). Surprising, magical and miraculous turns of events: Children's reactions to violations of their early theories of mind and matter. *British Journal of Developmental Psychology, 12,* 83–96.

Chase, M. (1944). *Harvey.* New York: Dramatists Play Service.

Chukovsky, K. (1925/1963). *From two to five.* Berkeley: University of California Press.

Clark, C. D. (1995). *Flights of fancy, leaps of faith: Children's myths in contemporary America.* Chicago: University of Chicago Press.

Cohen, D., & MacKeith, S. A. (1991). *The development of imagination: The private worlds of childhood.* London: Routledge.

Copple. (October 1991). Fantastic voyages. *Sesame Street Magazine.*

Davies, M. M. (1997). *Fake, fact, and television: Children's interpretations of television reality.* Mahwah, NJ: Lawrence Erlbaum.

Dennett, D. C. (1991). *Consciousness explained.* Boston: Little, Brown & Company.

Derryberry, D., & Rothbart, M. K. (1984). Emotion, attention and temperament. In C. E. Izard, J. Kagan, & R. Zajonc (eds.), *Emotion, cognition and behavior* (pp. 132–166). New York: Cambridge University Press.

Dierker, L. C., & Sanders, B. (1996). Developmental and individual differences in children's ability to distinguish reality from fantasy. *Imagination, Cognition and Personality, 16,* 25–49.

DiLalla, L. F., & Watson, M. W. (1988). Differentiation of fantasy and reality: Preschoolers' reactions to interruptions in their play. *Developmental Psychology, 24,* 286–291.

Dorr, A. (1983). No shortcuts to judging reality. In J. Bryant & D. R. Anderson (eds.), *Children's understanding of television: Research on attention and comprehension* (pp. 199–220). San Diego, CA: Academic Press.

Doyle, A. C. (1921/1872). *The coming of fairies.* New York: Samuel Weiser.

Dreyfus, H. L., & Dreyfus, S. E. (1986). *Mind over machine.* New York: The Free Press.

Dunn, J., Brown, J., Slomkowski, C., Tesla, C., & Youngblade, L. (1991). Young children's understanding of other people's feelings and beliefs: Individual differences and their antecedents. *Child Development, 62,* 1352–1366.

Estes, D., Wellman, H. M., & Woolley, J. D. (1989). Children's understanding of mental phenomena. In H. W. Reese (ed.), *Advances in child development and behavior* (pp. 41–87). San Diego, CA: Academic Press.

Farver, J. M., & Howes, C. (1993). Cultural differences in American and Mexican mother-child pretend play. *Merrill-Palmer Quarterly, 39,* 344–358.

Flavell, J. H., Flavell, E. R., & Green, F. L. (1983). Development of the appearance-reality distinction. *Cognitive Psychology, 15,* 95–120.

Flavell, J. H., Flavell, E. R., & Green, F. L. (1987). Young children's knowledge about the apparent-real and pretend-real distinctions. *Developmental Psychology, 23,* 816–822.

Flavell, J. H., Flavell, E. R., Green, F. L., & Korfmacher, J. E. (1990). Do young children think of television images as pictures or real objects? *Journal of Broadcasting and Electronic Media, 34,* 399–419.

Foulkes, D. (1982). *Children's dreams.* New York: Wiley.

Fowler, R. D. (November, 1986). The case of the multicolored personality. *Psychology Today,* 38–49.

Fowles, J. (1969). *The French lieutenant's woman.* Boston: Little, Brown & Company.

Fraiberg, S. H. (1959). *The magic years.* New York: Charles Scribner's Sons.

Freud, A. (1936/1966). *The ego and the mechanisms of defense.* New York: International Universities Press.

Freud, S. (1900/1965). *The interpretation of dreams.* New York: Avon Books.

Frith, U. (1989). *Autism: Explaining the enigma.* Cambridge, UK: Blackwell.

Gallup, G. H., & Newport, F. (1991). Belief in paranormal phenomena among adult Americans. *Skeptical Inquirer, 15,* 137–146.

Gardner, H. (1993). *Multiple intelligences: The theory in practice.* New York: Basic Books.

Garvey, C. (1977). *Play.* Cambridge, MA: Harvard University Press.

Gerrig, R. J. (1993). *Experiencing narrative worlds: On the psychological activities of reading.* New Haven, CT: Yale University Press.

Gil, E. (1991). *The healing power of play.* New York: The Guilford Press.

Gleason, T. R., Sebane, A. M., McGinley, J., & Hartup, W. W. (1997). *Invisible friends and personified objects: Qualitative differences in relationships with imaginary companions.* Poster presented at the biannual meeting of the Society for Research in Child Development, Washington, D.C.

Gleitman, H. (1991). *Psychology.* (Third ed.). New York: W. W. Norton.

Golomb, C., & Galasso, L. (1995). Make believe and reality: Explorations of the imaginary realm. *Developmental Psychology, 31,* 800–810.

Golomb, C., & Kuersten, R. (1996). On the transition from pretense play to reality: What are the rules of the game? *British Journal of Developmental Psychology, 14,* 203–217.

Gottman, J. M., & Parker, J. G. (eds.) (1986). *Conversations of friends: Speculations on affective development.* Cambridge: Cambridge University Press.

Harriman, P. L. (1937). Some imaginary companions of older subjects. *American Journal of Orthopsychiatry, 7,* 368–370.

Harris, P. L. (1994). Unexpected, impossible and magical events: Children's reactions to causal violations. *British Journal of Developmental Psychology, 12,* 1–8.

Harris, P. L., Brown, E., Marriott, C., Whittall, S., & Harmer, S. (1991). Monsters, ghosts and witches: Testing the limits of the fantasy-reality distinction in young children. *British Journal of Developmental Psychology, 9,* 105–123.

Harris, P. L., & Kavanaugh, R. D. (1993). Young children's understanding of pretense. *Monographs of the Society for Research in Child Development, 58*(1).

Harris, P. L., Kavanaugh, R. D., & Meredith, M. C. (1994). Young children's comprehension of pretend episodes: The integration of successive actions. *Child Development, 65,* 16–30.

Harter, S., & Chao, C. (1992). The role of competence in children's creation of imaginary friends. *Merrill-Palmer Quarterly, 38,* 350–363.

Harvey, N. A. (1918). *Imaginary playmates and other mental phenomena of children.* Ypsilanti: Michigan State Normal College.

Heath, S. B. (1983). *Ways with words: Language, life, and work in communities and classrooms.* Cambridge, UK: Cambridge University Press.

Heise, D. R. (1988). Delusions and the construction of reality. In T. F. Oltmanns & B. A. Maher (eds.), *Delusional beliefs* (pp. 259–272). New York: Wiley.

Hostetler, J. A., & Huntington, G. E. (1971). *Children in Amish society: Socialization and community education.* New York: Holt, Rinhart & Winston.

Hillman, J. (1975). *Re-visioning psychology.* New York: Harper & Row.

Hurlock, E. B., & Burnstein, M. (1932). The imaginary playmate: A questionnaire study. *Journal of Genetic Psychology, 41,* 380–391.

Imperiale, N. (1992 September 30). Imaginary pals say lots about kids. *Orlando Sentinel Tribune,* p. e1.

Jalongo, M. R. (1984). Imaginary companions in children's lives and literature. *Childhood Education, 60,* 166–171.

Jaynes, J. (1977). *The origin of consciousness in the breakdown of the bicameral mind.* Boston: Houghton Mifflin Co.

Jersild, A. T., Markey, F. V., & Jersild, C. L. (1933). *Children's fears, dreams, wishes, daydreams, likes, dislikes, pleasant and unpleasant memories.* (Vol. 12). New York: Teachers College, Columbia University.

Johnson, C., & Harris, P. L. (1994). Magic: Special but not excluded. *British Journal of Developmental Psychology, 12,* 35–51.

Johnson, M. K. (1988). Discriminating the origin of information. In T. F. Oltmanns & B. A. Maher (eds.), *Delusional beliefs* (pp. 34–65). New York: John Wiley.

Johnson, M. K., Hashtroudi, S., & Lindsay, D. S. (1993). Source monitoring. *Psychological Review, 114,* 3–28.

Kahlo, F. (1995). The diary of Frida Kahlo: An intimate self-portrait. (Introduction by Carlos Fuentes, essay by Sarah Lowe). New York: Harry N. Abrams, Inc.

Kalyan Masih, V. (1978). Imaginary companions of children. In R. B. R. Weizmann, P. J. Levinson, & P. A. Taylor (eds.), *Piagetian theory and its implications for the helping professions*. Los Angeles: University of Southern California.

Kavanaugh, R. D., Whittington, S., & Cerbone, M. J. (1983). Mothers' use of fantasy in speech to young children. *Journal of Child Language, 10,* 45–55.

Kaye, M. (1990). *The real tooth fairy*. New York: Harcourt Brace & Co.

King, S. (1977). *The Shining*. New York: Doubleday & Company, Inc.

Klein, B. R. (1985). A child's imaginary companion: A transitional self. *Clinical Social Work Journal, 40,* 272–282.

Kluft, R.P. (1984). Treatment of multiple personality disorder: A study of 33 cases. *Psychiatric Clinics of North America, 7,* 9–29.

Kluft, R. P. (1987). An update on multiple personality disorder. *Hospital and Community Psychiatry, 38,* 363–373.

Kottmeyer, M. (196). Fairies. In G. Stein (ed.), *The Encyclopedia of the Paranormal*. Amherst, NY: Prometheus Books.

Kriegsman, A. M. (1988 November 13). Paul Taylor: The long shadow of a master. *Washington Post*, p. G1.

Laurendeau, M., & Pinard, A. (1962). *Causal thinking in the child*. New York: International University Press.

Lazurus, A. (1984). *In the mind's eye: The power of imagery for personal enrichment*. New York: Guilford Press.

Leslie, A. M. (1987). Pretense and representation: The origins of "theory of mind." *Psychological Review, 94,* 412–426.

Lewis, C. S. (1955). *Surprised by joy: The shape of my early life*. New York: Harcourt Brace & Co.

Lillard, A. (1994). Making sense of pretense. In C. Lewis & P. Mitchell (eds.), *Children's early understanding of mind* (pp. 211–234). Hillsdale, NJ: Lawrence Erlbaum.

Lindsey, R. (1988 July 24). Promises to keep. *New York Times Magazine*, pp. 23–24.

Lynn, S. J., Pintar, J., & Rhue, J. W. (1997). Fantasy proneness, dissociation, and narrative construction. In S. Krippner & S. M. Powers (eds.), *Broken images, broken selves: Dissociative narratives in clinical practice* (pp. 274–302). Washington, D.C.: Brunner/Mazel.

Machtlinger, V. J. (1976). Psychoanalytic theory: Pre-oedipal and oedipal phases with special reference to the father. In M. E. Lamb (ed.), *The role of the father in child development* (pp. 277–305). New York: Wiley.

MacKenzie, N. (1965). *Dreams and dreaming*. London: Aldus Books.

Manosevitz, M., Fling, S., & Prentice, N. M. (1977). Imaginary companions in young children: Relationships with intelligence, creativity and waiting ability. *Journal of Child Psychology and Psychiatry, 18,* 73–78.

Manosevitz, M., Prentice, N. M., & Wilson, F. (1973). Individual and family correlates of imaginary companions in preschool children. *Developmental Psychology, 8,* 72–79.

Mauro, J. (1991). *The friend that only I can see: A longitudinal investigation of children's imaginary companions.* Unpublished doctoral dissertation, University of Oregon.

McCurdy, H. G., & Follett, H. (1966). *Barbara: The unconscious autobiography of a child genius.* Chapel Hill: The University of North Carolina Press.

Mead, M. (1932). An investigation of the thought of primitive children, with special reference to animism. *Journal of the Royal Anthropological Institute of Great Britain and Ireland, 62,* 173–190.

Miller, P. J., Hengst, J., Alexander, K., & Sperry, L. L. (in press). Personal storytelling as generic activity: Envisioning reality from a personal perspective. In C. Johnson & K. Rosengren (eds.), *Imagining the impossible: The development of magical, scientific, and religious thinking in contemporary society.* Cambridge, UK: Cambridge University Press.

Mills, A. (1992). *Are children with imaginary playmates and children said to remember previous lives cross-culturally comparable categories?* Paper presented at the American Anthropological Association, San Francisco.

Milne, C. (1974). *The enchanted places.* London: Eyre Methuen Ltd.

Morison, P., & Gardner, H. (1978). Dragons and dinsosaurs: The child's capacity to differentiate fantasy from reality. *Child Development, 49,* 642–648.

Murphy, L. B. *The widening world of childhood: Paths toward mastery.* New York: Basic Books.

Myers, W. A. (1976). Imaginary companions, fantasy twins, mirror dreams and depersonalization. *Psychoanalytic Quarterly, 45,* 503–524

Nagera, H. (1969). The imaginary companion: Its significance for ego development and conflict resolution. *The Psychoanalytic Study of the Child, 24,* 89–99.

Newson, J., & Newson, E. (1968). *Four years old in an urban community.* London: George Allen & Unwin.

Newson, J., & Newson, E. (1976). *Seven years old in an urban environment.* London: George Allen & Unwin.

Nicolich, L. M. (1977). Beyond sensorimotor intelligence: Assessment of symbolic maturity though analysis of pretend play. *Merrill-Palmer Quarterly, 23,* 88–99.

Nordlinger, J. (1997 August 11). The life of a lonely determined golfer. *The Weekly Standard,* p. 35.

Opie, I., & Opie, P. (1959). *The lore and language of school children.* Oxford: Oxford University Press.

Overton, W. F., & Jackson, J. P. (1973). The representation of imagined objects in action sequences: A developmental study. *Child Development*, *44*, 309–314.

Perner, J., Leekam, S. R., & Wimmer, H. (1987). Three-year-olds' difficulty understanding false beliefs: Representational limitation, lack of knowledge or pragmatic misunderstanding. *British Journal of Developmental Psychology*, *5*, 125–137.

Perner, J., Ruffman, T., & Leekam, S. R. (1994). Theory of mind is contagious: You catch it from your sibs. *Child Development*, *65*, 1228–1238.

Piaget, J. (1929). *The child's conception of the world*. London: Routledge and Kegan Paul.

Piaget, J. (1962). *Play, dreams, and imitation in childhood*. New York: Norton.

Pines, M. (September 1978). Invisible playmates. *Psychology Today*, 38–42.

Prentice, N. M., Manosevitz, M., & Hubbs, L. (1978). Imaginary figures of early childhood: Santa Claus, Easter Bunny and the Tooth Fairy. *American Journal of Orthopsychiatry*, *48*, 618–628.

Proctor, J. T. (1967). Children's reactions to Christmas. *Journal of the Oklahoma State Medical Association*, *60*, 653–659.

Putnam, F. W. (1989). *Diagnosis and treatment of multiple personality disorder*. New York: Guilford Press.

Redekop, C. (1989). *Mennonite society*. Baltimore, MD: Johns Hopkins University Press.

Rhue, J. W., & Lynn, S. J. (1987). Fantasy: Developmental antecedents. *Journal of Personality*, *55*, 121–137.

Rosemond, J. (1991). Boy, 2, continually asks,"Why?": His mother wants to know why. *Corvallis Times*. OR.

Rosengren, K. S., Kalish, C. W., Hickling, A. K., & Gelman, S. A. (1994). Exploring the relation between preschool children's magical beliefs and causal thinking. *British Journal of Developmental Psychology*, *12*, 69–82.

Roudane, M. C. (1990). *Who's afraid of Virginia Woolf?: Necessary fictions, terrifying realities*. Boston: Twayne Publishers.

Rozin, P., Markwith, M., & Ross, B. (1990). The sympathetic magical law of similarity, nominal realism, and neglect of negatives in response to negative labels. *Psychological Science*, *1*, 383–384.

Sakol, J. L., (1987). *The Royals*. New York: Congdon & Weed.

Salinger, J. D. (1953). *Nine stories*. Boston, MA: Little, Brown & Co.

Samuels, A., & Taylor, M. (1994). Children's ability to distinguish fantasy events from real-life events. *British Journal of Developmental Psychology*, *12*, 417–427.

Sanders, B. (1992). The imaginary companion experience in multiple personality disorder. *Dissociation*, *5*, 159–162.

Sartre, J.-P. (1940). *The psychology of the imagination*. London: Methuen & Co. Ltd.

Scarlett, W. G., & Wolf, D. (1979). When it's only make-believe: The construction of a boundary between fantasy and reality in storytelling. In E. Winner & H. Gardner (eds.), *New directions for child development: Fact, fiction and fantasy in childhood* (pp. 29–40). San Francisco: Jossey-Bass.

Schaefer, C. (ed.) (1979). *The therapeutic use of child's play*. New York: Jason Aronson.

Schaefer, C. E. (1969). Imaginary companions and creative adolescents. *Developmental Psychology, 1,* 747–749.

Seiffge-Krenke, I. (1993). Close friendship and imaginary companions in adolescence. In B. Laursen (ed.), *Close friendships in adolescence* (pp. 73–87). San Francisco: Jossey-Bass.

Seiffge-Krenke, I. (1997). Imaginary companions in adolescence: Sign of a deficient or positive development? *Journal of Adolescence, 20,* 137–154.

Seuss. (1957). *The cat in the hat.* New York: Random House.

Shweder, R. A., & Levine, R. A. (1975). Dream concepts of Hausa children. *Ethos, 3,* 209–230.

Siegel, R. K. (1992). *Fire in the brain: Clinical tales of hallucination.* New York: Penguin Books.

Siegler, R. (1996). *Emerging minds: The process of change in children's thinking.* New York: Oxford University Press.

Singer, D. G. (1993). *Playing for their lives: Helping troubled children through play therapy.* New York: The Free Press.

Singer, D. G., & Singer, J. L. (1990). *The house of make-believe: Children's play and developing imagination.* Cambridge, MA: Harvard University Press.

Singer, J. L. (1961). Imagination and waiting ability in young children. *Journal of Personality, 29,* 396–413.

Singer, J. L., & Singer, D. G. (1981). *Television, imagination, and aggression: A study of preschoolers.* Hillsdale, NJ: Lawrence Erlbaum.

Singer, J. L., & Streiner, B. F. (1966). Imaginative content in the dreams and fantasy play of blind and sighted children. *Perceptual and Motor Skills, 22,* 475–482.

Sorokin, P. (1957). *Social and cultural dynamics.* Boston: Porter Sargent.

Sperry, L. L., & Sperry, D. E. (1996). The early development of narrative skills. *Cognitive Development, 11,* 443–465.

Spock, B. (1974). *Bringing up children in a difficult time.* Boston: The Bodley Head.

Stoney, B. (1974). *Enid Blyton: A biography.* London: Hodder.

Subbotsky, E. V. (1993). *Foundations of the mind.* Cambridge, MA: Harvard University Press.

Subbotsky, E. (1994). Early rationality and magical thinking in preschoolers: Space and time. *British Journal of Developmental Psychology, 12,* 97–108.

Svendsen, M. (1934). Children's imaginary companions. *Archives of Neurology and Psychiatry, 2,* 985–999.

Taylor, B., & Howell, R. J. (1973). The ability of three-, four-, and five-year-old children to distinguish fantasy from reality. *Journal of Genetic Psychology, 122,* 315–318.

Taylor, M. (1988). Conceptual perspective taking: Children's ability to distinguish what they know from what they see. *Child Development, 59,* 703–718.

Taylor, M. (1997). The role of creative control and culture in children's fantasy/reality judgments. *Child Development, 68,* 1015–1017.

Taylor, M., & Carlson, S. M. (1997). The relation between individual differences in fantasy and theory of mind. *Child Development, 68,* 436–455.

Taylor, M., Cartwright, B. S., & Carlson, S. M. (1993). A developmental investigation of children's imaginary companions. *Developmental Psychology, 29* (2), 276–285.

Taylor, M., Gerow, L., & Charlie, C. (1998). A longitudinal follow-up of children with imaginary companions. Unpublished data.

Taylor, M., Kavanaugh, R., & Carlson, S. M. (1998). Adult memories of childhood imaginary companions. Unpublished data.

Terr, L. (1990). *Too scared to cry: Psychic trauma in childhood.* New York: Basic Books.

Tolkien, J. R. R. (1984). On fairy stories. In C. Tolkien (ed.), *The monsters and the critics, and other essays.* Boston: Houghton Mifflin.

Turkle, S. (1995). *Life on the screen: Identity in the age of the Internet.* New York: Simon & Schuster.

Twain, M. (1922). *The Mysterious Stranger.* New York: Harper & Row.

Ustinov, P. (1977). *Dear me.* Middlesex, England: Penguin.

Vandenberg, B. (1988). The realities of play. In D. C. Morrison (ed.), *Organizing early experience: Imagination and cognition in childhood* (pp. 198–209). Amityville, NY: Baywood Publishing Co.

Vonnegut, K. (1973). *Breakfast of champions.* New York: Dell Publishing.

Vostrovsky, C. (1895). A study of imaginary companions. *Education, 15,* 383–398.

Walton, K. L. (1990). *Mimesis as make-believe.* Cambridge, MA: Harvard University Press.

Warfield, F. (1948). *Cotton in my ears.* New York: The Viking Press.

Watkins, M. (1990). *Invisible guests: The development of imaginal dialogues.* Boston: Sigo Press.

Watterson, B. (1995). *The Calvin and Hobbes tenth anniversary book.* Kansas City: Andrews and McMeel.

Weaver, L. H. (1982). Forbidden fancies: A child's vision of Mennonite plainness. *Journal of Ethnic Studies, 11,* 51–59.

Wegner, D. M. (in preparation). *On purpose: The illusion of conscious agency.*

Wellman, H. M., & Estes, D. (1986). Early understanding of mental entities: A reexamination of childhood realism. *Child Development, 57,* 910–923.

White, J. , & Allers, C. T. (1994). Play therapy with abused children: A review of the literature. *Journal of Counseling and Development, 72,* 390–394.

Wickes, F. G. (1927). *The inner world of childhood.* New York: D. Appleton & Company.

Wilcox, S. A., & Woolley, J. D. (1989). *Children's evaluation of statements of belief as sources of information.* Paper presented at the biennial meeting of the Society for Research in Child Development, Kansas City, MO.

Williams, M. (1975). *The velveteen rabbit.* New York: Avon Books.

Wilson, S. C., & Barber, T. X. (1981).Vivid fantasy and hallucinatory abilities in the life histories of excellent hyponotic subjects ("somnambules"): Preliminary report with female subjects. In E. Klinger (ed.), *Imagery, Vol. 2: Concepts, results, and applications* (pp. 341–387), New York: Plenum Press.

Wimmer, H., & Perner, J. (1983). Beliefs about beliefs: Representation and constraining function of wrong beliefs in young children's understanding of deception. *Cognition, 13,* 103–128.

Wingfield, R. C. (1948). Bernreuter personality ratings of college students who recall having had imaginary companions during childhood. *Journal of Child Psychiatry, 1,* 190–194.

Winner, E., Gardner, H., & Silverstein, L. (1988). Creating a world with words. In F. S. Kessel (ed.), *The development of language and language researchers: Essays in honor of Roger Brown* (pp. 353–371). Hillsdale, NJ: Lawrence Erlbaum.

Winnicott, D. W. (1953). Transitional objects and transitional phenomena. *International Journal of Psychoanalysis, 34,* 89–97.

Woolley, J. D. (1995). The fictional mind: Young children's understanding of imagination, pretense, and dreams. *Developmental Review, 15,* 172–211.

Woolley, J. (1997). Thinking about fantasy: Are children fundamentally different thinkers and believers from adults? *Child Development, 68,* 991–1011.

Woolley, J. D., & Phelps, K. E. (1994). Young children's practical reasoning about imagination. *British Journal of Developmental Psychology, 12,* 53–67.

Woolley, J. D., & Wellman, H. M. (1992). Children's conception of dreams. *Cognitive Development, 7,* 365–380.

Woolley, J. D., & Wellman, H. M. (1993). Origin and truth: Young children's understanding of imaginary mental representations. *Child Development, 64,* 1–17.

Wright, J. C., Huston, A. C., Reitz, A. L., & Piemyat, S. (1994). Young children's perceptions of television reality: Determinants and developmental differences. *Developmental Psychology, 30,* 229–239.

Wullschläger, J. (1995). *Inventing Wonderland: The lives and fantasies of Lewis Carroll, Edward Lear, J. M. Barrie, Kenneth Grahame, and A. A. Milne.* New York: The Free Press.

Yawkey, T. D., & Yawkey, M. L. (1983). *Assessing young children for imaginativeness through oral reporting: Preliminary results.* Paper presented at the International Conference on Play and Play Environments: Research and Its Application to Play Settings, Austin, Texas.

Zolotow, C. (1961). *The three funny friends.* New York: Harper & Row.

Acknowledgments

THE idea of doing research on imaginary companions came to me while I was listening to Paul Harris at a meeting of the Society for Research in Child Development several years ago. He was describing a series of fascinating experiments on children's grasp of the distinction between fantasy and reality in the context of emotionally charged pretense involving monsters. I was familiar with the ground-breaking studies on imaginary companions by Dorothy and Jerome Singer and by Jennifer Mauro showing that imaginary companions were relatively common and psychologically healthy. As I listened to Harris's talk, I kept thinking about how to apply some of his ideas to a study of imaginary companions. Like the pretend monsters in Harris's study, imaginary companions elicit strong emotion (in the case of imaginary companions, it is love rather than fear). Just like the pretend monsters that Harris asked children to imagine in an empty box, imaginary companions are projected outside the head of the pretender. They take up space in the real world, requiring their own corner of the bed, their own chair at the dinner table. But in the case of imaginary companions, the fantasy is extended in time and masterminded by the children themselves, rather than being a one-time pretense coached by an adult experimenter. Did children absorbed in fantasies involving pretend friends ever start to think of these friends as real?

Since then, most of my research has been devoted to trying to answer this question and many others about pretend play and imaginary companions. Stephanie Carlson has been my intellectual partner in this work. It has been a very rewarding collaboration, and I thank Stephanie for all her effort, and insight, and for being the first person to read an early draft of this book. I am very lucky to have wonderful colleagues in Susan Gelman, Angeline Lillard, Jacqueline Woolley, and Deborah Legorreta, who have taught, challenged, and supported me. Their comments on this book, in particular, and on my research, in general, have been extremely valuable.

My colleagues at the University of Oregon have been willing for years to listen to my endless ramblings about imaginary companions. In particular, I have benefited from the thoughts and wisdom of Dare Baldwin, Beverly Fagot, Debbie Frisch, Sara Hodges, Lou Moses, and Anne Simons. Lew Goldberg couldn't remember much about his childhood imaginary companion, but he sure helped me a lot with statistics! I also appreciate the guidance Mary Rothbart provided on longitudinal design.

Many students have worked on various fantasy studies and provided lots of ideas, feedback, and critique. Over the years this group has included (among others) Bridget Cartwright, Carolyn Charlie, Tara Fisher, Rebecca Frankel, Alicia Grandy, Adele Kohanyi, Wednesday Lomas, Vicki Luu, Andrea Minton-Edison, Adrienne Samuels, Alise Tome, and Ken Tuttle. I am particularly grateful to Lynn Gerow, who has been a major contributor to this research. In the home stretch of preparing the final manuscript, Mark Sabbagh and Gretchen Lussier saved the day. I also want to thank all the other friends and colleagues who have assisted me in so many ways throughout the course of this project: sending me literary and scholarly references to imaginary companions, children's books about them, cartoons featuring them, stories about the imaginary companions in their own families, as well as lots of encouragement and enthusiasm. This supportive group of people includes Barbara Altmann, Sally Anderson, Holly Arrow, Ila Ausland, Jodie Baird, Marcia Barss, Mary Bennett, David Butcher, Kathie Carpenter, John Crabbe, William Davie, Robert Davis, Tom Dishion, Bonnie Esbensen, Ellie Flavell, Jennifer Freyd, Francie Green, Barbara Hort, Ray Hyman, Jeri Janowsky, Oliver John, JQ Johnson, Scott Monroe, Mose Moseley, Helen Neville, Briar O'Bryant, Mike Posner, Bruce Rogers, JJ, Nickolas, and Julia Scheri, Ramesh Srinivasan, and Cindy Veldhuis. I also want to acknowledge the important influence of my young friends, Caitlin and Elizabeth Monroe, who have never let me forget the importance of fantasy in children's lives.

Hundreds of children, parents, and other adults have participated in my research. Thanks so much for helping me learn about imaginary companions. I am very grateful for the generous support of the National Science Foundation. Part of the manuscript was written while I was an Erskine Fellow at the University of Canterbury in Christchurch, New Zealand. Thanks to Gill Rhodes and Ian McLean who were terrific friends and hosts in NZ, and were very supportive of this work. The conversations I had with Jeff Simpson, my office mate at Canterbury, made a lasting impression. Thanks also to his son Chris for a wonderful drawing.

My editor at Oxford, Joan Bossert, has encouraged me right from the time I first told her about my idea for this book over coffee. Her incisive editing dramatically improved the manuscript. I am very grateful to Nirmala

Darmarajah for smoothing the final stages of the publication process in many ways, and to Kim Torre-Tasso, the production editor.

Finally, special thanks goes to John Flavell, who taught me about cognitive development, and who has helped and inspired me throughout my career. Also to Bill Harbaugh for his emotional support and last-minute editing. And most of all, my love and thanks to Amber, who brought imaginary friends into our family, and so much more.

Permissions

Quote from "Breakfast of Champions" by Kurt Vonnegut. Permission granted by Dell, a division of Bantam, Doubleday, Dell Publishing Group, Inc.

Quote reprinted from *Broken images, broken selves: Dissociative narratives in clinical practice* by S. Krippner & S. M. Powers. Permission granted by Taylor & Francis.

Quotes reprinted from The Imaginary Companion by Humberto Nagera, *The Psychoanalytic Study of the Child*, 1969, Vol. 24. By permission of International Universities Press, Inc. Copyright 1969 by International Universities Press, Inc.

Index

Printed in the United States
28776LVS00001B/12